THE SEDUCTIVE IMAGE

TURNING POINT Christian Worldview Series
Marvin Olasky, General Editor

Turning Point: A Christian Worldview Declaration
by Herbert Schlossberg and Marvin Olasky

Prodigal Press: The Anti-Christian Bias of the American News Media
by Marvin Olasky

Freedom, Justice, and Hope:
Toward a Strategy for the Poor and Oppressed
by Marvin Olasky, Herbert Schlossberg,
Pierre Berthoud, and Clark H. Pinnock

Beyond Good Intentions: A Biblical View of Politics
by Doug Bandow

Prosperity and Poverty: The Compassionate Use
of Resources in a World of Scarcity
by E. Calvin Beisner

The Seductive Image: A Christian Critique
of the World of Film
by K. L. Billingsley

THE SEDUCTIVE IMAGE

A Christian Critique of the World of Film

K. L. Billingsley

CROSSWAY BOOKS • WESTCHESTER, ILLINOIS
A DIVISION OF GOOD NEWS PUBLISHERS

The Seductive Image.

Published by Crossway Books, a division of
Good News Publishers, Westchester, Illinois 60153.

Published in association with the
Fieldstead Institute,
P.O. Box 19061
Irvine, California 92713.

First printing, 1989

Printed in the United States of America

Library of Congress Catalog Card Number 88-71805

ISBN 0-89107-510-0

TABLE OF

CONTENTS

ACKNOWLEDGMENTS

Books, like film, are also a collaborative medium. I wish to thank the Fieldstead Institute and Marvin Olasky for tapping me for the project. The author also wishes to acknowledge the invaluable assistance of Dorothy Anderson, Ellen Gold, Evelyn Robinson, Edna Cavazos, Margie Duckrow, and José Salgado of the Serra Library System, along with the library staffs of Westminister Theological Seminary and Point Loma College. I greatly appreciate the assistance and inspiration of G. Randall Kuhl, Kenneth A. Myers, Harry M. Cheney, Sherwood E. Wirt, Robert J. Caldwell, Robert Royal, Michael Medved, Roberta Green Ahmanson, Jan Dennis, Lois Sibley, Stephen Schwartz, Roy M. Brewer, Joseph Farah, Mark Ferjulian, Jack Hafer, and David Horowitz. To them goes the gratitude, to me the responsibility for what follows.

I want . . . I want, everything I've ever seen in the movies!
(Accountant Leo Bloom, from Mel Brooks' *The Producers)*

If there's one thing I hate, it's the movies. Don't even mention them to me.

(Holden Caulfield, from J. D. Salinger's *The Catcher in the Rye)*

You can take Hollywood for granted like I did, or you can dismiss it with the contempt we reserve for what we don't understand. It can be understood too, but only dimly and in flashes.

(F. Scott Fitzgerald, *The Last Tycoon*)

INTRODUCTION:

Apologia Pro Liber Suo

Seven years ago, a director friend suggested that I "run, not walk" to see a new British film called *Chariots of Fire*. I saw the picture at my earliest convenience, liked what I saw, and recommended that friends give it a try. However, one Christian friend, though intrigued with the story, was not ready to slap on his Nikes and dash to the box office.

He first wanted to know whether it was a "Christian" film. The question surprised me, because the fellow watched plenty of prime-time television without applying any spiritual test. Neither had this question been raised when he and his wife took us to see *My Brilliant Career*, an Australian film they adored but which I found boring.

I replied that I didn't know whether *Chariots of Fire* was a Christian film, but that one of its major characters was a committed Christian. I thought this explanation would suffice, but it did not. One Christian character, my friend insisted, did not a Christian film make.

As the discussion unfolded, I raised the question whether there was any such thing as a specifically Christian movie. My friend was a still photographer of considerable talent. I asked him if the photos he took of trees and rocks were "Christian" pictures. If the subject of one of his portraits was a faithful pastor, would this automatically make it a Christian photograph? What if a Zoroastrian priest or atheist had taken the same photograph? Would it still qualify as Christian? Did he perhaps use Christian film or a Christian camera? Or, if a picture of the Grand Canyon was technically perfect, would this make it a Christian photograph? Were the photographs of Ansel Adams and Edward Weston, two artists my friend revered, "Christian" photographs?

Conversely, how about a picture of, say, Billy Graham, with his face cropped just above the eyebrows? What about an overexposed, out-of-focus shot of Chartres Cathedral, with a garbage truck parked in front? Would these poor efforts qualify as Christian pictures, even if a Christian took them? No clear answers to these questions emerged.

I then applied this line of reasoning to *Chariots of Fire*. I didn't know the religious beliefs of those who made the film, but I assumed they were not Christians, since few in the film business are. Nor were all the characters in the story Christian, and no one gets converted. Moreover, it is made clear that the Christian character meets an untimely demise.

My photographer friend was still not satisfied, but his sole answer to these arguments was to repeat his original question. I believe that at one point I asked if *The Ten Commandments* was a "Jewish film." We eventually called a truce.

I relate this incident at some length to show that any work on a highly subjective topic like cinema is a veritable minefield. The cinema, and criticism of it, is not science, theology, or an academic discipline, and there is nothing resembling a consensus. For example, some film historians and critics hail D. W. Griffith as a genius, and call his *Birth of a Nation* a masterpiece. Others regard him as a pompous charlatan and consider his work third-rate at best.

The problem can only be multiplied when the work is part of a series billed as coming from a Christian perspective. While this writer is a Christian, and believes that his co-religionists should develop a Christian worldview, the process is not without its perils and disagreements. Just as Aldous Huxley wrote that "science" was sometimes taken to mean the opinions of professors X, Y, and Z, some mistake a Christian worldview, or even "Christianity," as the opinions of Christians X, Y, and Z.

If there were a host of Biblical teaching on film—say, an Epistle to Hollywood—that would put an end to much controversy. But with such material lacking, the approach must be of a more general nature. Since interpretations differ, it should be no surprise that there is a wide diversity of opinion on what the Christian view of cinema is, or even if there can be one.

Some viewers, Christian and otherwise, find deep spiritual parables in such films as *E.T.* or *Star Wars*,[1] while others regard them as cartoons or "militaristic" propaganda. I once had some good things to say about Ingmar Bergman's *Fanny and Alexander*[2] and was taken to task by a Christian lady who said that even a "secular" newspaper had been more critical of the film's antireligious overtones than I had. (Curiously, thus warned, she went to see it anyway.) On another occasion, I rapped *Footloose* for its caricature of Christians,[3] only to find that my piece touched off hate mail from, among others, a minister's daughter.

This diversity among Christians does not mean that no attempt should be made to deal with this subject. Indeed, given the undeniable power of film, its proliferation during the last eighty years, and its elevated status in contemporary culture, the need for analysis would seem to be great.

Martin Esslin of the Arts Council of Great Britain, and former professor of drama at Stanford, notes that film, stage, television, and even radio are all part of the basic *dramatic* form of expression, which even extends to commercials. Since this form now surrounds us, Esslin contends, "we ought to be able to understand and analyze its impact on ourselves—and our children" because "the explosion of dramatic forms presents us all with considerable risks of being enslaved to insidious forms of subliminal manipulation of our consciousness."[4]

Astute observers of film such as Parker Tyler share this judgment. Writes Tyler: "Hollywood is a vital, interesting phenomenon, at least as important to the spiritual climate as daily weather to the physical climate."[5] I hold similar views, but make no claim that this work is *the* Christian view of cinema, and do not believe that there can be such an official view.

This book will attempt to help readers think about film, but will not do their thinking for them. It will not indulge in such wastes of time as counting the number of violent acts in *Rambo* or four-letter words and nude scenes in *Porky's*. It will not cite studies by Swedish psychologists purporting to prove or disprove whether films affect those who watch them. Common sense and simple observation should be enough to confirm that they do. If well-directed, well-written scenes of great power and beauty exalt the viewer, as everyone admits, it surely follows that poorly-written, poorly-directed scenes of squalor and depravity will to some degree degrade the viewer. How can it be otherwise?

It is inescapable that a book of this nature must include strictly subjective opinions and judgments about certain films, film techniques, and even film critics. The reader should not only feel free to disagree on such matters but is in fact encouraged to do so. I ask only to be given a fair hearing and taken seriously in my pronouncements *about* film, as well as judged fairly in my use of the data, Biblical and otherwise. As James Schlesinger noted, everyone has a right to his own opinion, but no one has a right to his own facts.

In this book, praise for a certain film or its director should not be interpreted as this writer's personal recommendation that all people see the work in question or approve of its content. Neither is it an approval of the beliefs or lifestyle of the director, writer, or any of the cast. Likewise, a caution to a prospective viewer is not necessarily a condemnation of any film, its maker, or those who appear in it.

I am a screenwriter, a member of the Writers Guild of America, and have worked on sundry film and television projects. I live near Los Angeles, cinema's Vatican. I count film producers, actors, and directors among my friends, and have spent time on location, as well as prowling about the studios. I consider that such experience, while limited, has provided some material worthy of passsing on. This book is not, however, a completely "inside" view of film. Screenwriting is far from my only occupation. My career has been something of a literary decathlon, largely motivated by economic concerns.

Though I have written about film for a number of publications, I do not aspire to be a professional film critic. Given the current state of the business, watching movies as a job would be, as far as I am concerned, a form of cruel and unusual punishment.

Neither do I write as an aficionado or "film buff." To be sure, I enjoy movies. When Woody Allen, in his film *Bananas*, has a triumphant Latin American revolutionary proclaim that the official language of his country will now be Swedish, I consider it a master stroke. I even found myself cheering when in the James Bond film *Living Daylights,* the Afghan *Mujahedeen* attack a Soviet base and prevail. *American Graffiti* takes me back to my teen-age years, and Horton Foote's *The Trip to Bountiful* makes me think of my mother, and even about God.

But, I should hasten to add, I am not panting for anything that *cinéastes* have to offer. My expectations of film are low, and I'm seldom disappointed. With few exceptions, the lives and opinions of film people, especially actors, do not interest me in the slightest. The truth is that actors are quite often boring people, interesting or funny only when they are playing someone else.[6] I believe that film trivia is just that, trivial. My basic posture toward film as a medium is increasingly skeptical, and any list of all-time favorites I could put together would be rather short. That said, I stress the medium's power, and add that to ignore it would be folly.

In these pages I hope to take a hard look at film as a medium and a business. This will necessitate some exploration of drama and its relation to the Christian faith. (However, the documentary mode will also be covered.) It will also mean asking some basic, general questions that often seem overlooked in the quest for specifics: Can film tell the truth? Do films reflect culture? What can film do well? What are its limitations, its dangers? How does American cinema portray religion? What, if any, are the politics of film? What will be the effect of the proliferation of film?

Some answers may already be known and if certain sections seem overly obvious, the author requests the reader's indulgence. This done, the author will attempt to explain what it all means, specifically for those in the Christian community. As it happens, more than a few in that community are dead set against movies. That is the subject of Chapter One.

PART ONE

CHRISTIANITY AND DRAMA

O N E

CHRISTIANS AND MOVIES

Even if it were possible for you to attend the movies without personal detriment, taking fire into your bosom without burning your clothes, you would still be an accomplice to an industry that is causing untold crime and moral degradation among the young people of our country.

(Stephen W. Paine, former president
of Houghton College and of the
National Association of Evangelicals, 1957)[1]

American Christians have never objected to film *as film.* Indeed, they have always made ample use of the medium for educational purposes. Every popular Christian author or speaker, it seems, has had his own film series. It is commercial, Hollywood fare that has brought objection. In 1957, the above-quoted Stephen Paine stated categorically that "We don't attend movies."[2] Carl McClain, author of the 1970 *Morals and the Movies,* wrote that "evangelicals do not patronize the movies."[3] Though cinematic abstinence has been most characteristic of the "holiness" churches of the Arminian tradition, such as the Wesleyans, Methodists, and Nazarenes, some in the Reformed tradition have followed suit. The following sections will explore three reasons why some Christians over the years have opposed Hollywood.

"SEPARATION"

Stephen Paine's *The Christian and the Movies* was a classic statement on the subject. And Paine, it should be noted, was not a backwoods preacher nor a theological mossback, but a careful academic and church official. For Paine, the cinema was "worldly" and Christians were to be "separate" from the world. Christians were not to support the movie industry in any way, even if it occasionally offered a picture worthy of attention, which he conceded to be the case.[4]

"Some careful Christians," Paine wrote, "find a very basic objection in the feeling that all acting is intrinsically wrong," that it is "essentially dishonest" for someone to "leave their personality" and "for a time to put himself into the personality of another."[5]

Here Paine was in essence providing a variation on the argument of second-century theologian Tertullian, who rejected the dramatic form as inherently evil. (Tertullian, let it be noted, also believed that sex, even within marriage, was sinful, and preferred the extinction of the race to its continuance by sexual means.) Paine agreed with this judgment on acting "in part," but went on to disagree with the idea that *all* acting or impersonation is wrong in principle, citing Jesus' parables, the art of storytelling, and missionaries who find impersonation and pictorializing indispensable to their ministry.

To the question "what harm in good movies?" Paine wrote that good movies were an "entering wedge," so much bait to set up the viewer for the hard stuff. He added that even in seeing such films one was still supporting the industry. He admitted that it was impossible to avoid some measure of support for what one does not approve, and that is certainly true. For example, a pastor may use part of his salary to blow away doves with his 12-gauge. Banks take one's money and lend it to racetracks and topless bars. The U.S. government uses taxpayers' dollars to extend soft loans to Communist dictatorships which persecute Christians and Jews. But Paine believed the movie business was a special case and called those who support it "accomplices."[6] Such support, he contended, must be avoided, even if the viewer was not adversely affected by what he saw.

Paine left the distinct impression that evil scarcely existed before the advent of the movie business. The use of a loaded word like "accomplices" implies that the entire enterprise is criminal. One wonders what he would write today, when *Porky's* has replaced *Rebel Without a Cause,* and when the FBI is investigating the penetration of the movie business by the Mafia.[7]

Interestingly enough, Paine also stated that in the areas of television and "cinerama," each person "will have to make up his own mind about these things in the final analysis."[8] That indeed would seem to be the case, and that is what this author believes people should do.

MORALITY

Other Christians over the years rejected "separation," but strove to remove from Hollywood productions all depiction of sexual activities, questionable language, and even reference to controversial issues. Some of these efforts may have been useful, but the Hays Office, the movie industry's self-censoring agency, cut from scripts even words which were found in the Bible such as "whore" and "virgin." It also forbade terms such as "wet nurse," "lousy," and "nuts," and descriptions such as "tom-cat" for a man. The "Code" of the Hays Office even forbade the mention of diapers and scenes involving the milking of cows. Any reference to venereal disease was also deleted. Criminals were not to be shown attacking the police.

Worse, the Code also declared off-limits such properties as Somerset Maugham's *Rain* and Evelyn Waugh's *Brideshead Revisited,* a moving story of a man who finds God, which has since been made into a mini-series. Logically and consistently applied, the Code would have condemned all of Shakespeare and vast stretches of the Bible.

An attitude which would even censor the Bible can only be called prudery. Such a posture is effectively anti-Biblical and hardly deserving of respect. Hortense Powdermaker was an anthropologist who had studied taboos in different cultures, including that of Hollywood. She wrote that "neither morality nor taste is achieved through the mechanical following of taboos,"[9] and most films made under the Code confirm that judgment.

The Code also demanded that criminals and wrongdoers be punished, which prompted Powdermaker to write that by so doing it excluded "the theme of redemption through repentance and God's grace." Moreover, she added, "both the spirit and the letter of the Code contradict the very core of Christianity, Christ dying to save erring mankind."[10] One might say that in straining at a gnat, the Hays Office swallowed a camel.

One other aspect of the response of some Christians to the movies needs to be addressed here.

ANTI-SEMITISM

The American film industry was founded by Jewish immigrants from Eastern Europe. Their almost complete dominance of the business drew many anti-Semitic attacks. Certified American heroes such as Charles Lindbergh railed against Jewish influence, and Hollywood notables such as Scott Fitzgerald and Errol Flynn were known to let loose anti-Jewish sallies in unguarded moments. Sadly, some fundamentalist ministers also betrayed Biblical teaching in this way.

The essence of the attacks from preachers was that wealthy Jews were using the film industry to weaken the moral fiber of the country. In some cases, the attackers equated Judaism and communism, a ludicrous charge in that communism is based on materialism and atheism.[11] These are canards similar to those found in classical anti-Semitic demonologies such as the *Protocols of the Elders of Zion,* and, like them, completely false.

One would be hard pressed to find people more dedicated to their new country than the early film moguls. As Neil Gabler points out, they believed implicitly in American values and wanted desperately to be regarded as Americans, not Jews. And some of them, such as Benjamin Warner, were most devout.[12]

There is plenty to criticize in films and the movie business. But Christians must reject anti-Semitism, which, as of this writing, is again rearing its ugly head. A group called the "Fundamentalist Army," headed by the Reverend R. L. Hymers, protested *The Last Temptation of Christ* by stationing themselves outside a Jewish producer's home and chanting, "Jewish money! Jewish money!" and performing a skit in which a Jewish producer whips and crucifies Christ. Ironically, some prominent local Jews also publicly objected to *Last Temptation.* Responsible Christian groups protesting the film rightly objected to Hymers' tactics.[13]

That nasty issue aside, it is noteworthy that none of the protesters of *Last Temptation* were calling for Christians to roll up their sleeves and make their own films on the life of Christ, or any other subject. We will return to this theme in later chapters.

RESPONSE

It is true that much of what is depicted in movies is often nihilistic from the standpoint of belief, immoral from the standpoint of behavior, trash from the standpoint of art, and incompetence from the standpoint of craftsmanship. That anyone, Christian, Jew, Buddhist, or even atheist, should avoid such works on those grounds is entirely justified. Pauline Kael of the *New Yorker* writes freely of film producers "polluting" America and the world.[14] Even the great dramatist George Bernard Shaw wrote that the "obvious destiny" of the cinema was to "promote the castigation by ridicule of current morality."[15]

It is also true, as Paine acknowledged from a variety of sources, that films are powerful and influence behavior, especially that of young people, who possess great powers of imitation. J. D. Salinger's Holden Caulfield, who is no fan of the cinema, confirms the tendency to imitate by confessing that "I hate the movies like poison, but I get a bang imitating them."[16]

Yet, myriads of people, young and old, who regularly attend movies are relatively unaffected by them. They go to the theatre, as they would to a basketball game or concert, watch *Bambi* or *Hoosiers,* are entertained, and for the most part that's the end of it. To assume that everyone will imitate what they see is practically to deny free will, spiritual discernment, or moral courage. As for "worldliness," that would seem to be more of an internal rather than an external matter.

"Do not conform any longer to the pattern of this world, but be transformed *by the renewing of your mind,*" says the relevant Biblical text.[17] I take this to mean that one's way of thinking is changed, which leads to this statement, in the same context: "For by the grace given me I say to every one of you: Do not think of yourself more highly than you ought, but rather think of yourself with sober judgment. . . ."[18] Hence, I believe, the essence of worldliness is not a question of abstaining from movies, cards, or dancing. Rather, the essence of worldliness is hubris, holding an inflated view of oneself or exalting oneself above others. Preventing that condition is a much trickier business than refusing to see *Ghostbusters* and chiding those who do.

In addition, the Apostle Paul writes to the Corinthian church that when he told them not to associate with sexually immoral people, he was referring to those *within* the church. He did not mean "the people of this world who are immoral, or the greedy and swindlers, or idolaters" because "In that case you would have to leave this world."[19] In effect, that is what groups such as the Amish have done. It is also, in effect, what Paine calls upon Christians to do.

It should be clear that what one is up against here is not merely the question of movies, but the cultural purviews of what is generally called fundamentalism. Much has been written on the subject in recent years, a great deal of it nonsense. And while this book is not a treatment of the wider discussion, the issues in question may be easily summarized.

Piety is a reverence for God expressed in good works and the cultivation of a devotional life, and as such is desirable. Piet*ism,* however, is a false asceticism which rejects anything outside of church attendance, work, prayer, evangelism, and Bible study as "worldly."[20] Like the Reformers, pietists stress the spiritual mandate and the spiritual side of life; but unlike the Reformers, they ignore the cultural mandate and the cultural side of life.

This is particularly true of the whole area of the arts and entertainment, though one notes that sports, ski trips, and motor homes seldom, if ever, present an ethical problem to those of pietistic inclinations. In similar style, drinking is taboo (Stephen Paine called movies "wet propaganda"), but one may overeat with impunity. The approach is sometimes called "legalism," a system of dos and don'ts which reduces Christianity to a list of rules. While this legalism is frequently connected to what is called the Religious Right, the Religious Left does the same with its lettuce boycotts and its calls for television to stop showing cartoons and do more reports on the homeless and organic gardening.

In any case, the concept of physical "separation" is simplistic and, at base, monastic. It is this idea which has led to the ghettoization of the Christian community, and the widespread identification of Christians as people who are always *against* something, who do *not* do certain things, and who are unsettled at the knowledge that someone, somewhere might be having fun. I am of the Reformed tradition and believe that fundamentalists have been unfairly, even viciously, criticized in recent times. But I also believe that many are deserving of criticism on this point, primarily from their fellow-Christians.

When philosopher Francis Schaeffer began to develop a Christian epistemology and concept of culture, many viewed him with suspicion, as somehow unspiritual or unfaithful. I agree with Schaeffer that his critics represented a stunted, unhistorical Christianity, which makes for stunted Christians who are afraid to pursue the truth wherever it leads, lest they fall off the edge of the earth.[21]

With Newton, Pascal, and others, I believe that all truth is God's truth. With Bach, Michelangelo, and Cervantes, I believe that art needs no justification. Hence, I believe there is no religious case against the movies, only against the abuse and misuse of them. If someone wishes to stay away, that is their decision, and their reasons for doing so must be respected, even if one does not agree with them. Those who stay away testify by their behavior that films matter a great deal indeed.

But those who abstain are not to judge their sisters and brothers who think differently.[22] Neither are they to imagine that their asceticism endows them with a superior spirituality. Indeed the Bible describes the one with the sensitive conscience in areas of nonessentials as the "weak" brother.[23]

In 1970, Carl McClain went so far as to write: "I submit that a frequenter of the theatre or movie house cannot at the same time be a spiritual force for good, a vital Christian leader or Sunday school teacher."[24] This is nonsense. It might be noted that, like countless pastors and seminary professors, outstanding Christian leaders such as John Stott and Os Guinness regularly see plays and movies. It would be fair to say that each has had much more influence for good than Mr. McClain, who lacked understanding of the dramatic medium. And long before film, there was drama.

T W O

WHAT IS DRAMA?

The play's the thing.
(Shakespeare, from *Hamlet*)

Drama, as we understand it, began when the Greek poet Thespis stepped out of a chorus and acted out the part of one of the characters in the story the chorus was telling. He is thus regarded as the first actor or "thespian." Greek lawgiver Solon denounced Thespis' invention, but it took hold and has survived some fearful assaults.

At the simplest level, a drama is a story about human conflicts and emotions, to be *acted* or performed on a stage, as opposed to being read in private. The Greek word *drama* means "action." Early plays were usually performed by one man. Aeschylus added a second character, and Sophocles a third, and by that time the dramatic convention was firmly established.

Using a "live" setting, the dramatist introduces his characters and sets up the problem or conflict, without which there can be no drama. Once the conflict has been set up, the individual scenes, subplots, and actions must push the story forward toward a resolution or *dénouement*, French for "end" or "unraveling" (French *noeud*= "knot").

Change, action, and conflict are key dramatic elements, and there is a sense in which all lives are dramatic. All people go through changes, and if the protagonist in a play or film does not change, there has been no drama. No life is without conflict or action, and few, if any, people have no antagonists. The best drama externalizes not only specific human conflicts, but the larger good versus evil struggle in various manifestations. It takes this struggle out of the abstract and gives it a presence, names, and faces.

A story that goes in circles makes for poor drama, or no drama. Similarly, the direction of life is forward, toward an end; life has a limited run. The tools and time of the dramatist are likewise limited, and so are the resources of every human being. Everything that happens in a play should mean something in terms of the overall story, just as the most seemingly insignificant events in human experience are often of the greatest moment.

Action may be the soul of drama, but tragedy and comedy are its thunder and lightning. In Greek drama, tragedy was the occupational disease of heroes, but it is an element from which no one is immune. Spanish philosopher Miguel de Unamuno knew this and penned a thick tome called *The Tragic Sense of Life*. One could argue that the great dramas, such as *Macbeth*, are tragedies. An example of a tragic film would be Peter Weir's *Gallipoli*, about Australian troops in the First World War.

Comedy, on the other hand, is more than revelry, slapstick, or the simple telling of jokes. True comedy is actually very serious business indeed and is a consequence of the Fall, which left human beings in a no-man's-land between the perfection they can conceive and the utter imperfection of what they are and do. Comedy operates in this zone, and is evidence of a purer, higher, but as yet unrealized state. We laugh when confronted with this gap, since, in our deepest selves, we know it to be so. A dog falling down is not funny, but a human being falling down inevitably gets a laugh, as both Red Skelton and Chevy Chase are well aware. Whether people admit it or not, we do not expect creatures made in the image of God, capable of composing *Messiah* and flying to the moon, to take a tumble. It seems beyond their dignity.

Many great humorists, it should be noted, were and are believers in God: Rabelais, Shakespeare, Gogol, Cervantes, Waugh, Muggeridge. It is the secular, materialist mindset that must take man and his predicament with stony seriousness. Unfortunately, a long sermonic tradition has caused North American Christians to associate wisdom with solemnity, and hence they sometimes miss the raging truth to be found amidst the laughs.

Since this is a book about film let me take two examples from that medium, the first from Lina Wertmuller's *Seven Beauties*. In one scene, Pasqualino, a fugitive, apparently believes himself invincible. He insults his pursuers and yells that they'll never take him alive, etc. But the instant he finishes saying this, a policeman calmly steps from his hiding place and puts a pistol to Pasqualino's head. "Okay, so I was wrong," the fugitive shrugs.

In Woody Allen's *Annie Hall*, a man spouts off to his girlfriend about Fellini and Marshall McLuhan, just loud enough so bystanders can hear. He is obviously quite impressed with himself. Allen's character endures the performance as best he can, but finally turns to the offender and tells him he knows nothing about Marshall McLuhan. The man defiantly replies that he is a professor of communications, at Columbia University no less, as though that settles everything. Allen does not argue but instead proceeds to usher Marshall McLuhan himself into the scene. The media guru calmly informs the professor that he understands nothing about his work and wonders how he ever got to teach anything. The pedantic windbag is totally deflated.

Isaac Bashevis Singer believed that the purpose of literature was to keep time from vanishing. To that end drama can also be an aid to memory, keeping alive cherished people or experiences in a world that changes all too rapidly, too often in ways one finds abhorrent. *I Remember Mama*, a Broadway play and a film, would be an obvious example of this type of drama. Tom Key's *An Evening with C. S. Lewis* would be another. Even Shakespeare, Shaw, and Wilde qualify, though these authors did not intend to write "period pieces." One of the things film can do much more convincingly than the stage is recreate the worlds of the past, though the stage is often better at reviving the people of the past. The spoken word, and verse in particular, are much more at home on the stage than the screen.

Drama can also be didactic, a teaching tool, but lectures or homilies are not in themselves dramatic, even if delivered with great fervor. If a dramatist of the stage or screen sets out to teach rather than tell a compelling story, both his story and his message often fall flat. If his ideas carry the characters rather than the other way around, his characters will be little more than stick figures. In a strictly didactic play, the dialogue will amount to the author speaking, and little else.

In drama, as in literature, the author has a godlike quality. He not only controls his work but should, like God, be everywhere present but nowhere visible. Too often the reverse is true.

People do not normally attend plays or films to be taught or lectured, and certainly not to be harangued. Audiences can sense when they are being fed propaganda and usually object, regardless of whether the message is social, political, or religious; indeed, perhaps especially if it is religious. I recall a review of the World Wide Pictures film *Time to Run*, which came billed as family entertainment, and which the reviewer fully expected it to be. But when, toward the end, he suddenly found himself being preached at by a screen-wide image of Billy Graham, he said he knew it was "time to run" and did so.

There are cases, however, in which the audience is there for the specific purpose of hearing propaganda, which allows the author to preach to the converted. In some agit-prop[1] plays people are encouraged to scream "Revolution!" or "Down with Zionism!" Examples of propagandistic "message movies" would include *Missing, Walker, The Last Emperor*, and *The Day After*, a piece of anti-nuke pornography which was coordinated with a vast propaganda campaign through the media and even in some schools.

The inherent weakness of message movies is that they are all black and white in a moral sense. There is never any doubt in the audience's mind as to whose side they should be on.

Scripture is full of paradoxes and unintended consequences: Dying, we live; losing our lives, we find them; in weakness we are strong. Adam Smith pointed out the unintended consequences of economic actions. Such laws and paradoxes also apply in drama. If a writer has a genuine story to tell, as opposed to a message to smuggle in, and is faithful in his storytelling and skillful in technique, the audience may get a message. In fact, they may get more and deeper messages than the author ever intended. But for that to happen, the work must be a compelling story, not a homily, and the characters must come to life in some real sense. It can't be a puppet show in which the author simply stands behind his characters with a bullhorn.

Just as there is no drama without conflict, there can be no drama if the *audience* is excluded. Drama, unlike prose literature, is a *public* form, the most "social" of the arts. Doubtless, many people attend plays or films for communal experience, for an escape from self. Film critic Roger Ebert contends that the best way to see a movie is not at home on one's VCR but in a large theatre packed with strangers. The mass response to the movie "makes it easier for us to join the communal experience, to enter into the film-going reverie and shut down our awareness of self."[2]

The dramatist should respect his audience—after all, their money keeps him alive—not pander to them, disgust them, insult them, or talk down to them. Audiences want to see people whose struggles are similar to their own, which is now, in the opinion of some, far from the case. Comedian Jay Leno says that at one time you could identify with characters in films such as *Old Yeller* or *The Summer of '42.* Now, he says, you go to a movie and hear people behind you saying things like: "You know, I killed a guy like that once."

The skillful dramatist will not leave the audience passive, but will make the folks work a bit. Agatha Christie was good at this and a master at bamboozling the crowd. Her play *The Mousetrap* has been running since the 1950s. *Absence of Malice* is a film that forces the audience to think. The dramatist who respects the audience will create a situation in which the people in the seats know more than the characters on the stage or screen, a most effective technique. In some cases, characters may be stationed in the audience, as in *Reserve Two For Murder.* Actual audience participation is possible with stage drama, and occasionally takes place with cult films such as *The Rocky Horror Picture Show.* Woody Allen managed a form of it in *The Purple Rose of Cairo*, though all the audience participation happened on the screen.

There is a downside to the public, communal dimension of drama. In a real sense, good drama depends on a good audience. Actors know full well that no two crowds are alike. With some groups, a subtle, nuanced line can bring down the house; with others it can bomb. A joke that one must explain is no joke at all, and drama provides no opportunity for explanation.

But it is the *fact* of the audience that gives drama a collective or herd dimension. Mass psychology, in itself, is neither good nor bad. It is a factor in the best oratory, and even in worship. But at times, mass psychology can induce a mob mentality.

Laughter, for example, can be positively infectious, with audience members not so much laughing at or with the actors as much as in imitation of others in the crowd. Such laughter, particularly at weak material, has been cited as one reason why a democracy can never work. An audience might cheer at a vicious joke made at the expense of, say, a nun. But a Roman Catholic spectator who found the joke not at all funny can only bear it in silence or walk out. There is no right of reply, unless one later attempts a critical review or writes another play in response. There is no turning the page, no closing the book. The crowd has spoken. Everything takes place in a restricted, artificial environment with its own rules. The author defines the debate, and the one who defines the debate usually wins.

I was once involved in a critique session for a play that portrayed all Southerners as ignorant bigots and slobs. Every one of them was a one-dimensional outtake from *Smokey and the Bandit.* When I suggested that this portrait was inaccurate and unfair (not to mention redundant), there was a burst of laughter. "Well, I guess that answers that," said the one directing the session. But of course that did not answer that; there was simply an audience reaction, which ultimately proved nothing. It was a miniature version of "The Phil Donahue Show," which is really a show-trial. Suppose that some racist wrote a play in which a character screamed that blacks were inferior. An audience of cheering Ku Kluckers and Nazis would hardly settle the point. In crowds, the majority rules, and the majority is not always right.

Popular film reviewer Roger Ebert recalls a rather nasty film titled *I Spit on Your Grave*, in essence a series of violent attacks on a young woman and her ensuing campaign of vengeance. His judgment of the film is about as subtle as the title; it was "a vile bag of garbage . . . sick, reprehensible and contemptible," an "expression of the most diseased and perverted darker human natures" (*sic*). But he found the audience more "profoundly disturbing" than the film.

The place was packed and the folks were "eating it up." After one brutal rape scene, someone shouted, "That was a good one!" One of the bad guys was retarded, and when his comrades forced him to attack the girl, the audience laughed. When the victim began to systematically and perversely slaughter her attackers—she disembowels one with an outboard motor—a female patron shouted,

"Cut him up, sister!" Ebert concluded that many members of the audience had "suffered a remarkable loss of human feelings," to the point that, if they believed what they were saying, they were "vicarious sex criminals." Perhaps that was why Ebert refrained from telling them that their behavior was disgusting, which he wanted to do. It would not have gone down, and they likely would have turned on him. The incident became "one of the most depressing experiences" of Ebert's life, and he left the theatre "feeling unclean, ashamed and depressed."[3] Readers have doubtless had similar experiences. I certainly have.

Television has the "studio audience," which does what it is told, and the canned audience of the laugh track. In *Annie Hall*, Woody Allen is a comedian and one of his friends, a television man, is shown editing his show. "Give me a big laugh here," he tells the sound mixer, when, in fact, nothing funny has occurred. "Don't you realize how immoral this is?" Allen says. The man has a point. Audiences can be dangerous, for dramatist and spectator alike. With few exceptions, those who produce television "comedies" have every reason to supply their own laughter. It is of more than passing significance that Hitler insisted that a live audience be present for his speeches. It was his form of the studio audience.

Prose literature, as opposed to drama, is a more private medium, in which matters are strictly linear and events happen one at a time. It is always "and then" or "meanwhile." But drama does not share this limitation; many things can be happening simultaneously on stage or screen, conveying a sense of realism and immediacy. The skillful dramatist exploits this property to the full. There are ways, of course, in which prose literature enjoys advantages over drama, and these will be dealt with in due course.

Drama, it should be stressed, is not mere spectacle. A circus, a comedian, a line of chorus girls, a battle of gladiators, or even a hanging may well have theatrical elements, but do not in themselves constitute drama. In drama, one thing leads to another, and eventually to a resolution. Hence, the question for the audience should be, "what next?" Spectacle lacks dramatic structure and meaning. The only question it raises is, "what else?" Aristotle argued that "those who employ spectacular means to create a sense not of the terrible but only of the monstrous are strangers to the purpose of tragedy."[4]

Drama also requires the willing suspension of disbelief on the part of the audience. For the dramatist, this means that he or she is in a real sense constrained by what the audience will accept. They must be won over, and if they leave the theatre, as they often do, saying, "I just didn't believe it," then the work has failed. The tougher and more discerning the audience, the harder the dramatist will have to work, and the better the final product will be. On the other hand, if the dramatist perceives that the audience has low standards and scant discernment, the temptation is to dodge hard work and substitute "everything the traffic will allow," as Irving Berlin perceptively put it in his song "There's No Business Like Show Business." Under present conditions, it seems that dramatists, especially filmmakers, have little cause for alarm since the traffic currently allows for just about everything.

For the audience, suspension of disbelief should outline some rather stark boundaries and limitations for the dramatic medium. W. Somerset Maugham, one of the most successful playwrights of his time, comments:

> For the drama is make-believe. It does not deal with truth but with effect. . . . The importance of truth to the dramatist is that it adds to interest, but to the dramatist truth is only verisimilitude. It is what he can persuade his audience to accept.[5]

Similarly, Alan Rudolph, a film director and colleague of Robert Altman, states rather cynically that "truth is whatever gets the most applause."[6]

Good drama can stir emotion, elicit fond memories, crystallize an historical situation, and bring characters to life. It can make incisive comments on social conditions, beliefs, and customs, and send an audience into riots of laughter at the posturings of the "human condition." It can entertain and in some cases enrich. Or, it can fail to do all this and often does so. But drama is not Real Life or Ultimate Truth, and this is particularly true of film. "The cinema is not a slice of life," said Alfred Hitchcock, "it is a piece of cake."[7] And in the final analysis, drama is one person's representation of reality.

THREE

CHRISTIANITY AND DRAMA

Stage plays are the most petulant, the most impure, impudent, wicked, unclean, the most shameful and detestable atonements of filthy Devil-gods.

(St. Augustine)[1]

Objections to the dramatic medium did not begin with Stephen Paine, nor with the Puritans, nor even with the Christian Church. Long before Christ, Plato wrote that plays unduly stirred passions and obscured reason, and banned players from his ideal republic.[2] Literary historian Joseph Krutch notes that even in the actual governments of the ancients there were many statues which implied that the "the theatre was regarded at best with suspicion," and adds that distrust of the theatre is "perpetual."[3] That has certainly been the case in the Church.

"There was never a moment from the fourth century downwards," writes Percy Scholes, "when some or other leaders of the Church were not fulminating against the stage." He adds that it was quite an ecumenical attack, with Independents, Catholics, Presbyterians, Baptists, and Anglicans relentlessly flailing away and essentially saying the same thing.[4] The Council of Arles in A.D. 314 produced a Canon Law that excommunicated theatrical players, and this remained in effect in France until relatively recent times.

In early times, the connection of Greek drama to Dionysian ritual was a point of contention. But if, as some have contended, the use of drama in pagan ritual discredits the medium forever, then altars are also discredited, or perhaps ritual itself. One notes, however, that both altars and rituals, with different content of course, played a large role in Old Testament worship. The law against graven images would not seem to apply, since, as Francis Schaeffer has pointed out, the Old Testament Temple and Tabernacle contained virtually every variety of representational art. It was the *worship* of such images, or the use of them to represent God, that was forbidden.[5]

Though the Old Testament forbade the indulgence of pagan ritual, there is no specific "thou shalt not" regarding drama as a form of storytelling. Francis Schaeffer noted that God instructed the prophet Ezekiel to repeatedly perform what amounted to a simple drama, as a warning to Israel.[6]

Tertullian argued that it is immoral for someone to pretend to be someone else, because in such a position he must tell lies. Those who, like Paine, follow Tertullian on this point, claim to find support in the Bible.

The Greek term for a stage player was *hypocrite,* derived from *hypocrisis,* the acting of a part. The term is also related to the masks worn by actors. Jesus accused the Pharisees of being "hypocrites," and some have taken this as a condemnation of drama. This interpretation, however, requires considerable liberties with the text. Jesus' criticism was that the Pharisees were not doing their proper duty before God, but merely playing the role. Like stage players, they put on a mask—in their case, a mask of self-righteousness.

The lesson seems abundantly clear: religious leadership should be sincere, and is not the proper arena for feigning qualities one does not have. Religious leaders should not say one thing and do another. For example, if a minister fervently preaches marital fidelity on television, he should not hide in cheap motel rooms and copulate with whores.

Contrary to what many moderns suppose, the ancients were not stupid people. As Paul Johnson has contended, "In many ways an educated man in the 1980s was less equipped with certitudes than an ancient Egyptian in 2500 B.C.," who at least had a "clear cosmology."[7] Every ancient who ever saw a play understood that the theatre was a convention and willingly suspended his or her disbelief. But suspension of disbelief should not apply *outside* of the theatre, and that is surely what Jesus was getting at. If he wanted to condemn drama, actors, or their audiences He surely would have done so directly. Indeed, when Jesus condemned, He did so plainly and without any ambiguity whatsoever: "generation of vipers," "blind guides," and so on. He resorted to the enigmatic—and often highly dramatic—medium of parables to communicate the mysteries of the Kingdom, not to condemn.

It is also of some interest that the Apostle Paul, while in Athens, made no condemnation of Greek theatre, and certainly never petitioned the emperor to ban plays. Paul even quoted some of the poets, of the day.[8] The stage was a primary forum for the poets, with verse being a staple of theatre until recently.

Origen, another early Christian theologian, believed, like Plato, that plays inflamed lusts, and this set the tone for what was to follow.

THE PURITANS AND THE STAGE

> Plays are banished for a time out of London, lest the resort unto them should ingender a plague, or rather disperse it, being already begone. Would to God these common plays were exiled altogether, as seminaries of impiety, and their theatres pulled down, as no better than houses of baudrie. It is an evident token of a wicked time where players wax so rich that they can build such houses.
>
> (Rev. William Harrison, rector of Radwinter, 1572)[9]

Puritan and Elizabethan England produced a tide of religious invective against the theatre, as exemplified by such delicately titled works as Arthur Bedford's *Serious Remonstrance on behalf of the Christian Religion against the Horrid Blasphemies and Impieties which are still used in the English Playhouse*. And who could resist picking up William Rankin's *A Mirror of Monsters, wherein is plainly described the manifold Vices and spotted Enormities that are caused by the infectious sight of Plays, with the descriptions of the subtle slights of Satan in making them his instrument*. The title page of William Prynne's massive *Histrio-Mastix* carried on for a full page, much of it in Latin.

One would like to ask these authors: "But what do you really think?" After such titles, why bother to write the book? The style resembles the "high concept" idea of the film business, which encapsulates the whole story in the title.

The attacks on the stage and actors, particularly by clergy, remind one of current moral criticism of South Africa by liberals and leftists. The fever pitch of it seems to suggest an impeccable and exclusive righteousness in the critic. The sheer bulk of it implies that no evil exists anywhere else, and that the author possessed deep, inside knowledge of the subject, which may well be doubted in many cases. The one-sidedness of it evidences unfairness, which further hints that the case is not strong. The timing of it suggests that there was no evil before the stage or apartheid came along. As good Calvinists, the Puritans knew otherwise. Reverend Harrison's notion that plays caused plagues smacks of superstition. If sin brought instant judgment, who could stand? And as the Gospel According to Luke notes, those killed when the tower of Siloam fell on them were not "more guilty than all the others living in Jerusalem."[10]

It should be stressed that the Puritans did not object to drama *as drama* but to the abuse of the *theatre,* and to the acting profession. A primary concern was the performance of plays on Sunday, but outside of that, as professor Henry Morley notes, "there remained no very substantial grounds of offense."[11] John Northbrooke, perhaps the first systematic critic of the theatre in England, actually encouraged plays in certain settings, such as schools. This is not a man who shares Tertullian's objections that plays were inherently immoral. Likewise, the 1642 ordinance that shut down the London stage expressed no objection to plays as plays, but thought it best to stop them temporarily, in view of impending civil war.

But while the London stage was temporarily shut down, plays continued to be written and published, with no objection from the authorities. Moreover, it was during the Puritan era that opera came to England and began to flourish. Some have cited this as an example of Puritan and English hypocrisy; one could enjoy the stage as long as one called it something else, and had the characters sing instead of talk. There would appear to be some merit in the charge. However, there is more on the positive side.

A case can be made that there were professional actresses before Shakespeare's day, but the normal practice was for boys to play women's parts. However, during the Puritan era, women became acceptable on the boards. A certain Mrs. Coleman played the part of Ianthe in *The Siege of Rhodes,* 1656, and was openly listed in the *dramatis personae.*[12] As for other "entertainments," the Puritans were especially fond of music and were not adverse to dancing. Neither were they teetotalers, as is commonly believed.[13]

The thrust of the Puritans' objections was the perception of indecency and profanity, both in the stage material and in the lives of the actors. To discredit drama by pointing to the lifestyles of professional actors is a rather *ad hominem* approach. Here is the argument in syllogistic form: Errol Flynn was a movie actor; Errol Flynn led a licentious life; therefore, movies are bad. One hears the same about jazz: Charlie Parker was a jazz musician; Charlie Parker was a heroin addict: therefore jazz music is evil. Needless to say, not all actors or musicians are libertines or drug users, far from it. But to those fond of this *non sequitur,* that fact counts for little.

Actually, it is not drama or music in themselves, but probably the unsettled nature of life on the road that contributes to the rather imbalanced lives characteristic of *some* actors and musicians. The same could be said of soldiers or salesmen, or anyone who tends to move around a lot. But stationary folks have similar difficulties.

I once worked in an automobile factory and noted that the repetitive, stultifying jobs and resulting boredom inclined many toward apathy and alcoholism. And the interior decor did not conduce to good morals. Workers had papered the walls with *Playboy* centerfolds, and woe betide the one who complained about the situation, much less tried to alter it.

Certain construction trades are known for heavy drinking and heavy partying, both on the job and off. As for lewdness, women know full well what happens when they jog past a building site. But the trades themselves are not thereby discredited. Neither would the behavior of some workers be sufficient grounds for declaring the field off-limits to Christians, either as a consumer or a producer, any more than the liaisons of Jimmy Swaggart and Jim Bakker raise questions about the medium of preaching. The fact that some American congressmen have been crooks, womanizers, or pederasts should not deter anyone from voting or running for office. Neither does it mean that Congress should be abolished or temporarily shut down.

As to the content of plays, there persists a mentality which believes that what an author records or shows, or what an actor dramatizes, is necessarily what he or she *approves*. Such is hardly the case. If it were, the Bible is in serious trouble, since it records, often in great detail, fratricide, mass murder, dismemberment, homosexual gang rape, incest, vengeance, betrayal, drunkenness, and much, much more. Some of its major characters are notorious liars, and some of its heroes—David and Moses, for example—are murderers. In David's case, he is also an adulterer, though a repentant one. In March 1970, Lord Platt wrote in the *Times* of London that the Old Testament was a "horror story," and urged that it be "proscribed as totally inappropriate to the ethical instruction of schoolchildren."[14]

The Puritans have often been singled out for abuse, but they were far from the only ones engaged in theatre bashing. In 1704, Queen Anne issued a proclamation against "Indecencies and Abuses of the Stage." The House of Lords thanked her for "restraining the playhouses from immorality."[15] Playwright Ben Jonson periodically scorned what he perceived as the swinish tastes of the English stage, its patrons, and its critics.

While Prynne, Bedford, *et. al.* are certainly lurid, consider the following: "It is vulgar and barbarous drama, which would not be tolerated by the vilest populace of France or Italy . . . one would imagine this piece to be the work of a drunken savage."[16] The work in question is Shakespeare's *Hamlet,* and the critic is Francois Marie Arouet, more commonly known as Voltaire. To be fair to Shakespeare, one should add the verdict of Mme. de Stael on Voltaire's *Candide,* which she thought "written by creature of a nature wholly different from our own . . . laughing like a demon or an ape at the misery of this human race with which he has nothing in common."[17]

In another writer, Shakespeare aroused "an irresistible repulsion and tedium," and to ascribe any merit to the bard was "a great evil, as is every untruth." The famous playwright, in this man's humble opinion, was "not an artist" and was, in fact, of the "lowest and most immoral" tendencies.[18] The critic is none other than Tolstoy, author of *War and Peace* and *Anna Karenina.*

Consider also this: "Their plays run to extremes in idea, vulgarity, excessive sensuality, abnormality of all kinds." The writer is Sydney

W. Carroll, president of the London Critics Circle, and also a successful theatrical manager, writing about the American stage in 1932. One of his chief targets was Eugene O'Neill.[19]

The modern critic of the Puritans should also note that in 1910, the board of trustees of the burgeoning and progressive California city of Hollywood banned movie theatres from its boundaries, even though there were none in the area at the time.[20] Marxists are the last ones who should be pointing a finger, since they often operate or defend genocidal governments which ban not only plays but religion, books, and even independent thought.

DRAMATIC SITUATIONS IN THE BIBLE

The bulk of the Bible is straight narrative—in short, storytelling. Poetry also gets a lot of space. The Bible is not, as it is often unfortunately regarded, an almanac of wise maxims and proof-texts. The verse and chapter numbers are entirely arbitrary and were not contained in the original texts. Indeed, Scripture's most highly theological sections are letters.

As mentioned, God instructed Ezekiel to perform a didactic drama. In addition, the book of Job shows a clearly dramatic structure and consists mostly of speeches. It could be adapted for the stage with little difficulty. And there are other strongly dramatic situations in Scripture.

The story of Joseph in the book of Genesis is a thoroughly dramatic tale, particularly when the brothers come to Egypt in search of food. At that point, the reader knows more than they do. The tale also has a happy ending.

So does the book of Esther, in which no reference to God is found. In this highly dramatic story, goodness and justice also triumph. Haman, the antagonist, is hanged on the gallows he prepared for Mordecai, a satisfying resolution indeed. It would make a compelling film, but to my knowledge it has never been attempted, even though it could be done for a fraction of the cost of *The Greatest Story Ever Told.*

Some of the more successful dramas, especially on film, have been of families: *The Godfather, Ordinary People, Brideshead Revisit-*

ed, On Golden Pond, and many others. There is much material along these lines in the Bible. The chronicles of David's family, in particular, contain more than enough compelling material for a fifteen-part mini-series; or, at least, a feature film.

Baptism and Communion are also highly dramatic. They are visible, highly symbolic demonstrations of spiritual truths and experiences; they must be *acted* out. By washing His disciples' feet, Jesus dramatized the attitude they were to take toward one another, that of the servant. Jesus' parables were perfect novels in miniature, many with highly dramatic content, living characters, riveting dialogue, and not always a happy ending. His teaching method was *story,* not abstract theological discourse. The people carry the ideas, which makes for good drama.

There is a sense in which a church service is dramatic, not that the minister is a performer and the congregation an audience, but rather that the performance of both—i.e., their lives and their worship—is evident to a higher but unseen audience, God. The Puritans' call for a "city set on a hill" is very much in this spirit.

Needless to say, the most effective preachers are those who can make Biblical truths and characters "live," which often involves acting the part.

THE DOGMA IS THE DRAMA

More than a few Christian thinkers have conceived of God in artistic terms, and regarded the creation as an ongoing drama, with a vast cast of characters, innumerable subplots, and all sorts of conflicts: truth versus falsehood, God versus the Devil, good versus evil. The whole production is heading toward a resolution known only to the Author, but foreshadowed in the Apocalypse, where He is the Author *and* Finisher, the Alpha and the Omega.

What makes this drama different is that the Author has seen fit to become human, to be born among His characters, then to work, suffer and ultimately die at their hand. G. K. Chesterton attempted to dramatize this in his play *The Surprise,* in which the author first performs the action through puppets, who faithfully execute his every command. Subsequently, a shift is made to living, self-willed men and women who manage to make a mess of things. From offstage the author cries: "What do you think you are doing to my play? Stop it! I am coming down."

As Dorothy Sayers writes, "The Christian faith is the most exciting drama that ever staggered the imagination of man—and the dogma is the drama." The central doctrine of Christianity is a tale of "the time when God was the under-dog and got beaten, when He submitted to the conditions He had laid down and became a man like the men He had made, and the men He had made broke Him and killed Him." Moreover, "nobody is compelled to believe a single word of this remarkable story." The divine Dramatist has set out to convince us.[21]

I believe this view has much to commend it. Certainly, it is more satisfying than the dreary conceptions of scientism, or to such ethereal notions as the "Life Force" or "Ground of Being." It is in my mind superior to the view of God as a kind of transcendent doctrinal statement, which is rather common among evangelicals.

Whenever a dramatist performs his craft, he is only doing in miniature what the ultimate Author has already done on a grander scale. The characters are all composites of those the Author has created. There is only one true Creator. The rest of us just rearrange.

RELIGIOUS DRAMA

Down through the ages, the Church has never been totally opposed to drama. Roswitha, a Saxon nun who lived around A.D. 1000, wrote plays about the Christian martyrs. The Middle Ages saw the rich tradition of the mystery plays which dealt with religious themes. The "passion plays" still enacted in various places around the world are a legacy of that tradition, and are welcome in an increasingly secularized age. There are Christian theatre troups, such as the Lamb's Players, who perform in parks and in prisons with great effectiveness, and not always to deliver a message. The Los Angeles branch of the Salvation Army produced a highly professional and thoroughly enjoyable musical called *Eva,* about Evangeline Booth.[22]

Malcolm Muggeridge recalls that after a performance of *Godspell,* an Anglican bishop in gaiters leapt to his feet and shouted: "Long live God!"[23] Evidently the fellow was not a theological heavyweight.

THE CASE FOR ART AND ENTERTAINMENT

I once contended in an article that human beings need entertainment,[24] only to be challenged by a reader: "Where does Mr. Billingsley find that in the Bible?" I'm not sure, but it is likely somewhere near the verse that sets the speed limit for the state of Alaska, or the one that explains gun registration in Maine, or the passage that outlines Western policy toward Colonel Qaddafi. In other words, it's not in there, just as there is no Biblical proof-text for myriads of things people do and use—aquatic theme parks, motor-homes, and Sunday schools, for example.

I believe that art needs no justification, that the capacity for art is one important area of distinction between human beings and animals. That human beings need entertainment seems palpably obvious from my study of history, observation of human beings in various cultures, and my own experience. Puritan writer William Perkins wrote that at times, "recreation may be more necessary than meat."[25]

Any Christian who has performed or watched a puppet show, a "skit night," a gospel "magic show," or bathrobe pageant at Christmas or Easter confirms that judgment. One might add that sports is entertainment—highly dramatic at that—and that Christians who watch or play sports also testify that human beings need entertainment. Many male American Christians are theological ignoramuses, but still capable of reciting the exact slugging percentage of their favorite baseball star. Indeed, church services have been altered to accommodate football games. Perhaps the reader who challenged me attends such a church.

None of this is to say that all the offerings of stage and screen are worthy of attention. Neither is it to say that the dramatic medium is particularly suitable for religious experience. These themes will be developed in the next section.

PART TWO

THROUGH A LENS DARKLY

FOUR

PICTURES THAT MOVE, PICTURES THAT TALK

A Must See!
(Omnipresent blurb)

Early in the new century, about 1905, Bill Miner emerges from a thirty-year prison term to find that the world he knew has disappeared. The stagecoaches he used to rob have been replaced by trains, and horses must vie with noisy contraptions called automobiles. The carnivals and circuses that roamed the land now have competition, because there is also a new form of entertainment that has the folks buzzing: pictures that move. Though short on cash, the ex-con must see what all the fuss is about.

Miner enters a nickelodeon. The lights go down and a crude projector flashes *The Great Train Robbery* on the screen, with accompaniment from a live piano player. The old boy watches in wide-eyed amazement. He had been thinking about going straight and settling down, but the experience so inspires him that he buys a revolver and begins to rob trains himself. This testimony to the attraction and power of film is from the 1982 film *The Gray Fox*, and might not be an exaggeration.

In 1933, at the nadir of the Depression, *King Kong* opened in New York. Impoverished New Yorkers managed to dig up $89,931 in four days to see the picture. At the time, it was a record for attendance of an indoor attraction.[1] And it was not exactly a limited run; *King Kong* is reportedly playing somewhere in the world at all times, to this day.

The 1950s movie *Rebel Without a Cause* featured scenes of teenagers slashing tires. Actor-director Dennis Hopper, who was involved in the making of this film, recalls that after the picture's release, there were hundreds of tire slashings in places where such acts of vandalism had never happened before.[2]

Both Lenin and Stalin claimed that they could easily turn the world to communism if they controlled Hollywood. While that might be an exaggeration, there are some notable converts via the cinematic route. French actor Yves Montand has admitted that he never read a word of Karl Marx, but had been converted to Marxism by Sergei Eisenstein's *The Battleship Potemkin.*[3] That film was commissioned by the Soviet government and, as Malcolm Muggeridge has noted, was "part of the holy writ of all good Leftists"[4] during the 1930s. Goebbels praised *Potemkin* as a model for Nazi cinema.[5] It should be added that Mr. Montand has since severed his relations with the Left, but his experience is another testimony to the power of film.

I recall watching a crowd spilling out of *Close Encounters of the Third Kind* looking like they had been in some sort of revival meeting. Clearly the film had religious significance for many. And for a time after the trend-setting *Flashdance*, the good women of Beverly Hills *et environs* would appear in public wearing torn sweatshirts and other appurtenances of slob chic. Needless to say, they seldom looked as good as the svelte welder/dancer in the film. Marlon Brando's *The Wild One* caused the same sort of fashion breakthrough, with leather jackets becoming *de rigueur*.

It is safe to say that everyone who has regularly attended movies can testify to their power. Images, words, and music add up to a powerful combination, in a sense larger than life, and certified big magic indeed. David Puttnam, producer of *Chariots of Fire*, writes that "Far more than any other influence, more than school, more even than home—my attitudes, dreams, preconceptions and pre-conditions for life had been irreversibly shaped five and a half thousand miles away in a place called Hollywood."[6]

A BRIEF HISTORY OF CINEMA

Some observers have seen intimations of film in Plato's analogy of people in a cave unable to see those passing by, only their shadows, which the cave-dwellers take for the real thing. A closer model would be the attempts of ancient cultures to tell stories with pictures. Actually, the very first motion pictures did not attempt anything so grand as telling a story; one of the earliest sequences showed a man named Fred Ott sneezing. The year was 1889.[7]

There is a sense in which movies are the offspring not so much of drama or literature but of interest in mechanical and technological matters. Leonardo da Vinci's *camera obscura*, the still camera in an elementary stage, was another step toward the cinematic form, as was the "magic lantern" invented by Athanasius Kircher, a Catholic priest, in approximately 1650.[8] (Swedish film director Ingmar Bergman titled his recent autobiography *Lanterna Magica*.)

It is perhaps of some significance that other early precursors of film were toys such as persistence-of-vision gadgets. One of these was the zeotrope, a revolving drum with images that presented the illusion of motion. Film director Francis Ford Coppola (*Apocalypse Now*) named his now-defunct San Francisco operation American Zeotrope Studios. There is a sense in which "optical illusion" is still valid, because films are a series of stills which pass through the projector faster than the eye can detect the breaks. The end result appears to be continuous motion.

The major cinematic breakthroughs came in the mid-1800s: the development of still photography, the invention of celluloid roll film by George Eastman, and the kinetograph or cinematograph, an early motion picture camera largely developed (though not invented) in France by August and Louis Lumière, whose last name, ironically enough, means "light." The pair have been dubbed the "Light Brothers."

A development of great importance was the invention of film editing in 1903. Interestingly, before the advent of editing, films had been largely about "factual" subjects. However, after editing, which allowed for almost limitless alteration, they began to drift towards fantasy.[9]

France and England figured largely in early motion picture progress, and Nestor Almendros argues that France is the "home of film."[10] George Méliès made his famous film *A Trip to the Moon* in 1902. It was perhaps the first attempt at a science fiction picture. But right from the beginning, filmmakers were more fascinated with crime. Audiences went wild over Edwin Porter's *The Great Train Robbery*, though not all took up train robbing like Bill Miner.

No one was more obsessed with the pictures that moved—"flickers" they were sometimes called—than Americans. Early films were popular at church socials, and even replaced vaudeville during a performers' strike in 1902.[11] They were also a big hit in saloons, where they have since given way to "Monday Night Football" on big-screen television. Penny arcades and nickelodeons showed films accompanied by live musicians such as the one in *The Gray Fox*.

Although the French and English pioneered early film technology, it was in the United States where filmmakers were making what might be called quantum leaps. David Wark Griffith has been called the creative father of film. He developed the "mask," a shield placed over the lens to alter the shape of the screen image. A form of this is still used when the point of view (POV in screen jargon) is through a telescope or binoculars. Griffith also developed the "Iris effect" in which an adjustable aperture spreads or pinpoints light. Other Griffith innovations include the pan shot, in which the camera moves sideways, and the tracking shot, in which the camera moves closer to or away from the subject. The close-up and fade-out were also Griffith's ideas.

Griffith used these tricks in works such as the aforementioned *Birth of a Nation*, which some have called "the most important film ever made."[12] While that judgment is hardly shared by film *cognoscenti*, few would disagree that things were not the same after Griffith's major *opus*.

Without at this point getting into the argument whether the cinema is "art," it does have much in common with other forms. A movie can serve as a canvas for a director to make a personal statement. Like music, films have a kind of tonal structure, and, like literature, they tell stories and flesh out characters. However, unlike other art forms, films are expensive to produce.

Before Griffith came into his own, films, though popular, were considered a rather trivial form of entertainment, an extension of

Coney Island, and hence not worthy of major investments. Griffith broke the money barrier. His *Birth of a Nation* cost $125,000, less than the cost of one (Lite) beer television commercial in the 1980s, but a staggering amount of money at the time. In terms of 1980's dollars the film cost at least $50 million. The epic required six weeks of rehearsals and nine weeks of shooting, not to mention the thousands of men, women, and animals involved.

Many early American filmmaking efforts took place in the eastern part of the country, where Thomas Edison, a pioneer of cinematographic equipment, was suing independent producers for infringement of the patent on his kinetoscope, a peep-show kind of gadget that used a film loop. Edison formed a trust with companies that used his innovations, and there were raids, lawsuits, and even riots involving upstarts who used bootleg gear. These "pirates," as they were called, began to make films in Florida, Cuba, and California, which became the favorite site because of its ideal climate and topography. Though the Edison monopoly followed them there, they were ultimately unsuccessful and the trust was finally busted.

Cecil B. De Mille, while living in a barn at the corner of Vine and Selma in Hollywood, made *The Squaw Man*, starring Dustin Farnum (after whom actor Dustin Hoffman is named) for $15,000. The picture earned $225,000.[13] The year was 1913. By 1925 Hollywood was a veritable film factory, with the following companies churning out the footage: Paramount, United Artists, Columbia, Warner Brothers, Universal, Fox, and Metro-Goldwyn-Mayer.

The first press publicist employed by the film companies was lured away from the Barnum and Bailey circus. His name was Harry Reichenbach and his first assignment was *The Return of Tarzan*, which he promoted by renting a hotel across from the New York theatre where the picture opened, and ordering fifteen pounds of raw meat to his room. Upon delivery the waiter discovered a full-sized lion sitting on the table and shrieked in horror. As intended, the event made headlines.[14]

By 1940, Americans were streaming into theatres with such romantic names as the Bijou, Odeon, and Palace. Movies were the eleventh largest industry in the United States,[15] and they always had plenty of raw material to work with. Myriads of actors and actresses from all quarters came to the new boomtown and jammed the streets, even for jobs as extras. There were so many in the early days, in fact, that the Chamber of Commerce took out an advertisement that showed a crowded street scene in Hollywood and stated:

> Don't try to break into the movies in Hollywood until you have obtained *full, frank and dependable information* from the Hollywood Chamber of Commerce (Hollywood's Great Community Organization). It may save disappointments. Out of 100,000 persons who started at the bottom of the screen's ladder of fame only five reached the top.[16]

The names of the fortunate five were not mentioned, and it seems certain that many more than that had in fact "made it." But one thing was clear: the "flickers" had found a home.

Much was still going on, of course, in other parts of the world. For example, Russian filmmakers such as Eisenstein developed the montage sequence, a rapid series of images, sometimes superimposed or revolving around a central image. Nazi propagandist Leni Riefenstahl (*Triumph of the Will*) mastered the technique of putting cameras on moving tracks for her 1936 film *Olympia*, which many consider a great work, in spite of Riefenstahl's role as court hagiographer for Hitler. However, Hollywood was where the special effects breakthroughs took place, the birthplace of *Superman*. It was the movie mecca of the world, and, for the most part, remains so.

As long as movies were silent they would always be considered inferior to the live theatre. Some were prepared to live with the disparity. In 1925, D. W. Griffith stated "quite positively" that a century hence, "all thought of our so-called speaking pictures will have been abandoned."[17] He was off by ninety-eight years. Though *The Jazz Singer* of the mid-1920s was not technically the first "talkie," it was the first movie to integrate sound into the actual narrative of the film. From there it was upward and onward to full sound, which paved the way for headier fare such as *Citizen Kane*, a cinematic attack on media tycoon Randolph Hearst.

The period from the advent of the talkies until the dawn of television has been called film's great era of communication. Newsreels were shown before feature films, with this meager footage constituting a narrow window on the world for those not otherwise informed.

This is not to say that this was cinema's Golden Age, simply that it was the only game in town as far as moving, talking pictures were concerned.

Very early, movie magnates realized the power of their product. In 1930 the Association of Motion Picture Producers Inc. of California, along with the Motion Picture Association of America, adopted the Motion Picture Production Code. Its preamble stated:

> Motion picture producers recognize the high trust and confidence which have been placed in them by the people of the world and which have made motion pictures a universal form of entertainment.
>
> They recognize their responsibility to the public because of this trust and because entertainment and art are important influences in the life of a nation.
>
> Hence, though regarding motion pictures primarily as entertainment without any explicit purpose of teaching or propaganda, they know that the motion picture within its own field of entertainment may be directly responsible for spiritual or moral progress, for higher types of social life, and for much correct thinking.

The enforcing agency of the motion picture industry was the Hays Office, named after William H. Hays, who had been Postmaster General during the Harding administration, hence his nickname "General." He was also an elder in a Presbyterian church. Jack Vizzard, a former Jesuit and employee of the Hays Office, states that "the Code was an instrument designed to present reality on the screen not as it *was*, but as it *should be*."[18]

That the relatively young movie industry survived the Depression suggests that American audiences wanted neither reality as it was nor the way it should be. They wanted fantasy, they wanted escapism, and got plenty of it, at least what the General would allow. The Code lasted into the early 1960s and was eventually replaced by the present rating system. It can be argued that it has also been replaced by a different, unwritten code, which is more strictly enforced than the original. This theme will be dealt with in due course.

The former censor Jack Vizzard, while preferring the present setup, notes that "it behooves us not to confuse mature material with the effluvia of adolescence," and recalls that when the Code was finally eliminated, one jubilant producer exclaimed: "We've achieved the ultimate. At last we can say s---!"[19] Thus speaks a man of truly modest goals. It would be hard to consider such a person an artist.

THE AGE OF SHOW BUSINESS

> Hollywood is engaged in the mass production of prefabricated daydreams. It tries to adapt the American dream, that all men are created equal, to the view that all men's dreams should be made equal.
>
> (Hortense Powdermaker)[20]

Evidence suggests that the camera, not atomic energy, is the true defining force of the present age. The first eighty years of commercial cinema produced some twenty thousand films in the United States and Britain alone. If laid end to end, the footage for *all* films combined would doubtless be well on its way out of the solar system. This supply could only be in response to a great demand. Human beings, unlike animals, cannot live on bread alone. Movies meet some of their psychological or even spiritual needs, and are a difficult habit to break. Commercial filmmakers, like cigarette companies and distilleries, are basically catering to a habit.

The advent of the video cassette recorder (VCR) initially caused the moguls some alarm, but they have learned to love the device, which is responsible for over a billion dollars a year in rentals and has probably guaranteed their industry a bright future.[21] One consequence has been the decline in walk-in theatres, once huge and luxurious, but many of which are now little more than concrete bunkers in shopping center parking lots, and roughly the same size as the nickelodeons where the first crude "flickers" made their debut.

But the wild proliferation of film has had a far more serious result, what the French call a "cinematic culture," in which many people are unaware of almost everything that hasn't been the subject of a movie. Stephen Spielberg, the Pete Rose of the box office, is such a person. As Richard Grenier has observed, Spielberg shows little evidence of having read anything. But he is in the best Hollywood tradition. When Vivien Leigh, star of *Gone With The Wind,* heard a band strike up, "Dixie," she exclaimed, "Oh, they're playing that song from our picture."[22] There is much evidence that the United States, at present, leads the world in the advancement of cinematic culture.

The United States Congress has invited actresses Jessica Lange, Sissy Spacek, and Sally Field to testify on agricultural matters, based on their roles in, respectively, *Country, The River,* and *Places in the Heart.* Jane Fonda, who has used her movie fame to appoint herself Aerobics Instructor-in-Chief, has also made an appearance on The Hill. At least one university features a Barbara Streisand Chair in Women's Studies. One professor at Dartmouth College took his literature class to see *Broadcast News*, which, in spite of whatever merits it might have, is most definitely not a book. Perhaps someday George Lucas will be invited to lecture NASA on spacecraft design, or Richard Chamberlain (TV's "Doctor Kildare") will share his surgical expertise with the Harvard Medical School. The possibilities are endless. Unfortunately, dramatic talent is not fungible, and only in a film-drenched culture could actors be taken seriously simply for the roles they play.

Elia Kazan, one of the preeminent filmmakers of the 1950s and early 1960s (*On the Waterfront, Gentleman's Agreement, A Streetcar Named Desire, Viva Zapata, The Last Tycoon,* and many others), notes that film is now "the language of mankind." In sports, for instance, the director cuts to a close-up of the one who has been involved in a key play, or to the audience, to capture the emotion.[23] The same forces are in play with camera coverage of the news, and of Congress and Parliament.

Professor Neil Postman of New York University has authored a thoughtful book called *Amusing Ourselves to Death: Public Discourse in the Age of Show Business*,[24] and it seems hard to deny that he is right about the nature of our times. This is indeed the age of show business, and it seems certain that the show will go on. That is some cause for concern, for reasons outlined in the following chapter.

FIVE

THE LIMITATIONS OF FILM

The camera cannot catch reality any more than (and perhaps less than) the painter. Indeed, it was this very dilemma that enthralled the cubist painters . . . they wanted to paint not what they could see, but what they knew was there, lurking beneath the deceptive membrane of visibility.

(Virginia Stem Owens)[1]

GOD, RELIGIOUS FIGURES, RELIGIOUS EXPERIENCE

The eye is a glutton for frontiers, but, as Christians believe, reality does not begin and end with the visible. They ever must believe a lie, says Blake, who see with, not through the eye. In fact, for the Christian, ultimate reality lies in the transcendent, in what is *not* seen.[2] Unfortunately—or, perhaps, fortunately—film crews cannot enter those precincts.

God is invisible and cannot be shown on stage or sceen. Film characters and television preachers may talk about God, but one doesn't *see* God; one sees *them*. Hence, there is a sense in which God is *de facto* excluded from drama. In cinema, God can never be more than an out-of-scene character or perhaps a voice. And the Incarnation does not solve all the problems.

For example, it requires more than the usual suspension of disbelief to accept Max Von Sydow as Jesus Christ. With eyes bluer than Paul Newman's, Von Sydow looked more like a Scandinavian decathlete than a first-century Palestinian Jew. As Harry and Michael

Medved note in their book on Hollywood flops, there were more than a few doubting Thomases regarding the casting for this role. One critic wrote that the Swedish Von Sydow never varied his expression of mild suffering, "as though he had a pebble in his sandal."[3]

There is some consolation for the Christian, because films about the life of Mohammed have a bigger problem: Islamic law forbids any attempt to show a representation of their prophet. Even his shadow is out of bounds. With such fatal limitations, Moustapha Akkad's *Mohammed: Messenger of God* managed to lose some $30 million. Richard Grenier's 1983 novel *The Marrakesh One-Two* was a comic treatment of a movie about Mohammed, likley based on Akkad's efforts. In this tale, the filmmakers depended largely on reaction shots. Mohammed was reportedly a short man, but the filmmakers had people looking up at him, as though he were Kareem Abdul-Jabbar.

Spiritual experience is also a tall order for cinema. Such experience, although it has outward manifestations, is essentially internal, a matter of the heart. If done for purposes of exhibition, it is hypocrisy. Even religious acts such as fasting, for example, are not intended to be public demonstrations of piety, but, as Jesus said, to be practiced secretly, before God.[4] Faithful church attendance can be filmed, but does not make for exciting drama.

Orson Welles is reported to have said that the movies would never be able to show a man praying to his God. While attempts have been made, none of them "play." On film, prayer comes out as a soliloquy, which doesn't always work on the screen. Or, it looks as if the one in prayer is still half-asleep. As those who cruise the television channels and briefly linger on Christian stations know full well, the overall effect, though unintentional, tends toward the comic, or even self-parody. The same is true of the depiction of worship; it either renders the worshiper boring or slightly odd. Big screen or little screen, both tend to trivialize everything they touch.

Even the Billy Graham films obey the unwritten rules on religious experience. The executives of World Wide Pictures, a branch of the Billy Graham Evangelistic Association, are aware that the new Christian life of the convert is not dramatic. Accordingly, World Wide's movies concentrate on the pre-conversion life of the protagonist when, in the words of the old hymn, he was "sinking deep in sin." Once the protagonist becomes a Christian, the story is effectively over and does not become the subject of a sequel, since religious experience doesn't play.

Some might point to *Chariots of Fire* as an exception, and it does raise interesting questions. Under present conditions, what could be more of a non-issue than refraining from sports on Sunday? One would be hard-pressed to find many North American Christians who shared this conviction. Most believe that sports is not work on the sabbath, but a form of relaxation. Taken by itself, the question is about as exciting as watching paint dry. And in the case of Eric Liddell, it only works because it raises a dramatic question about the Olympics and forces him to make a decision. The audience wants to know: will Eric run or won't he?

On this point the filmmakers took considerable liberties. Liddell knew about the Sunday heats for months in advance, and trained accordingly. In the film, he is boarding the boat for the channel crossing when a newsboy calls out, "Eric, do you know your heat is on a Sunday?" The sprinter then looks as if he suddenly heard that his sister had fallen ill, or discovered that his wallet was missing. Similarly, the Jewish runner Harold Abrahams was not motivated by a resentment for anti-Semitism. Indeed, economist P. T. Bauer, a Hungarian of Jewish background who emigrated to England and attended Cambridge at the same time, says that anti-Semitism was not at all in evidence, and that the picture presented in *Chariots of Fire* is entirely false.[5]

Fortunately, Eric Liddell did get to read Scripture in this film, which portrays the "Flying Scotsman" accurately. This writer finds it difficult to think of another film character so motivated by religious conviction. Such characters are rare, but not entirely banished from the screen.

Missionaries make periodic appearances in film, but one suspects that their appeal to producers is more because they live in exotic foreign locations and work with exotic foreign people than anything else. And in these situations, the religious characters are often involved in overt acts that play better on the screen. Medical work, for example, not only involves action, but a good deal of crisis and emotion as well. But it is not, strictly speaking, religious experience.

This is not to say that the effective portrayal of religious experience is impossible, only that the medium does not naturally lend itself to such portrayals, and that it requires considerable skill to pull it off. Horton Foote (*Tender Mercies, The Trip to Bountiful*) is one of the few who are up to the task.

T. S. Eliot enjoyed Chesterton's Father Brown stories, which dealt effectively with religious experience, and even carried religious messages. But "when the same effect is aimed at by zealous persons of less talent than Mr. Chesterton," wrote Eliot, "the effect is negative."[6] One could say the same about Mr. Foote, as compared with many efforts at "religious" movies by zealous persons of less talent.

To compound the problem, religious hypocrisy *does* play well, because it involves the gap between the ideal and the actual, and shows religious characters *doing* things they have forbidden to others. *Elmer Gantry* would be a classic example.

But with true religious experience beyond the scope of the lens, and with certain types of characters only dramatically interesting when they do wrong, the cinema will be forever imbalanced on the subject of religion.

ART ON THE SCREEN

Artistic experience is likewise elusive. Moving pictures are supposed to *move,* and the screen cries out for *action.* A writer crashing away at a typewriter just doesn't make it. Neither does a sculptor chipping at a statue, or a painter dabbing at a canvas. The creative process is, like religious experience, internal and rather mysterious. This is one point on which prose literature is superior to film.

Consider this description from Malcolm Lowry's *Under the Volcano*: "High overhead sailed white sculpturings of clouds, like billowing concepts in the brain of Michelangelo."[7] The only way to capture this on the screen would be to have someone read it, and filmmakers do not like narration.

One effective treatment of artistic experience was the film *Amadeus.* The scenes in which Mozart dictates to Salieri are particularly effective. The film's score made manifest what was going on in the great composer's mind.

Another exception might be a film about the stage *(A Chorus Line, The Producers),* about television *(Tootsie),* or about film *(All That Jazz, Hooper).* Film is a house of mirrors, a medium absorbed with itself, and this is a subject that may be handled with expertise and enthusiasm. But it is the action and the subject, not the creative process itself, that are appealing. Generally speaking, the creative experience doesn't play on the screen.

THE LIFE OF THE MIND

When compared with the human mind, the most state-of-the-art technologies of film come off rather poorly. In fact, the comparison is quite ludicrous. The pictorial and imaginative powers of the mind are truly awesome. It is the mind that is engaged when one reads a novel. Something rather different happens with film.

Richard Brooks, director of *Sweet Bird of Youth* and *Lord Jim,* notes that, to comprehend the printed word, the language must first be translated by the brain. "Therefore, the *primary* reaction in reading a book or watching a stage play is an *intellectual* one." If everything else is right, he adds, an emotional response may follow. Movies, on the other hand, are the "exact opposite." They consist of "an arrangement of images," which take precedence over words. "Therefore, the primary reaction to a movie is *emotional,*" and if the images are effective, "then the audience may also achieve an *intellectual* response"[8] (original italics).

Then again, they may not; and if they do, the intellectual response may well be false, based as it is on a string of arbitrarily chosen images, with the musical score alternately highlighting or editorializing. Take *The Sound of Music,* for example. It presents Austria in the late 1930s as unified against a Nazi takeover, when, in fact, most of the population was vigorously pro-Nazi. Hitler simply marched in and took the place, without firing a shot, and the people stood up and cheered.

I take Brooks' statement as something of a confession. It is precisely this emotional primacy, part of the very nature of film, that gives the medium such potential for manipulation. Rare is the novel that can move the reader to tears, but quite often, there's not a dry eye in the theatre.

Literature can play to the vast powers of the mind. It can refer to other books or to history with equal ease. It can effectively allude to almost anything outside the scene. Film, however, can only refer to itself. Its range is limited by the camera's lens. And someone must decide where to point that lens.

The novel is well suited for the portrayal of thought. In Dostoyevsky's *Crime and Punishment,* Raskolnikov's ruminations as he prepares to kill his landlady are truly frightening. The reader gets right inside the student's hothouse mind. In a movie, the scene would not be much different from those in *Halloween* or *Dressed to Kill.*

Film, unfortunately, does not portray thought very well. The only practical way is with the voice-over, but this has its limitations. Alfred Hitchcock used it effectively in *Psycho* to reveal one character's conscience, but most filmmakers don't even make the attempt, likely because their characters lack consciences. Like cavemen, filmmakers and television news directors tell the story primarily with pictures. Words are a device to be used as sparingly as possible.

For example, director John Ford advised his students to direct as though their films were silent, to convey the story by action so that even a deaf person could follow.[9] The concept borders on mime. Elia Kazan was one of those students and contends that many of the best films "can be seen without dialogue and be perfectly understood." He adds that even the music is more important than anything in the movie "except the pictures."[10] It is also of some significance that Fellini dubs in all of his dialogue after the fact, and his movies are more "talky" than American pictures.

I recall hearing a review of *Rambo*, in which the critic said that he didn't mind a character talking with an accent, as long as it was a human accent. Jay Leno is not far off the mark when he says that Stallone and Schwarzenegger have opened the acting profession to those who couldn't get in when speech was a requirement. It was never a big requirement in any case.

Without the ability to portray thought, film finds it difficult to philosophize or handle complex issues. It is good at detail but weak on meaning. Screen characters often lack their full human dimensions, including and perhaps especially a conscience, let alone an intellect. With few exceptions, film is mostly mindless and often juvenile. Of far too many films one could say what Bernard Levin wrote of Franco Zeffirelli's version of *Othello*: "For the eye, too much; for the ear, not enough; for the mind, nothing at all."[11] I also recall a statement of

Walter Matthau that movies were made by morons, for morons. In similar style, H. L. Mencken remarked that movies were "entertainment for the moronic majority."[12]

This might be considered an overstatement by a man not noted for delicacy, but consider that in 1938, W. Somerset Maugham wrote that "intellectually, the theatre is thirty years behind the times, and the intelligent, owing to its poverty of thought, have largely ceased to frequent it."[13] If the works of Shaw, Coward, and O'Neill could be thus described, one wonders what Maugham would say about *Saturday Night Fever* or *Bright Lights Big City.* He might say that contemporary commercial films are effectively *anti*-intellectual, and for that judgment there is some evidence. In some cases, they do insult the audience, both with their puerile dialogue and their outrageous gaffes.

For example, in *Monsignor,* a criminal is on the phone in New York City making some sort of shady deal. He looks at his watch and makes a brief calculation as to what hour it might be on "Costa Rica time." As it happens, Costa Rica and New York are in the same time zone.

In the more recent *No Way Out,* the hero is trying to chase down a gift made to a government official. His strategy is to print out reams of files and search for the name. While he does this, someone else is exploring evidence that will expose *him.* Who will find the key clue first? Anyone in the hero's position of an intelligence officer would know that even a cheap personal computer could instantly find the name he needed, or else tell him that it wasn't there. But that would spoil the excitement.

In *Heaven's Gate,* a man trapped in a burning cabin scrawls an explanatory note, carefully signing his name so that there will be no doubt as to his identification. The filmmaker was apparently unaware that paper burns.

In *Shoot to Kill,* an FBI agent tracks a killer into Canada, where the local police become his collective factotum. Guns blazing, he tracks down his man. As a native of Canada, I can assure the reader that the situation is ludicrously impossible; American cops are not allowed to run wild north of the border.

Canada, in fact, barely exists in the movies. It is the "Great White North," or "The Northwest." In Hollywood films, the motto of the "Northwest" Mounties is, "We always get our man." Actually it is, *Maintien le Droit,* or, in the other official language, "Maintain the Right." And the Mounties do not always get their man.

Then there are the distorted national, ethnic, and professional stereotypes: the simple northern woodsman, the hypocritical preacher, the greasy Latin, the crazed general, the malevolent Oriental, and the prevailing incumbent, the fanatical Arab. There are enough outright stupidities and distortions of this type to fill many books. The title of one film, *Stop Making Sense,* seems a fitting summation for cinematic trends. Unfortunately, the power and presence of film makes such gaffes and stereotypes acceptable, or at least less noticeable.

A commercial filmed in Paris by veteran cinematographer and director Nestor Almendros involved a tourist running into a train station only to find he had lost his wallet. To elicit a romantic sort of ambience, the director included clouds of steam, in spite of the fact that French trains have been electric for years. When informed that there were no steam engines in France, the director insisted that no one would notice, and no one did, not even the French. The commercial was well-received and ran for months.

Almendros said that he learned two lessons. One, that Americans' "cinematic imaginations are formed by old Hollywood movies," and thus they were conditioned to expect steam. Second, and more important, "On the screen, the style of an image is more powerful than its history or its logic."[14] In other words, style over substance is an ironclad rule of the screen.

One of film's current heavyweights believes that films are inherently reductionist. Oliver Stone, who has written and directed movies as diverse as *Scarface, Midnight Express, Conan the Barbarian, Salvador,* and *Platoon,* states that

> movies are different from what you [as a journalist] do. You try to clarify. In the movies, I think we deal more with obfuscation. It's what I said earlier about films being subversive. You can be on the nose in print, but when you're on the nose in movies, it goes over the top. Movies always involve reduction.[15]

Reductionism is certainly different from what literature does. John Updike argues that prose is the true hero of the novel. Or, in the case of Tolstoy and Solzhenitsyn, the protagonist is truth. As Henry James noted:

> The deepest quality of a work of art will always be the quality of the mind of the producer. In proportion as that intelligence is fine, will the novel, the picture, the statue partake of the substance of beauty and truth.[16]

That is not quite the case in the vast majority of films. Intelligence goes begging. Images, bigger than life, carry the day. A flood of visual delights drowns thought; style swallows substance. The stars have it.

At this point one might try a brief test: how many speeches from films had anything profound to say? How many did one find intellectually challenging? How many can one even remember? Did any of them, as Ben Stein says in *The View From Sunset Boulevard,* challenge the assumption that the unexamined life is the only one worth living?[17] Or was it all standard boilerplate and biodegradable pap?

One script that stands out in this writer's memory was that of *Network,* a movie in which characters actually said words like "untenable" and "wanton fiscal affront." Film is the medium for the Century of the Common Man, and a commercial film is supposed to be for this elusive Everyman. The use of words Everyman might not understand is cinematic heresay. *Network* not only broke this rule, but its characters actually made reference to historical figures such as Moses, Savonarola and Che Guevara. In particular, I remember the speeches of Peter Finch as Howard Beal, the mad prophet of the airwaves. I could probably recite his eloquent denunciations of television, with which I substantially agree. The writer was the late Paddy Chayevsky, also responsible for *Marty,* a most touching film. There are not many like him, and if someone else had presented the project, it would likely have been turned down.

GOODNESS ON THE SCREEN

It is hard to deny that goodness can be effectively portrayed on the printed page. C. S. Lewis was attracted to works such as George MacDonald's *Sir Gibbie,* even though they were not of the first rank in literary quality, because he found goodness in them. In prose, "good" characters come alive. But this is not the case with cinema. Beyond its troubles with religious, intellectual, and artistic experience, the cinema also has a hard time with simple goodness, which, for some strange reason, does not translate well to the screen.

Simone Weil noted that there was nothing so beautiful or wonderful, or so full of perpetual ecstasy as the good. Conversely, she saw that evil was dreary and boring. However, Weil noted that in worlds of fantasy such as the cinema, it was the other way around. In such forums, "fictional good is boring and flat," she wrote, "while fictional evil is varied and intriguing, attractive, profound, and full of charm."[18]

A "good" character in a dramatic film will often come off as a busybody, or phony, perhaps boring, and often naive. The kind, good-hearted Melanie, for example, from *Gone With the Wind,* is a pillar of drabness next to the dashing Scarlett O'Hara, whose duplicity and machinations are highly dramatic. One can easily predict how Melanie will behave, but what will that impetuous vixen Scarlett be up to next? One could make the same comparison between the stately and platitudinous Ashley Wilkes and the, as Scarlett called him, "black-hearted varmint" Rhett Butler, a character of far greater interest.

To be sure, this is a rather old example, but one with which most filmgoers will likely be familiar. Unfortunately, one gets the feeling that "good" characters, even in minor roles, have been blacklisted from films since the 1960s. It was about this time that the cult of the anti-hero began. *The French Connection* might be an example because in the film even the cops have all kinds of kinky habits. It is *film noir* in a moral sense.

There are, of course, exceptions. A favorite of mine is *Goodbye Mr. Chips,* based on the novel by James Hilton. The story concerns the life of a teacher named Mr. Chipping, a character based largely on Hilton's father. The first film version appeared in 1939 starring Robert Donat, whose Mr. Chips beat out Clark Gable's Rhett Butler for the Oscar. Peter O'Toole played the lead in a 1960s semi-musical version with Petula Clarke in a supporting role. As a highly biographical and episodic tale, the story is not dramatically strong. I believe it is the essential goodness of the central character, and the way that goodness is expressed, that carries the day. Chips is loving, but not soft; wise, but not arrogant; old-fashioned, but always willing to listen and to change if he is wrong. His life combines victory and tragedy and evokes true pathos, not cheap sentimentality. And Chips is also a highly symbolic character, a reminder of a gentler, nobler time, a permanent fixture in a changing world. In that sense, the film is profoundly conservative. Many viewers recognized a Mr. Chips character from their own experience. Critic John Simon, who praises few films, admitted that the movie (O'Toole's version) moved him to tears.[19]

Horton Foote's *Trip To Bountiful* abounded in characters who were kind, honest, and polite. Moreover, some of them have little plot value and spend time talking about their favorite birds. Another mentions how much she loves her husband. And yet, they are all compelling. The audience can say with some certainty that they know people like that. Foote's earlier *Tender Mercies* also managed to capture goodness, that fugitive from the silver screen.

SUMMARY

Goodness, religious experience, the creative process, and intellectual life constitute a considerable part of human experience. Film's inability to portray them effectively means that it is a severely limited medium indeed. Perhaps one reason this is seldom noticed is that film does a powerful job with those facets of life for which it is eminently suitable. To those we now turn.

SIX

WHAT FILM DOES WELL

THE TECHNICAL DIMENSION

In a technical sense, the reductionism of film is an advantage because it strips narrative to the bare essentials: action and dialogue. All descriptions are superfluous, and the subtleties and nuances for which the novelist strives may be accomplished with a few establishing shots, say, of New York City, the Pacific Ocean, the Himalayas, a ramshackle New Orleans flat, an aircraft carrier. The camera does its job well, and film is strong at conveying a sense of place. For that alone, not much suspension of disbelief is required.

Brian de Palma's *The Untouchables* was in my opinion a weak and occasionally ridiculous film, but its re-creation of the Chicago of old was most convincing. Tougher tasks have been accomplished. Films such as *2001: A Space Odyssey* and *Outland* catapult one into space, while *Farenheit 451*, based on Ray Bradbury's fine novel, created a bleak, futuristic world all its own. That particular film also did a good job with the written and spoken word.

Others succeed at conveying sheer distance, which only the rare novel, such as Tolstoy's *War and Peace*, manages to pull off. Simply bouncing people around the globe doesn't get it done. Within the inherent limitations of the screen, film does quite well with space. *Never Cry Wolf*, for example, captures the vast reaches of the Arctic, but also moves in for "macro" close-ups. The screen handles the switch from the general to the specific with ease.

"Moving" pictures are most suited to action, much more so than the stage. In fact, if the characters and story fail to convey sufficient action, it is the audience that will move—out the door. But the filmmaker has everything on his side. He can strap a camera to a train or an F-14. As a glance at *Top Gun* will verify, the results are spectacular. He can speed the action up, a technique often used in fight scenes, or slow it down. As one reviewer remarked, *Chariots of Fire* pretty much exhausted the ways of showing people running.

Time differences do not present the filmmaker with great difficulties. He can cut to different story lines involved in his plot and subplot, even if these are years or even centuries apart. These cuts can be as brief as several seconds, which would simply not work well on the stage or in a novel. For example, *The Godfather* intercuts a mobster's recitation of baptismal vows with quick, violent vignettes of his underlings, acting on his orders, breaking virtually all of those vows. It is a powerful sequence. *Cabaret* used similar techniques. *Breaker Morant* made effective use of flashback in its portrayal of a court case.

Film time is not the same as real time, or even stage time. A film can stretch a dramatic moment much longer than it would actually require. This is the case with Eisenstein's famous sequence of the Odessa steps, an event which never happened. But film time can also be faster than real time, and make its leaps with the greatest of ease.

The documentary film is probably superior to print in its ability to convey a speech, interview, or conversation. For this specific purpose, film is probably the most authentic medium, provided the material comes in its context, without editorial cuts. It is the closest thing to an exact replica. Gestures, facial expressions, changes in tone, hesitations, body language—all the nonverbal communication—is immediately evident on the screen but sometimes missing from the page. Former State Department official Richard Perle told Congress that one Soviet official, when he insistd that the American SDI ("Star Wars," in its media pejorative, another confirmation of cinematic culture) program be confined to the laboratory, bracketed his hands in the form of a box. This, said Perle, would not be evident in the transcript, though it indicated the Soviet position as much as anything the official said.

It should be added that a great deal depends on how the interview or speech is filmed, because camera angles make a great difference. One can always tell who the villains are on "60 Minutes" because they are invariably shown in extreme close-up, which makes almost anyone seem unsavory, especially under the hot lights. And of course the interviews are highly edited.

To understand the power of an Adolf Hitler, it helps to see and hear his speeches on film rather than simply read them. With the maniac glare, gesticulations, and "special effects" of a live audience and the trappings of *son et lumière*, the aura of evil around this man becomes suddenly palpable, in a way that the page cannot convey.

And while the cinematic medium is weak at portraying thought, it is good at getting inside people's fears. Dream sequences and reveries have long been favorite techniques and are generally effective. *I Never Promised You a Rose Garden* would be one example. On the screen it is a short jump from the real to the unreal. Hence the medium is also comfortable with fantasy, everything from Disney's *Fantasia* to *The Princess Bride*. One notes that animation is now combined with conventional films, as in *Who Framed Roger Rabbit?*

As Richard Barsan concludes, "In short, the motion picture artist is a magician in almost complete control of some of the artistic problems which have confronted other artists for centuries."[1] He has at his command what Evelyn Waugh called the "vast enchanted toyshop" of the studio,[2] and everything the investors' millions can provide. He can hire the best talent in the world and populate the set with thousands of extras and animals.

This is not to imply that the techniques outlined above are beyond the reach of other mediums, nor that they are always used honestly. It is simply a brief outline of what film happens to do well, subject to human limitations and imperfections.

THE QUESTION OF CONTENT

While film has a difficult time with serious ideas, it takes readily to lighter, trivial subjects. Generally speaking, cinema is comfortable with the superficial (the James Bond films), the puerile (*Porky's, Animal House*[3]), the talky comedy (*Tootsie*), and, of course, flat-out stupidity and slapstick such as *The Jerk*, an astonishingly unfunny film.

Film excels at amusement, a word which is seldom analyzed. To "muse" is to think or ponder. The prefix *a* changes the meaning entirely, as in "theist" and "atheist." To be *a*mused is therefore not to think, or to be prevented from thinking. This is what film does best in a host of ways. As Bernard Shaw noted, "The cinema keeps its victim fascinated as by a serpent's eye."[4] This seems to be what audiences want, to forget their troubles; and in most cases, who can blame them?

When the commercial cinema ventures into slightly deeper waters, it tends to stick to the well-marked trade routes. Crime, for example, is probably the most enduring theme of the cinema. Crime always plays well, perhaps because it gives the audience the sense of being a witness, of possessing inside information, or even of being an accomplice. Sometimes it seems that producers make a special effort to inject crime into a story. Somerset Maugham's *Christmas Holiday*, for example, is a simple story about an English schoolboy in Paris, but its film version involves an American pilot and an escaped convict. Crime sets up the most commom and overt good-versus-evil conflict, allows for the triumph of the good, and makes for a tight resolution, with no loose ends. The Good Guys win, the Bad Guys lose. Clean up the bodies and on to the sequel.

Accordingly, policemen, detectives, and private investigators have been standard film protagonists, serving as either heroes or as a *deus ex machina*.[5] The current and longest running incumbent is Clint Eastwood, who understands the widespread perception that, in real life, criminals get away with murder. In fact, in Mr. Eastwood's home state of California, the perception is entirely accurate. For example, in 1984, one Bernard Lee Hamilton stabbed, mutilated, and decapitated a San Diego woman. Though a jury found him guilty and ruled that he should be executed, a higher court overturned his death sentence a year later. Justice Otto Kaus wrote in a majority opinion that the murder could have been accidental or at least unintentional.[6] Robespierre would doubtless take heart at the decision. His intention was to purify society.

Mr. Eastwood knows how outraged people are by such travesties of justice. Hence, in Dirty Harry films, murderers do not escape with impunity, and audiences approve.

The screen also does a marvelous job with war. Battle scenes always play well, the bigger and noisier the better. In *Blazing Saddles*, a semi-retired gunfighter called the Waco Kid laments that, in his day, he "killed more people than Cecil B. De Mille," but Akira Kurosawa's

Ran could give the old magnate a run for his money. Many were slain by fire and sword in that magnificent picture.

War plays on the screen because it follows the rules of drama and includes the audience. While Clint Eastwood knows that audiences want to see justice done, Sylvester Stallone and Chuck Norris understand that people want an opportunity to cheer. They give it to them, in the most corny and lame-brained packages, but with plenty of bang for the buck. The folks love it. It might also be noted that when crowds cheered the battle scenes in *Platoon*, which they did with great enthusiasm, they were not approving the politics of Oliver Stone but simply applauding the action. Orwell observed that one may dislike tin soldiers, but tin pacifists don't make the grade.

While film's efforts at the transcendent and supernatural fail with the good, they are often a positive triumph with evil. The occult, the irrational, the evil all seem to come naturally to the cinema. Film easily evokes the reality of evil. The power of a film like *The Exorcist* is likely due to the fact that it raised the question of demonic possession, but failed to explain it away scientifically or psychologically. According to some reviews, there wasn't a dry seat in the house. Producers know that audiences will not tolerate boredom but don't mind being frightened. Accordingly, the Devil and his minions get frequent casting calls, from *Macumba Love* to *Angel Heart*.

Characters under the influence of goodness tend to be self-controlled, normal, and boring, while characters under the influence of evil are out of control, abnormal, and interesting. They perform acts that are cinematically exciting, and the wilder they are, the more the overweening sense of evil is magnified. The Biblical demoniac who lived among the tombs is a more compelling character for cinema than Nicodemus, a well-meaning but rather dense fellow.

And if they don't mind being frightened, on occasion audiences don't mind being sickened or outraged; just don't leave them indifferent. The commercial cinema has always showed a fondness for guts and gore, but lately it has become a staple. Witness the meal of "chilled monkey brains" in *The Temple of Doom*, along with the parade of slasher movies such as *Friday the 13th*. The Monty Python troupe has often spoofed this tendency. They show a victorian tea party, as filmed by Sam Peckinpah, noted for violent westerns. The proceedings turn into a bloodbath. In another show, a Python reviewer (Eric Idle) states that next week we'll be seeing John Wayne's latest film: "Buckets of Blood Pouring out of People's Heads." It's a clever joke, but since *Bonnie and Clyde*, this material tends to satirize itself.

In its quest for the visually interesting, film tends to go for the lowest common denominator. What Malcolm Muggeridge said about education could also apply to the cinema. Untold millions are spent on films, as they are on schools, but what do we often get from this orgy of spending? "The resort of any old slobbering debauchee anywhere in the world at any time—Dope and Bed."[7] As even the most casual observer can testify, the cinema is quite good at portraying sex, particularly when the liaison is illicit. Orson Welles is also reported to have said that the movies would never be able to show a man making love to his wife. It is usually someone else's wife, or husband. The medium excels at fondling its audience. Sex, not occultism or horror, is the mysticism of the screen. And it is guaranteed to affect every viewer in the audience.

Film critic Pauline Kael (after whom a villain in the film *Willow* is named) titled one of her books *Kiss Kiss Bang Bang*. She explained that she saw those words on an Italian movie poster and considered them "perhaps the briefest statement imaginable of the basic appeal of the movies." She added that "this appeal is what attracts us, and ultimately what makes us despair when we begin to understand how seldom movies are more than this."[8] Anthropologist Hortense Powdermaker noted that South Sea islanders who had been exposed to the movies put them in two categories: kiss-kiss, and bang-bang.[9]

One typical movie gambit is to make a pretense of condemning something, say, the lust and sadism of the Roman Coliseum, while simultaneously placing the audience in the position of the original spectators. *Star 80* purported to be a serious statement of the perils of the porn trade, but took great care to serve up a generous helping of flesh. The one virtue of real pornography is that, unlike *Star 80*, it does not pretend to be anything else.

Simone Weil had it right; in the world of fantasy, goodness is dull and flat, but evil is intriguing and full of charm. Nothing seems to verify Weil's statement more than film. *Dirty Dancing* pulled in the crowds, but who would pay to see a picture called *Wholesome Dancing* or *Normal Times at Ridgemont High*?

In real life, a drunk is a pathetic and sometimes dangerous

creature, but on the screen he or she most often emerges as a harmless clown. In like manner, there is scarcely a screen prostitute who is not a reservoir of folk wisdom. Tavern brawls are ugly, hateful affairs, but on film they seem like great fun.

Nestor Almendros notes that "one of the dangers of film is precisely its ease. Everything tends to seem prettier through the lens."[10] Why this should be so is not readily apparent, but it seems to be bound up in the nature of things that film is best at showing the downside of life. Coupled with its relative impotence to convey goodness, a rather skewed picture is certain to emerge.

SEVEN

BASIC QUESTIONS ABOUT MOVIES

The profit motive is the final arbiter in Hollywood, the ultimate and unanswered determinant of all behavior.

(John Gunther)[1]

WHY ARE MOVIES MADE?

The normal response to this question might be similar to the reasons for a novel or even a nonfiction book. (Why not "fact" and "nonfact" books?) Some individual, possibly talented, probably misguided, begins with an artistic vision, or wants to make a "statement," tell a story, or criticize some perceived injustice. He carries the artist's load, that great shapeless chunk of experience, and works on it long and hard, until it acquires definition. Or perhaps she or he is simply taken with the technique of the craft. She can't explain it, but simply "has to" write.

With film, such romantic considerations are secondary, and in most cases don't apply at all. I recall asking a producer why one aggressively stupid film, the name of which now escapes me, got made in the first place. He replied without hesitation that films are made for one reason: there is money to make them. Nothing in my experience since that time has caused me to doubt this statement in the slightest. In the beginning there is money, or there is no film. First comes the deal: terms are fixed, stars signed; the movie comes later and is in some cases almost an afterthought. But money rules. You don't "self-publish" *Raiders of the Lost Ark* and screen it for your friends and relatives.

The money rule applies whether the film is a commercial thriller for theatrical release, a kung-fu flick for foreign markets, *Teenagers in Heat* for the spring break crowd, or *The Life and Times of Billy Sunday*, starring Pat Boone and Amy Grant and pitched to the religious market. Somebody must pay.

Total costs for the average commercial film approach $20 million, a 400 percent increase since 1977. In the late 1940s, studio executives used to boast that every picture was a success, that they all made money,[2] but that is no longer the case and was probably never true in the first place. Gone are the days when audiences would shell out money for anything; there is simply too much choice in the field of entertainment for customers to subsidize hokum like *Howard the Duck* or *1941*.

Michael Cimino's gargantuan epic *Heaven's Gate* practically bankrupted one studio, and the makers of *Ishtar* squandered some $40 million, mostly on the expense of shipping crews to exotic North African locations. Actually, most of it could have been shot in the desert near Yuma, Arizona. That might have saved the budget, but not the film, a gobbling, squawking turkey if there ever was one. In film, you don't always get what you pay for, and this dictum applies to both producers and consumers.

It is possible to beat the system. Robert Townsend is reported to have made *Hollywood Shuffle* for about $100,000—still not exactly pocket change—most of which he borrowed on credit cards. Though this film has some hilarious vignettes, I suspect that it was the budget as much as the content of the movie that garnered the glowing reviews. Nevertheless, Townsend probably deserves an award for sheer willpower, an indispensable quality for a filmmaker.

Films are made because there is money to make them, and because they are intended to make money. Indeed, they must if the enterprise is to carry on. The true code of this world works this way: a "good" film is one that returns a profit; a "bad" film is one that does not. When producers refer to their wares, the term is "product." When a film's shoot has ended, the movie is "in the can," in the same sense that Alpo dog food or Ragu sauce are "in the can." On Oscar night, people get awards for "service to the industry," with "industry" being the operative word. As Hortense Powdermaker observed, "In Hollywood, money is always more important than man."[3] One can make a case that it is also more important than ideology.

For example, John Gunther's observation that bitterly opposed political factions buried the hatchet to work on lucrative projects was made at a time of vicious strife. More recently, striking screenwriters did not picket the Academy Awards broadcast because, in the words of Guild president George Kirgo, "that ceremony honors the entire industry."[4] Thus, thesis and antithesis in some cases join to form a new synthesis, for the benefit of all.

I am not saying, I should hasten to add, that the commercial cinema is to be judged negatively simply because it *is* a business, which exists, like all others, to make a buck. The success of the movie business simply reflects the regular, uncoerced decision of many people to see movies, just as they do sporting events. If people would pay five dollars to watch philosophers philosophize or editors edit, then they too could demand top dollar.

Unlike Christian writers such as Jacques Ellul and Tony Campolo, I don't believe that money is evil in itself. (Strange that, believing this, these people don't give their books or videos away free of charge.) I am an opponent of government encroachment on private life, and am particularly opposed to subsidized "art." However, I wish to emphasize the commercial dimension of cinema because, ultimately, film is a consumer issue.

Hollywood is a business community, not an artistic colony. Similarly, the Cannes Film Festival has a lot of glitter but is basically a place where deals are made, primarily for foreign distribution rights. Mel Brooks made the point in his remarkably unfunny *Space Balls*, in which the dolls, T-shirts, and other assorted junk based on the movie are ready for the shelves before the tale ends. "Merchandising!" says Brooks; that is what it is all about. He is right.

Films are the primary merchandise, but there is much more. As it happened, a package of cheese I purchased yesterday included colorful stickers based on the new George Lucas movie *Willow*, which a local reviewer took great delight in panning this morning. Without any doubt, *Willow* dolls, comics, and posters are on the way to replace the cuddly Ewoks and "E.T." toys of years past. Lucas, a capable filmmaker, has taken much criticism for hucksterism, some of it doubtless deserved. But he is far from alone. Hamburger stands now flog mugs plastered with cartoon figures from *Who Framed Roger Rabbit?*

A number of "placement firms" specialize in getting products into the movies. Nabisco paid $100,000 to have its Baby Ruth candy bar shown in *The Goonies*. Stephen Spielberg asked the makers of M&Ms for permission to use their product in *E.T.*, but was turned down. Spielberg then turned to another company, whose sales increased some 65 percent after their candy got screen exposure.[5] Films are also expected to promote singers, sell records, and even sell a lifestyle.

Religious films, such as those produced by the Billy Graham organization, are not entirely exempt from the merchandising game. While their producers consider the films a part of their ministry, they are sometimes released in standard theatres and one must pay to get in. The pictures do make money, sometimes quite a lot. Similarly, the offerings of Gospel Films are surely not considered "commercial," but part of their evangelistic outreach program. There is, nevertheless, a charge to rent them. Films made by other religious organizations are sometimes used to sell such materials as books and Bible study courses. As with religious publishing, there is a tension between ministry and business. In some cases, the enterprise is considered a ministry when it is time to pay the help, and the scale is a fraction of the going rate. But when the customer wants the product, it is all business.

To again allude to Irving Berlin, there's no *business* like show *business*. Aside from the joys of the craft, the plaudits, the awards, etc., there are certain advantages for the film impresario. Department store chains such as K-Mart and Sears are in the habit of refunding money for goods which are defective or even unsatisfactory to the buyer. But neither producers nor theatres return money to dissatisfied patrons. You pay your money, you take your chances. Not so in other industries. The manufacturer of a defective toaster will be sued if the product zaps children with electricity when they pop in an English muffin. An unsafe car may cost a manufacturer millions in liability claims. But unless he slanders someone or defrauds his investors or workers, a producer is pretty much in the clear with consumers. Even if the picture causes nausea and vomiting—by no means an impossibility—there is little recourse for the victim.

Some years ago it emerged that Alex Haley's *Roots* had lifted sections from a book called *The African*, written, ironically enough, by a white author, who sued for plagiarism. The matter was settled out of court and received little play in the media. Presidential aspirant Joseph Biden spoiled his chances by adopting, almost verbatim, a speech by British Socialist Neil Kinnock. The picture is somewhat different in the film business.

No author openly rewrites the novel of another, using the same title, no less, but films are remade all the time. One can lift entire scenes from others' works, but in film this is called "offering tribute," or "paying homage," to another artist. Entire film stories seem to be fair game. *The Big Chill* was a blatant rip-off of John Sayles' *Return of the Seacaucus Seven*. There were bits and pieces of *Network, Roller Ball* and *Logan's Run* in *Running Man*, with Arnold Schwarzenegger. Clearly, the standards are lower; you can get away with more in film.

And in what other industry can you demand millions of dollars for the television rights to your annual awards banquet? The prizes handed out at this ceremony also boost the value of the product. A Best Picture Oscar can increase the gross earnings of a film by $10 million dollars.[6] Little wonder that so many want to "get into the act."

WHO GOES TO THE MOVIES?

Filmmakers are in the business of satisfying their patrons, and hope to induce them to see the product more than once. Teenagers are practically the only group that will do this, and Hollywood perceives its major audience in the fourteen- to twenty-year-old group.

Thomas Pollock of Universal Pictures confirms that for the last decade, the philosophy of most studios was "to make movies for people between the ages of 15 and 30."[7]

Every year since 1969, the Motion Picture Association of America, the group that rates films, has sponsored an audience survey by the Opinion Research Corporation. The report for 1984 found that people over sixty comprised only 3 percent of movie audiences. Response in the fifties and forties range was similarly low. The 30-39 bracket made up 18 percent, 5 percent more than those in their twenties. But the 16-20 group formed a solid 23 percent of the audience.

The most recent survey shows that teenagers have dropped from

32 percent to 25, and also shows an increase in ticket purchases in the above-forty bracket. Though there may be a trend toward older audiences, Thomas Pollock adds that the percentage of teenagers seeing movies is as high as ever, but there are presently fewer teenagers and more people over forty.[8]

There is some justification for saying that, with few exceptions, American commercial cinema is an adolescent medium. In the world of entertainment, and even popular journalism, "adult" is usually a synonym for adolescent.

HOW FILMS ARE MADE

Assuming there is money to make a film, some property must be acquired. This may involve the purchase of film rights for a novel, biography, or nonfiction book. Or, it may be simply a concept pitched verbally by a screenwriter or producer. (Producers have been known to refer to a completed but unpurchased screenplay as a "concept.") The concept may be as threadbare as some new special effect or gadget, around which the film will be centered. *Tron*, for example, used computer graphics. It may even be an animal, such as Rin-Tin-Tin, who earned millions for his handlers.

One suspects that *Jaws* was partly motivated by the availability of a mechanical shark. I recall a television interview with Paul Newman in which he was asked to comment on the state of his profession. He replied that it was hard to be proud of a trade in which the biggest attractions were two robots and a shark. He does have a point.

In some cases, a prominent actor is contractually obliged to act in a film as the result of a previous deal, and one will be written as a "vehicle" for him, or even for a fictitious dramatic character. One sometimes sees in credits that the story is "based on characters created by" someone.

Some observers wonder why Hollywood bothers to purchase rights at all, since the final product is so often different from the book. Richard Grenier sees strong parallels between *Ishtar* and his 1983 novel *The Marrakesh One-Two*. However, Grenier considers the movie so terrible that he doesn't know whether to call his lawyer or take the Fifth Amendment.

Not all properties purchased make it to the screen. *The Spike*, a best-selling novel by Arnaud de Borchgrave and Robert Moss, was once ready to go, with Christopher Walken and James Mason in lead roles. But then problems arose, not least among them the death of James Mason. A thousand things can go wrong, and Murphy's Law (whatever can go wrong will go wrong) applies in Hollywood as in no other place.

It may sober some who aspire to the trade that a single studio, Fox, receives approximately ten thousand screenplays, books, treatments, or verbal pitches every year. Of these, less than one hundred are put into development and only twelve movies actually made.[9] The total number of ideas or properties pitched in a given year is doubtless well into six figures. In Hollywood, everyone's mind swarms with ideas for movies.

Critic Roger Ebert, who also writes for the screen, defines a sequel as a "filmed deal."[10] But there is a sense in which all movies are filmed deals, because many deals must be made before anything hits the screen.

After the property is purchased, squads of studio lawyers leap into action documenting the fine print of the deal and checking out the property to see if there are possibilities of plagiarism or libel. Practically all successful films attract a plagiarism suit. The descendants of Bonny Parker and Clyde Barrow sued Warner Brothers on the grounds that the film *Bonnie and Clyde* slandered their ancestors.[11]

Assuming the purchased property is "a go," the producer will then hire a director and screenwriter. These are not the only people he hires, of course, but they are the most important. The director often plays a major role in casting. The writer will start with a "treatment," a prose description of the major characters and what will happen in the story. Following the treatment, there will be at least three drafts of the screenplay by the original writer. Several other writers may be hired to rewrite or polish the screenplay. Scenes may be rewritten or added on location.

The film is never shot in the order found in the story. To save money, all the shots at a particular location are done at one stretch, whether they occur at the outset of the film or the end. This means that an actress may be playing a love scene at 10 o'clock, then, five minutes later, shrieking at her brother-in-law. One morning may transform her from a blossoming *ingenue* to a burnt-out slut.

Location shooting, it should be noted, is hard work for everyone involved. Shooting often begins at the crack of dawn. At the end of the day, usually at least twelve hours long, actors often tumble exhausted into their Winnebagoes or hotel rooms, but still must learn their lines for tomorrow. The director has a shooting schedule, and if he falls behind or goes over budget, he can be fired. Then there are the unions to deal with. The whole operation is in every sense a "production," and to pull it off at all is something of an accomplishment.

The films of Woody Allen and Clint Eastwood are always completed on time, and always come in under budget, to the unalloyed delight of producers and investors. That is one reason why these men get to make movies. Whatever one thinks of their films, they know what they are doing. This quality is usually called professionalism.

Once the shoot is complete and the film in the can, post-production work begins. The editor who cuts the film enjoys a great deal of power, and often has enough varied footage to make the story walk on all fours. A great deal of squabbling goes on as to who approves the "final cut." An actor who believes she turned in a sterling performance may find her work, in an often-used phrase, "on the cutting room floor." Sound effects must also be dubbed in and the musical score, titles, and credits added. This done, the whole thing is "mixed" and the final print readied. The producer now has a "product," but the battle is not yet over.

A new film may be subjected to test screenings. A sound editor friend informs me that an audience from Beverly Hills High School recently hooted some lame comedy right off the screen. If a test screening is unfavorable, the movie may be recut. At the first screening of Bill Cosby's *Leonard Part 6*, nobody laughed and, worse, nobody clapped when the star appeared. It was then cut a second time.[12]

A film that does not pass muster at a test screening may also be scrapped. Just as there are rooms full of screenplays which have been purchased but never produced, there are vaults of films which have been produced but never released. Michael Cimino's *Heaven's Gate*, one of the most expensive properties in film history, was never given a general release. At one point, studio executives suggested that Cimino's footage be chopped up and sold as picture postcards![13] Sometimes, however, movies rise from the dead.

Heaven's Gate is currently offered in a video format for some

$60.00, remarkable in that, as Jay Leno has noted, they couldn't get anyone to see it for five dollars. The 1982 low-budget *Gypsy Angels* featured Peter Lawford and Carol Wayne, but failed to be released. Why would such a picture be sent forth to market six years later, as is rumored to be the case? It turns out that the film includes some risque scenes involving Vanna White of television's "Wheel of Fortune." Apparently she is enough of an item that the film's major backer, Jack Bicknell of the Pizza Hut chain, believes it can make some money.[14]

If a test screeening is favorable, it may affect the release date or the advertising budget. Certain changes may have to be made to affect the picture's rating. Teenagers are the prime audience and flee from "G"-rated fare like vampires from a cross. Thus, producers may want to work in some four-letter words, sexual innuendoes, or acts of violence to avoid the "G" kiss of death. Other films must be altered if producers hope to avoid an "X" rating, since audiences avoid such pictures. *Last Tango in Paris*, with Marlon Brando, was the last "X"-rated movie to be produced by a major studio, though others come close to earning the classification. Filmmakers may want to change an "R" rating to "PG," if they think it will help at the box office.

Sometimes a test screening will be for the purpose of selling or defending a picture to a certain segment of the audience. Studios hired consultants to pitch *Chariots of Fire* to a perceived religious market. That film was eventually co-distributed through World Wide Pictures. Disney did the same for *Something Wicked This Way Comes*, but with less success, even though they brought in evangelist Rex Humbard and former *Christianity Today* editor Harold Lindsell, and even gospel singer Doug Oldham. The result was part salesmanship, part church service, and part gospel concert.[15]

Some attempt was made to peddle Clint Eastwood's *Pale Rider* to the church market. (The protagonist in that film, played by Eastwood, was an enigmatic character called "Preacher.") The producers of the embattled *The Last Temptation of Christ* hired Tim Penland, a Christian consultant who has made Roy Rogers movies, to ease religious objections about that picture.[16] Penland, however, has since quit, and began protesting the film himself.

If the product is still a go, it faces the final tests of the critics and the box office. Only then can it be determined what the "bottom line" will be, whether the film is "good" or "bad" by Hollywood standards.

The entire process from start to finish can take years and involve hundreds of people. This raises an important but neglected question that forms the subject of the next section.

WHO IS THE AUTHOR OF A FILM?

The novel is a writer's medium. The individual wordsmith comes up with the story, does the casting, wardrobe, and dialogue. She can change the point of view, and move the scene to Saudi Arabia or Khartoum as it suits her, with no increase in production costs. The stage play is also a writer's game, though the director and, of course, the actors are also indispensable.

In the literary community the writer is king, but in the film and television community, he is more or less a serf, as any writer who has dared to go on location will verify. I once made the mistake of showing up when one of my television scripts was being shot. In casual conversation with the lead actress, it emerged that I was the author of the screenplay. She loved the story but was totally unimpressed. I thought she might send me out for coffee and donuts.

Some directors, in fact, forbid writers from coming on location. The late Jackie Gleason would not even talk to his scribes, and made them slip their material under his office door. There is a long-standing Hollywood joke about an attractive but rather dim girl from the hinterlands who attempted to boost her acting career by bedding writers. She did not become a star.

Here are some of the writers who have plied their trade in Hollywood, by country: Germany: Thomas and Heinrich Mann, Leon Feuchtwanger, and Bertolt Brecht. England: Somerset Maugham, H. G. Wells, P. G. Wodehouse, Hugh Walpole, Graham Greene, J. B. Priestley, Cristopher Isherwood, and James Hilton. United States: F. Scott Fitzgerald, Ernest Hemingway, Thornton Wilder, Nathaniel West, John Steinbeck, William Faulkner, Zane Grey, Irving Stone, and Raymond Chandler. In short, this is as talented a group of literary *samurai* as has ever been assembled. But the screen shows little evidence of their brilliance, and no one refers to a "Nathaniel West film." David Niven laments that this storehouse of brilliance was "watered down, wasted, or filtered out by megalomaniac producers," with the result that little of it even reached the screen.[17]

As Elia Kazan has noted, what the screenwriter produces is more architecture than literature.[18] This is not to say that a script is easy to write; indeed, screenwriting is difficult. I would compare a screenplay to an instruction manual, with many of the instructions ultimately discarded and the final product nearly unrecognizable. Little wonder that so many screenwriters opt to become directors if given the chance. Screenwriters do not own the copyright on their material, and the director or those working for management can alter it at their preference and usually do, for various reasons.

Phil Alden Robinson spent a year writing *Rhinestone*, taking care to avoid clichés. As often happens, the project got moved around town, and the script wound up being rewritten by Sylvester Stallone, who changed everything and even added clichés.[19]

Multiple Choice, my first produced screenplay,[20] dealt with industrial espionage. In the tale, a man named Byron Malling, an employee of a defense contractor, is checking out new houses because he is banking on a promotion. But the promotion goes to a rival. To get back at the company, Byron considers selling off some company secrets. To show his anger at being rejected, I cut from a business meeting to an extreme close-up of a grim-faced Byron smashing a racquetball and mercilessly driving his older opponent all over the court. As it turned out, the producer, Ammi Productions of Panorama City, had difficulty renting a racquetball court, and substituted a jogging scene. It just didn't play.

In the story on which *The Killing Fields* is ostensibly based, a man named Dith Pran escapes the murderous regime of Pol Pot. He is the hero and the Khmer Rouge are the clear villains. However, in the hands of neo-Marxist director Roland Joffe, the story became an anti-American tract, a dishonest piece of 1960s revisionism, and a screen version of William Shawcross's book *Sideshow*, which blamed the United States for the Cambodian genocide. The hero of the film version is not so much Dith Pran but an American journalist of pronounced leftist sympathies. The film ends in absurd fashion, to the strains of "imagine there's no heaven . . ." Pure Lennonism.

Since films are so expensive, in the larger, strategic sense, cinema is a producer's medium. The same could be said for television. The producer might be compared to a member of the Joint Chiefs of Staff, charged with making the Big Decisions that can make or break a campaign. However, in the *tactical* sense, it is the director who is the true "author" of a film. He may not have control of the budget, but on the set he calls the shots. He is the general.

The military analogy has been used many times. Orson Welles was fond of saying that a poet needs a pen, a painter a brush, and a filmmaker an army. Producer Martin Bregman agrees that "making a film is like going to war."[21] In Evelyn Waugh's *The Loved One*, the central character, Dennis Barlow, is a poet who has been discharged from the British military and comes to California to help write the life of Shelley for the films. However, in Hollywood, Dennis "found reproduced, and enhanced by the nervous agitation endemic to the place, all the gross futility of service life."[22] It so offended him that he fled and took a job at a pets' cemetery and briefly considered going into the ministry.

Indeed, major studios do resemble military bases much more than they do factories. They are sprawling places, with certain sections off-limits and locked up tight. They teem with activity, but, as on a military base, there is no discernible product such as there is with Ford Motor Company. The "cans" of film may go out unseen, in the trunk of a Toyota, like secret orders. In addition, the pecking order is starkly defined. The director commands the big batallions and the strategic armaments.

Elia Kazan, who knows whereof he speaks, contends that the director's "vocabulary" of pictures, shots, angles, images, cuts, and other tricks are what get the story across, not the writer's dialogue.[23] Orson Welles agreed that the director is the *auteur* of the work, and went so far as to say that "theatre is a collective experience; cinema is the work of one single person."[24]

I do not entirely agree with the *auteur* theory, developed in France in the publication *Cahiers du Cinema*. It is the *writer*, after all, who has invented the story and the characters, and plotted the action. Unfortunately, Crown Books does not buy or sell screenplays. Neither can the writer give final life to his creation, and one must recognize these realities, even if one doesn't like them. In the words of Mike Medavoy of Orion Pictures, once you select a director, "you're relinquishing control to somebody else's vision."[25] This applies to writers, executives, and producers alike.

Hamlet is always listed as "a play by William Shakespeare." The director may get mentioned, but it is not "his" play. Film ads sometimes show the director's name above the title, as in "Richard Attenborough's film, *Gandhi*," even though someone else may have written the thing, thus confirming Lillian Hellman's contention that "movies always belonged to one man—the director."[26]

This issue concerns much more than who gets credit and top billing. Indeed, it lies at the core of how film should be interpreted. When someone picks up the novel *The War of the End of the World*, he readily understands that what he is about to read is a reflection of the views and experience of the author, Mario Vargas Llosa. However, television and film are things one *watches* and appear to be a window on life, with crowded street scenes, aerial shots of real cities, and all the other tools of cinematic realism. Such surface realism often serves to disguise deeper fantasy.

Because of what they show, and because it is understood that many people work on a film, viewers do not always assess the final product as the vision of *one person*. They sometimes fail to understand that the actors, the hundreds of extras, the musicians, and all the technicians do the director's bidding.

In short, audiences often fail to recognize the author, and this must limit their understanding. I believe this failure is reflected in such phrases as "This movie can't make up its mind. . . ," "This movie sets out to entertain us but. . . ," and so on, often used by popular film critics such as Gene Siskel. It is as though the movie had a life of its own. It is the *author*, the director, who can't make up his mind, and who sets out to entertain us.

Taking into account the original material, if any, the movie is not necessarily anything more than a representation of what its "author" thinks and believes. That is why I do not believe that films "reflect society," much less the "dreams and nightmares of a nation." To believe that either film or television represents the American people is tantamount to believing, in Ben Stein's words, "that a taste for snuff movies or Beluga caviar was the general taste of a nation."[27]

I believe that films reflect nothing more than the views, visions, and postures of a small, elite community, ultimately a few hundred people, must of whom live in the western part of the Los Angeles basin. To those sunny *environs* we now turn.

PART THREE

THE DREAM FACTORY

EIGHT

THE FILM COMMUNITY, THE FILM BUSINESS

No game licenses are issued in the reserve where the great pachyderms of the film trade bask and browse complacently. They have no suspicion that in most of America and in the whole of Europe, the word "Hollywood" is pejorative.

(Evelyn Waugh)[1]

It was neither unkind nor presumptuous, wrote Evelyn Waugh, to write critically of Hollywood. He perceived such criticism as necessary in large part because "morally, intellectually, aesthetically, financially, Hollywood's entries are written huge in the household books of every nation outside the U.S.S.R."[2] Were Mr. Waugh writing today, he would add the U.S.S.R. to the list. In the spirit of *glasnost,* there is an active interchange and collaboration among Soviet and American filmmakers, and Soviet themes are "hot."[3] (At this writing *Red Heat* is being released, starring Arnold Schwarzenegger as a Moscow cop.)

One could add that critical analysis of Hollywood is scarce, since many so-called "inside" stories often descend into gossip and name-dropping. More often it is the *outsider* who shows himself capable of seeing what it all means.

Mr. Waugh briefly analyzed the Hollywood of the late 1940s and made some judgments as to how the nature of the place and its denizens affected the product. Hortense Powdermaker brought her training as an anthropologist to bear on the movie colony. Neither one had the slightest desire to be part of the movie world, and hence wrote without inhibition. Insiders, or even local journalists, sometimes hold back because they entertain hopes of getting into or advancing in the business. In some cases, however, outsiders became insiders, and vice versa, and their observations are also valuable.

Ben Stein's *The View From Sunset Boulevard* focused on television, but practically this makes little difference since many of the same people and facilities are involved, and the outlook is essentially the same. Television magnate Norman Lear, for example, who figured largely in Stein's work, was also the producer of *The Princess Bride,* a popular film written by William Goldman. Mark Litwak's 1986 *Reel Power* probed the innards of the film business, based on over two hundred interviews with prominent actors, agents, executives, writers, and directors. But before delving into that business, here are some observations about where the business takes place.

LOS ANGELES

> Los Angeles [is] probably most horrible town in the world, enveloped in hurtful smog, all roads; a truly corrupted distorted place. One feels it at once on arrival.
>
> (October 31, 1962, diary entry of Malcolm Muggeridge)[4]

Los Angeles is a city "out" west, tucked in a corner of the United States, leading some to call it a "sunny Siberia." It sits in an amphitheater of mountains, further isolated by the Pacific Ocean on one side and the desert on the other. From this outpost, it is some three thousand miles to the nation's business and theatrical center in New York and the same remove to the political capital of Washington, D.C. The intellectual citadels of London and Paris lie across another ocean, some six thousand miles away. They might as well be located in southwestern Uranus for all they affect developments in Hollywood. Clearly, even in the age of instant communications, Los Angeles is not in the center of the world, except of course in the unreal world of the cinema, and even that is changing. It is a place apart, as denoted by tags like "tinsel town," "lotus land," "dream factory," and so on, which do not apply to Newark or Dubuque. However, one occasionally hears such pejoratives as "where the debris meets the sea," which might also work with New York or even Miami. But there is only one Los Angeles.

The city is a sprawling, amorphous mass that has an unreal, movie-set quality to it. There are few old buildings and little evidence of links to the past. Subdivisions and shopping malls suddenly appear, as if thrown up overnight. Even areas such as Watts are clean and neat when compared with similar neighborhoods in the East. Cars do not rust, and there is no mud or dirt in the streets. Many, if not most, of the people come from somewhere else. Thousands arrive daily, but in spite of the nearly perfect climate, there are few people mingling in the streets in the style of New York. In Los Angeles everyone spends their travel time in the automobile. One sees many people conducting business over their cellular phones while stuck in freeway traffic. In short, it is a different sort of place, and quite unique, as Richard Henry Dana noticed in the previous century. Then and now, it is hardly representative of America.

THE MOVIE COLONY

> In Hollywood we learn about life only from each other's pictures.
>
> (Frank Capra)[5]

There is only one Los Angeles, and only one movie colony, which goes by the generic name of Hollywood, even though it includes several cities. Many movies are also made in Paris, Rome, and Toronto, but nowhere does the film business define the place as it does in Hollywood, a company town.

It is not exactly the case that, as Waugh contended, no one in this region cares what happens beyond the mountains, but it is certainly true that the movie community is an isolation ward, and that in an already isolated city. Waugh compared the inhabitants of the film colony to monks in a desert oasis whose lives revolved around a few shrines: studios, hotels, and one restaurant. Those who frequent these haunts perceive the outside world primarily in terms of box office.

Mark Litwak, a New Yorker, came to Hollywood from a background of law and politics. He found himself a curiosity at cocktail parties, simply because he came from outside the fold. His eager listeners were "curious about what the outside world was like."[6] Evidently they didn't know much about it and seldom strayed from the shrines, except to go on location. In fairness, it might be noted that for a popular actor or actress to appear in public may well involve risk and embarrassment. During a television interview, Paul Newman told how someone had asked him for an autograph while he was at a urinal. This is the price one pays for celebrity, and such people cannot be blamed for staying inside and hanging out with their own.

The insularity of the community is strengthened by the fact that there is practically nowhere else to go for those who want to be in the business, especially actors. Only the wealthiest and most famous can afford to live elsewhere and commute.

Ben Stein observed that those who make film and television have little, if any, contact with the larger mass of people around them, particularly poor and working people. Film people tend to live in the affluent areas in the western part of the city, where the net worth of some residents might match the GNP of a small Caribbean nation.

In this small, elite community, the cinematic culture reaches its apogee; this is a colony totally immersed in film, with its own jargon. Here one speaks of "leveraging" someone and having one's agent call someone else's agent. It is true that people say "let's do lunch," but this rather novel use of "do" is not unique to Hollywood. A neo-Stalinist theologian from Argentina named José Míguez Bonino wrote a book called *Doing Theology in a Revolutionary Situation.* He might feel right at home in L.A., where he could "do" both lunch and theology with Martin Sheen.

The film colony is a congenial place, but the surface friendliness often masks a reality of intense rivalry or manipulation. Behind the warmth lies such questions as "what can I get from this person?" or "what does he want from me?"

The rhetorical mood of choice is the continuous hyperbolic, an ongoing tide of glowing adjectives. But such language must be decoded and kept in scale. If a producer showers your script with hosannas for half an hour, it might have a chance. If she calls your project "interesting," it means she hates it. She is saying, in effect: "get out of my office immediately and never bother me again." In a documentary, *Hollywood's Favorite Heavy,* Ben Stein recalls producers breaking forth in a geyser of praise for his ideas, even bringing in the secretaries, and asking Stein whom he would like to see cast in the lead roles. Everyone agreed that this was going to be a big smash. Then, Stein said, he would never hear from that person again. In truth, that is the way it happens.

American liberals are fond of brandishing statistics showing that a small percentage of powerful people control the vast portion of the nation's wealth. While this sort of study is often tendentious and fraudulent, such analysis holds with film, and with popular culture in general: the bulk of it is controlled by a small politburo which has little contact with the outside world and comparatively sparse knowledge of it. Indeed, it has always been that way.

THE STUDIO SYSTEM

> When Zanuck announced that the people were bored with lust and massacre in films, it meant that he personally was bored with them.
>
> (Alva Johnston on movie mogul Darryl F. Zanuck)[7]

Attempts at monopoly control of the film business existed from the earliest days of cinema. Edison's failed attempt at domination has been noted, but at one time the big Hollywood studios practically held a *de facto* monopoly. Under what was called the roster system, studio moguls signed personnel to long-term contracts and dictated their acting assignments. Recalcitrant actors or writers could be fired or suspended without pay, and the other studios colluded to keep them out of work until they did what they were told. It was practically a chattel system that Hortense Powdermaker saw as worse than slavery in psychological terms, since its inmates, particularly the actors, *chose* to be part of it, selling themselves to the highest bidder.[8] In addition, the studios owned extensive chains of theatres, thus controlling both ends of their operation. But this tidy racket was not to endure.

A successful 1945 lawsuit by actress Olivia de Havilland led to changes in the roster system. In what became known as the Paramount decision, independent film exhibitors sued eight major studios for anti-competitive practices. The independents prevailed after a long struggle, and in 1948 the Justice Department forced the studios to sell off their theatres.

In terms of film content, these developments did not portend the dawning of a new day. Indeed, television was already encroaching on film's turf, and some of the changes would have been made anyway. And the studios survived; they simply could no longer do whatever they wanted with the raw material. And while one set of power brokers lost some of its clout, another group was on the rise.

THE AGE OF THE DEAL

> When Henry Wallace proclaimed this to be "The Century of the Common Man," he was as wide of the mark as only an ambitious politician can be. This is still, and will be to its bitter end, the Century of the Middle Man.
>
> (Peter Ustinov)[9]

The end of the studio system spawned an army of hustlers, middlemen, and assorted flesh and influence peddlers in various guises but usually known as agents. Without their total control over personnel, studios are forced to compete for talent. Agents, in turn, control that talent, and therefore wield tremendous power. Something similar to a studio system is taking place with agencies: they have been consolidating into a few large entities who dominate the scene. At present, there are four which play that role.

Probably the most powerful is CAA, the Creative Artists Agency, headed by Michael Ovitz. Mark Litwak makes a strong case that Ovitz is the most influential person in Hollywood, even though he is not a star, producer, director, or studio executive. CAA has five equal partners, each of whom reportedly makes over $1 million a year. CAA also boasts forty-five agents and some seven hundred clients, including Paul Newman, Jane Fonda, Robert Redford, Dustin Hoffman, and Sylvester Stallone. Studios need CAA cooperation if they are to gain the services of such people, who are certified "box office material." And CAA policy is to represent only the top talent.

The CAA took over a preeminent position once held by the William Morris Agency, which handles Walter Matthau and other stars. Another important company is ICM, International Creative Management, the agency for Jennifer Beals, James Garner, Carol Burnett, and others. InterTalent, an upstart offspring of CAA, has recently been making some inroads.[10]

These agencies have unsurped many of the studios' most important functions. They develop and package talent, screen story ideas, put together deals for movies, and sometimes even handle the financing. Agents with the big players liken their job to working for the CIA. Indeed, they report that the studios come to *them* asking what people and projects they have available. Studios also keep key agencies secretly apprised of their production schedules and prospective projects.[11] Thus, it is not so much a question of the tail wagging the dog but rather, who is the dog?

PUBLICISTS

In addition to the agents that negotiate their deals, movie stars employ special agencies to handle their public relations. The Rogers and Cowan Agency handles Sylvester Stallone, Bruce Willis, Cybill Shepherd, and Paul Newman. The PMK firm handles Sally Field, Chevy Chase, James Garner, Debra Winger, Robert Redford, Tom Hanks, Woody Allen, and some sixty other leading actors, each of which has a New York and Los Angeles publicist. PMK managed the publicity for *Big*, *Willow*, and *Colors*.

Because these agencies control access to the stars, they wield tremendous power and can easily "leverage" the press and television. They won't let actors talk to just any journalist or publication, or appear on just any show, but favor those which display their clients in the best light. Pat Kingsley of PMK states that "We're only interested in doing articles that help the career."[12]

The appearance of a star on a magazine cover just before their movie opens is usually the result of a deal struck between that publication and a publicist. This kind of publicity is often crucial to the success of a film, with the "middleman" playing a key role. The other ways publicists are important will be dealt with in due course.

THE NEW STUDIOS

> I am frequently assured by visitors that the studios are "morgues," that they are "shuttered up," that in "the new Hollywood," the "studio has no power." The studio has.
>
> (Joan Didion)[13]

The major Hollywood studios are: Columbia Pictures, Walt Disney Studios, Paramount Pictures, Orion Pictures, 20th Century Fox, Universal Pictures, MGM/UA Communications Company, and Warner Brothers. Many of these are owned outright by corporations such as Gulf-Western, the parent of Paramount.

Even after the studios lost much of their clout, they still had the playing field largely to themselves, even if they couldn't lay down all the rules. As the *Los Angeles Times* recently put it:

> For eons and eons, Hollywood—the movie capital, where the River of Bankability flowed with glitz and celluloid—had been ruled by the Major Studios. All was calm in the land between the Sea of Red Ink and the Ocean of Profit.[14]

To put it in Marxist terms, the studios, whether independent or major, still control the "means of production," the vast array of expensive equipment it takes to make films, particularly the post-production equipment, which is now state-of-the-art computer gear. The primary means of production is money, and the financing of films is still the studios' major role.

The major studios also dominate distribution, holding multi-picture deals with the various theatre chains. They can afford to maintain regional offices around the United States, and their budgets allow for massive advertising. In most cases, they control the sales of movies to the pay television market. Some of the greatest profits of the majors come not from the movies they produced themselves, but from distribution of works done by independents. These cannot hope to equal the majors' marketing clout, and usually try to swing a distribution deal of some sort. If they fail, their works will likely be confined to smaller "art" cinemas or to the video market.

Important independent studios include: Lorimar, the Cannon

Group, Crown International, Samuel Goldwyn Co., Island Pictures, Transworld Entertainment, Blake Edwards Entertainment, and Lucasfilm Ltd., the producer of *Star Wars*. Some of these independents are not located in Los Angeles. George Lucas moved his operation to northern California for the specific purpose of getting away from Hollywood, which he considers a "foreign country."[15] But practically all independents must do business in Hollywood in one form or another. The number of independently produced movies was only sixty-five in 1980, but rose to 267 in 1986, an increase of over 300 percent.[16]

In short, while the agents may hold important cards, it still falls to the studios to make the important decisions. We now turn to that very special kind of person who decides whether a movie will ever become more than a script or an idea.

STUDIO EXECUTIVES

> Less brains are necessary in the motion picture industry than in any other.
>
> (Lewis Selznick, in testimony to Congress)[17]

> NOBODY KNOWS ANYTHING.
>
> (William Goldman's chief axiom of Hollywood)[18]

Though film executives are paid vast amounts of money, they are essentially hired help and can be disposed of at any time. Indeed, they often are. Mark Litwak contends that it is entirely possible for an executive to survive a year at a studio simply by turning down everything that comes to him. He may be fired when it comes to light that he produced nothing, but his chances of being picked up by another studio are good.[19]

As writers, actors, and directors never hestitate to point out, those who decide whether a movie lives or dies are from the *business*—not from the artistic—side of cinema. Unfortunately, the opinions of those from the artistic side on studio executives are not printable in a book such as this, but fortunately Evelyn Waugh's are. Waugh described the studio bosses as "empty-headed" and "quite without any purpose at all," in the artistic or political sense. In addition, such people "read nothing" and actually despise literary considerations. As a novelist, Waugh was "shocked" by their hostility to ideas and their "complete inability to follow a plain story."[20]

Hortense Powdermaker perceived movie executives as a highly superstitious, anti-intellectual group motivated by the belief that "success or failure is contagious through contact, a sort of sympathetic magic."[21] The script of one successful movie was 203 pages, leading an executive to decree that *all* scripts should be 203 pages, thereby terrorizing many a studio typist. The studio bosses were (and are) gamblers, who relied heavily on luck and "the breaks," a process Powdermaker compared to primitive animism.[22] In Hollywood, she added, "almost no one trusts anyone else, and the executives, particularly, trust no one, not even themselves."[23]

While this may sound extreme or dated, Mark Litwak's 1986 portrait bears strong parallels. At present, agents do much of the reading of screenplays and treatments. Studio people will seldom read anything sent over the transom, largely for legal reasons, lest someone subsequently claim that the studio stole the idea. But even once it gets by the agents, little reading takes place on the executive level.

A filmmaker must "pitch" an idea to an executive, and this does not take place in a literary form. The executives want the basic concept, which must be summarized in three short lines, or even in the title. This is known as "high concept," and the title *Back to the Future* would be one example. Four words encapsulate the whole film. Comedian Jay Leno is not far off the mark when he states that the ongoing series of slasher movies (*Halloween, Friday the 13th*, etc.) are not so much films as advertising slogans. He speculates that one will be called *Turkey* and advertised as: "Now it's his turn to do the carving." Some insiders contend that high concept is already passé, and that the slogan or jingle is now the rule.

This is what executives want, not details of the story, which only confuse them. In addition, they have little time, handling as they do some 150 telephone calls a day, most from people who believe their business is of the utmost importance.

The executives' frame of reference, it should be stressed, is not literature or the real world, but *film*, particularly films which have made money. Perhaps the most ironclad rule in Hollywood is that what makes money will be imitated. These men are under tremendous pressure to produce a marketable product, and will readily cannibalize or rob graves to do it.

Apparently, the makers of the highly successful movie *Aliens* pitched it as *Jaws* on a spaceship. The executives readily understood, opened their checkbooks, and were amply rewarded. *Outland* was pitched as *High Noon* in outer space. Critic Roger Ebert once commented that *The Breakfast Club* was "*Porky's,* written by Eugene O'Neill." Perhaps that was how it was pitched. Other ideas have been successfully sold before the originator even had a completion to his story.

Veterans of pitch session say that if it takes more than thirty seconds to get the message across, chances of success are slim, and if the entire session lasts more than five minutes, the verdict is quite likely to be negative.

The one doing the pitching must not only be concise, he must abide by the rules of film and be passionate. He is performing a conjurer's trick, eliciting visions of past films and big profits. He must push the right buttons and stir emotion and excitement in the one audience that really matters: the men with the money. It often makes a great difference if the "pitcher" is calm and collected, capable of inspiring confidence.[24]

As for the ability of studio bosses to read the public, it is worth recalling that Louis B. Mayer opposed *Mutiny on the Bounty* because he believed that the public disapproved of rebels, and turned down cooperation with Walt Disney's Mickey Mouse project on the grounds that all women were afraid of mice. Irving Thalberg thought talking pictures were a fad, and, when confronted with the story of Scarlett O'Hara, said that no Civil War picture had ever made a nickel.[25] William Goldman is right. In the movie business, nobody knows anything, at least for certain.

STARS

I'm not an actor, I'm a movie star.

(Peter O'Toole, in *My Favorite Year*)

A friend once told me how, even though he tried, he could not appreciate NHL hockey. I suggested he go to an arena and have a stab at skating. After he had mastered that, in both forward and backward directions, he might try maneuvering a little black disk down the ice and into a heavily guarded net, while five other people were trying to make him part of that ice. This process completed, I told my friend, he might appreciate the nuances of the sport.

Likewise, acting is a difficult and demanding profession, and those who think otherwise should consider auditioning for, say, the role of Stanley Kowalski in a community theatre production of *A Streetcar Named Desire*. The ladies could have a go at Blanche Du Bois. In a way Mademoiselle Du Bois is typical of a film actress in that she is a person who depends on the kindness of strangers.

Out of some eight thousand members of the Screen Actors Guild, only about 15 percent are working at any time. Of this small group, only a select few can lay claim to "star" status.

The term "movie star" is probably the most notable contribution of the cinematic culture to the *lingua franca*. As a group and as individuals, stars also wield tremendous power. The star's share is often a major part of a movie's budget. Sylvester Stallone gets over ten million per film, paid up front. Such enormous fees are usually apart from the actors' share of the profits. Motion picture deals sometimes depend on the signing of a major player, and their refusal could cause the project to crumble. Once a project gets going, the behavior of a star can make it or break it.

On the set of David Puttnam's *Revolution,* Al Pacino stayed in a seventy-foot motor home and every day had smoked salmon brought on location by motorbike. The movie's budget swelled, and the film eventually bombed.[26]

Actor Bill Cosby conceived the idea for *Leonard Part 6* and held approval of script, casting, costumes, sets, music, and the final cut. In other words, it was practically his home movie. Director Paul Weiland said that Cosby's power "swept away" all his cinematic judgments, but added, "Who were we to argue with the biggest star in the world?"[27]

The career of a star is generally a lot faster on the way down than on the way up. So much depends on who is hot, and even Academy Awards are no guarantee of continued success. In addition, film breaks the dramatic tradition of the stage, in which acting was a craft requiring a lifetime to learn and in which playwrights reserved the best parts for mature players.

Movie moguls, on the other hand, are on a continuing quest for youth. Rare is the actor who maintains "star" status for more than a decade, which makes it of more than passing interest that Clint Eastwood has endured since the 1960s with little sign of fading away.[28]

The stable of stars, along with who is an item at any given time, is an important factor in determining what the public will see.

DIRECTORS

Few jobs are as demanding as that of the film director, but directors were once glorified technicians subject to strict control from executives. Since the advent of the *auteur* theory, however, they are a major creative force. Once the director gets his hands on a project, it becomes subject to his or her creative vision. Critics such as Pauline Kael of the *New Yorker* have accused various directors of equating megalomania with art.

Sometimes the director gets everything he wants, as in Michael Cimino's *Heaven's Gate,* budgeted at some seven million, but which wound up costing nearly forty million. Observers have speculated that if someone had not put a stop to it, Cimino would *still* be out spending money by the truckload. He shot 1.5 million feet of film and printed 1.3 million, which works out to some 220 hours, or the equivalent of over one hundred feature films. It would take some ten days to see it all. Of the 8,047 still photos taken on location, some four thousand were shots of the director and his crew. An early version of the film included a battle scene an hour and a half long.[29] It wasn't so much a film as a gargantuan act of self-indulgence.

The choice of director sometimes determines which star will appear in a picture, because actors have people they prefer to work with, often because they make them look good, or because they share political views. The director is part of the "attachments" of a "package" when it gets pitched. Writers are also wise to be "nice to the star," by giving him or her as much play as possible, preferably in the area of their strengths.

Getting to be a director is a difficult task, and once one is in the trade, it is still difficult to find steady work. Only about 10 percent of those in the Directors Guild are working at any given time. One could describe these cinematic generals in the words of an old recruiting poster for the United States Marines: the few, the proud.

PRODUCERS

We have already outlined the importance of the producer. He is responsible for Major Strategy, like the Joint Chiefs. The demands and pressures of the job are enormous, encompassing everything from conceiving the project in the first place to stroking the stars, to working with the studio on distribution or flogging the picture on late-night talk shows. Little wonder that producers' careers tend to be short. Few survive longer than ten years. In many cases, longevity depends not on the producer's particular talents, but on his connections with stars, executives, and directors. In other words, as in most Hollywood precincts, it depends as much on who you know as what you know.

Insiders say that there are not more than twenty producers regularly getting films on line. Further, they contend that if such producers do not hang out with the big players at Spago's restaurant they will soon be out of the club.

With producers, one could adapt another Marine recruiting slogan: "Maybe you can be one of us." But the odds are that you can't.

WRITERS

> Writers aren't people, exactly.
>
> (F. Scott Fitzgerald, *The Last Tycoon*)[30]

Screenwriting is an essentially thankless task in Hollywood, even though there exists a possibility of great financial rewards. And that possibility often brings the accusation of "sellout." In J. D. Salinger's *The Catcher in the Rye,* Holden Caulfield says of his brother D. B., a screenwriter, that he is "out in Hollywood, being a prostitute."[31]

Although he cooks up the plot and dialogue, the writer's role tends to get lost in the "collaborative process," and he is generally treated as a second-class citizen by "the industry." Quite often, he is defrauded of money or credit, and even when he gets paid, he doesn't "own" the result of his labors and may not recognize the product on the screen, even if his name is there.

Though the writer has many good reasons to despise the business side of the film trade, he is actually not a writer in the true sense, but half a filmmaker. He must possess dramatic sense and be able to project the action on the screen of his imagination. Not everyone has these gifts, and many excellent novelists and nonfiction writers have flopped terribly as dramatists, on stage or screen.

On the other hand, some have made a successful transition from journalist or even film critic to screenwriter. Darryl F. Zanuck hired Frank Nugent of the *New York Times,* who had blasted many of his films, to look over scripts. Nugent went on to collaborate with John Ford and to write such pictures as *She Wore a Yellow Ribbon* and *The Quiet Man.*[32] Peter Bogdanovich (*The Last Picture Show*) is another convert from the critical community.

The writer is also an entrepreneur; he sells not labor but a product. He is constantly competing with his fellow-unionists. As Ben Stein puts it, "He is actually down there in the pit with the clawing agents and businessmen."[33] As Hortense Powdermaker noted, the influence of commercial values on the writer is more powerful than the influence of the writer's talent on the business.[34]

One does not simply join the Writers Guild. Entry is based on a points system for work already performed in the industry. However, many, if not most, of those who get in never manage a second sale. Only half of the Guild's membership is working at any given time, and an elite core of writers tends to dominate the important projects. Jay Leno jokes that when the present writers' strike is over, only 80 percent of the Guild will be unemployed.

William Goldman (*Marathon Man*), Sterling Silliphant (*In the Heat of the Night*), Robert Towne (*Chinatown*), and Horton Foote (*To Kill a Mockingbird*) are about the only "name" screenwriters that come to mind. Robert Bolt (*A Man For All Seasons*) might be another. Their attachment to a project could help it get done, or attract others to it. In the final analysis, few are the ventriloquists who put words in the mouths of the stars.

UNIONS

Not everyone is aware that the standard product they see on the screen is union-made from start to finish, with everyone from the caterer to the director to the extras to the projectionist being a member of a union or guild. At the time of this writing, my own union, the Writers Guild of America, West, Inc., has practically shut Hollywood down, though its primary effect has been in television.

Roy M. Brewer was once the most powerful union official in Hollywood. In fact, a case can be made that, as the international representative for Alliance of Theatrical Stage Employees, he was the most powerful *person* in Hollywood.[35] Such was his clout that he could, in effect, tell the moguls whether they could make a picture or not.

While present union power does not approach such levels, it is something to be reckoned with. They still have power to determine who works, and the primary consideration is not talent but one's status with the union. If *Days of Heaven* had been shot in California, the unions would not have permitted cinematographer Nestor Almendros, an outsider at the time, to do the job. As it turned out, Almendros' work on that film won an Academy Award.[36]

As Almendros notes, Hollywood unions are invariably of a Luddite mentality; they resist new innovations. For example, they prefer old-style gear heads on cameras to the new hydraulic models, eschew large editing screens for ancient moviolas, and prefer large awkward dollies over a smaller, maneuverable model developed in Italy. Further, they prefer the hard way of doing things in order to protect themselves. If the job were simplified, outsiders could more easily gain access to the ranks.[37] Many film innovations, by the way, such as lighter, portable cameras, were developed in Europe but in some cases perfected in the United States.

A union crew sometimes tells a director what he can do, and if they sense that he doesn't know what he is doing, they have been known to give him a hard time. It is not likely that they would cooperate on a picture with an anti-union point of view. That is likely one good reason why no such pictures emerge from the commercial cinema.

The opinions of producers and executives on Hollywood unions are generally unprintable in a book such as this. Film bosses sometimes choose a foreign location for shooting precisely to get away from the unions, and one suspects that George Lucas held similar motives for getting out of town altogether.

AT HOME WITH FAMILY AND FRIENDS

> We don't go for strangers in Hollywood . . . unless they're a celebrity. And they'd better look out even then.
>
> (F. Scott Fitzgerald, *The Last Tycoon*)[38]

Hollywood has been compared to a sealed vault that locks some in and keeps others out. Before he developed his craft in Europe, the aforementioned Nestor Almendros had a stab at Hollywood. There, he perceived "the almost insurmountable wall that surrounds American filmmaking,"[39] and earned his keep washing dishes. Almendros is now welcome in Hollywood, but tends to stay away from the place.

In America, the stars of popular culture receive the adulation that other societies reserve for royalty. The Hollywood community, in particular, is a kind of hereditary aristocracy, abundantly peopled with the relatives of those from an earlier day. As Mel Gussow notes, the early moguls—Zukor, Mayer, Cohn, Warner, *et. al.*—"like European royalty, mixed their families in marriage."[40] Though this is no longer the rule, the family connection cannot be denied. There are the Fondas, the Sheens, Liza Minelli, Chris Lemmon, Michael Douglas, and a host of others. In The Industry, nepotism rules.

In Waugh's *The Loved One,* Megalopolitan Studios fires Sir Francis Hinsley, a veteran of twenty-five years of successful service, and transfers his projects to a cousin of the publicity director's wife, who has just hit town. Such things happen. Sylvester Stallone picked his brother, a mediocre musician at best, to score *Staying Alive*. The closest political parallel would be John F. Kennedy's appointment of his brother Bobby as Attorney General. Paul Hogan hired his son Brett as a writer on *Crocodile Dundee II*, and it showed. Some gain work as the wives, husbands, or consorts of others.

That such people are often quite talented is beyond dispute; less credible is their claim that they would have done just as well without the attachments of Mom, Dad, or whoever. One suspects that they wouldn't have. It remains true that, as Theodore Taylor put it, the best way to make or be in films is to "have a father, uncle, brother, cousin, or wife who owns a studio, or at least runs it."[41]

Aside from the family connections, film people swing many of their biggest deals not in smoke-filled board rooms, or even over the telephone, but on the golf course or at parties. It is business between friends, and takes place where outsiders seldom tread. It does indeed depend upon who you know.

BARRACUDA TIME

The whole industry is built on phony accounting.

(David O. Selznick)[42]

One should not be too hard on either David Selznick or the movie business for the above revelation, which I recently shared with a resident of Hollywood. "So what?" he replied, "the whole *country* is based on phony accounting." He does have a point.

In Hollywood one sometimes hears it said of a movie that "everybody got paid," hence it was a "good shoot" or generally a good production. But everybody does not always get paid.

Unions formed in Hollywood largely because management has hundreds of ways to shaft the help, and often does so. Stars and directors are frequently in litigation over their share of video or foreign rights. The Writers Guild's "Unfair" list includes hundreds of names. In addition to their grievances with management, writers quarrel with each other over screen credit and with directors over projects.

According to Mark Litwak, one veteran producer paid himself a $1 million fee on a picture, and also made off with $1.5 million by making payments to himself through phony crew members. He even listed his dog as an "associate producer," for a fee of $50,000. Amazingly, he is still in the business.[43] So are some big-name directors who squandered much more. In any other business or community, they would be out.

While the above example is not the norm, there are plenty of fast-buck artists scrambling for money, and just generally a lot of back-stabbing, and genuine rip-offs, what insiders call "barracuda time." There is a sense in which, behind the tinsel, it's a jungle out there.

The eponymous main character of John Fowles' novel *Daniel Martin* is a British playwright who has made the journey to Hollywood. At one point he muses.

> The commercial cinema is like a hallucinogenic drug; it distorts the vision of all who work in it. What is at stake behind the public scenes is always personal power and prestige, which reduce the industry to a poker-table where every player must, if he is to survive, become some kind of professional cheat, or hustler. Success is always with the two-faced; and one can no more enter the game innocently than a house with BORDELLO in neon lights across its front. That its madams, pimps, whores and bullies masquerade publicly as "distinguished" directors and stars, famous producers and agents, simply shows how much there is to hide.[44]

Fowles' character goes on to wonder why so few decent films were made in the country which had the most opportunity, and why the sparse evidence that film could be art came primarily from outside the English-speaking world.[45] Elsewhere, Daniel Martin tells a woman set on being an actress that she is in "the sickest art of them all . . . where cretins have always ruled and always will."[46] One suspects that such sentiments represent the author's views, but that he found them too heavy-handed to put in nonfiction form. While not going all the way with him, one can agree that the speeches bear considerable verisimilitude.

Any community that has the power to package and promote also has the power to discard and ignore. In Waugh's macabre tale of Hollywood, old Sir Francis, after his own abrupt dismissal, remembered a colleague named Leo who, though once the darling of the industry, had "died with his bill unpaid in the Garden of Allah hotel."[47] A common phrase in Hollywood, from both labor and management, is, "You'll never work in this town again."

The Hollywood crowd, which likes to throw around terms such as "warmth" and "caring person," is not always composed of those who, in the words of "We Are the World," make a brighter day. During the present WGA strike, several writers were forced to put their homes up for sale, but were hiding the fact "in order not to show weakness that might later hurt them in status-conscious Hollywood."[48] Explained one writer who, quite typically, would not be identified, "When people learn that someone's having a problem, their first reaction is to turn away."[49] Hortense Powdermaker noted that in Hollywood, "a man out of a job is usually a man out of friends."[50] And since most people who aspire to the film business have left their support network of friends and relatives in the hinterland, that can be a serious problem.

AVOIDING THE HEAT

Hollywood is obsessed with awards and ceremonies, as though the community felt a deep need to tart up the business in order to convince itself and everyone else how wonderful it is. In fact, the pretentiously named "Academy" of Motion Picture Arts and Sciences was established in 1927 to confer respectability on a scandal-ridden industry.[51] Since that time, the mood seems to have been that of Dodo in *Alice in Wonderland,* who gushes, "*Everybody* has won and we all must have prizes."[52]

Film people are public figures and must cope with the critics. However, the critics have little effect on careers, and if they did, John Simon would have long ago have put an end to that of Barbra Streisand, whom he says is "repellent . . . knock-kneed and ankleless, short-waisted and shapeless, scrag-toothed and with a horse face centering on a nose that looks like Brancusi's Rooster cast in liverwurst. . . . Streisand remains arrogantly, exultantly ugly. . . . And she is no actress."[53] It actually gets worse, but Streisand carries on unscathed, and she is more likely to be remembered than Mr. Simon.

Adverse reviews do not generally affect the box office. If they did, *Dirty Harry* and *Red Dawn* would have been sent to an early grave instead of pulling in huge returns. Conversely, *Cry Freedom* was a box office loser, though widely praised in the prestige press.

As for the gossip rags, these can often help a star gain support, however scandalous or fraudulent the reports. It is true that at one time a hint of scandal could ruin a career, but those days are long gone. Harry Brand, press agent for Fox, speculates that if a star were caught in a sexual liaison with an ape, not only would it fail to cause a scandal, but "it might create a vogue."[54] In short, film people endure few of the rigors of public life in other places.

In Washington, for example, politicians must face tough questions from squads of hostile journalists, many of whom view themselves as the official opposition and whose barely disguised desire is to bring down the government. In Canada and Britain, contrary to what is often supposed, the political scene is far more vicious. While honorable members of Parliament are speaking, there are cries of "Resign!" and brutal heckling that would bring calls for censure in Congress, where the proceedings are a model of decorum. Stars, on the other hand, have it easy.

The publicists mentioned earlier control access to their clients, and part of their job is to keep them from the media when they don't want attention. As for their exposure, if a journalist portrays the star in a bad light, they will be denied access. This is why so much writing about movie stars and Hollywood is usually puffery, sometimes hagiography, and always bulked with clichés. It is, in a phrase, promotional literature, ad copy written with an eye to the publicist, whose favor will be needed in future to get those gorgeous faces on the cover. Politicians have press spokesmen, but cannot "leverage" the media in this fashion.

Then there is the laid-back television talk show, where a star relaxes in a soft chair while a congenial host squeezes banalities out of her like toothpaste:

"You've been filming in Monte Carlo, Lori?"

"Yeah, Johnny. It's a kinda weird place you know. One day the funniest thing happened . . ."

Pauline Kael never appears with say, Daryl Hannah, to offer such comments as "You know, of course, that you are a dreadful actress." And Barbra Streisand would never sit beside John Simon, though a clever promoter could probably sell tickets for such a match.

As it stands, the whole enterprise is actually a glorified commercial, in which clips are shown, to the guaranteed approval of the studio audience. As Waugh commented, in Hollywood "all is a continuous psalm of self-praise."[55]

SUMMARY

Long-standing critics such as Stanley Kauffmann perceive that American film is in a state of crisis,[56] which can be quickly verified at just about any theatre at any time. Throughout America, many ordinary people, particularly parents, wonder aloud why Hollywood can't make any decent movies. The rules of the film business and the nature of the film community largely answer that question.

In her lengthy study of Hollywood, anthropologist Hortense Powdermaker outlined the "democratic" mentality, which involves the freedom of thought, the availability of choice, and an awareness of alternatives "based on both imagination and knowledge."[57] Her underlying concept of man is one of a free moral agent, able to undertake thought, accept some choices, and reject others.

On the other hand, Powdermaker wrote, others perceived man as a passive being, without ability to choose, and hence a creature to be manipulated "by a powerful few who claim omniscience." These powerful few discourage spontaneity, cultivate conformity, and try their hardest to exclude the alternatives. She called this outlook "totalitarianism."[58]

Powdermaker also noted that totalitarianism involved the pursuit of power for its own sake. She saw that movie moguls had so much money that it became meaningless to them. Their primary pursuit then became power and prestige, and she cited examples in which film people had used their power to control and humiliate others. Applying these criteria to Hollywood, she concluded:

> Hollywood represents totalitarianism. Its basis is economic rather than political, but its philosophy is similar to that of the totalitarian state. In Hollywood, the concept of man as a passive creature to be manipulated extends to those who work for the studios, to personal and social relationships, to the audiences in the theaters and to the characters in the movies. The basic freedom of being able to choose between alternatives is absent.[59]

The result of this state of affairs was "business inefficiency, deep frustration in human relations, and a number of unentertaining second and third-rate movies."[60] These observations were made some forty years ago, when the studio system still flourished, and there is more creative freedom now. But there can be no doubt that the basic premises are still firmly in place. The business is inefficient, relations are still frustrating, and far too many movies are third-rate and not entertaining. People are still viewed as property and the audience as suckers. In like manner, John Fowles' character sees something "ominously stereotyping, if not positively totalitarian," in the machinery of the cinema.[61]

From these rules, as described above, it follows that it is not necessarily the most talented who will meet with success, or even get a chance to show what they can do. Should that come about, their creativity will necessarily be limited by the rather narrow purviews of the business, which submits art to accountancy. And no one gets to work simply because they believe in the Christian religion or Jewish religion, are members of the Republican, Democratic, or Communist Parties, or are known as a saint or even a "nice person." Neither does "having something to say" make any difference. It doesn't work that way. It takes many years to learn the ins and outs of the business and to acquire the requisite leverage. And it is precisely the business side that is not covered in film school, where they hand out diplomas, not power. Without such knowledge and power, it is nearly impossible to succeed in Hollywood.

In the final analysis, it is the most aggressive, those who know the politics of the business, those with family connections, the manipulative, the packager, the promoter, the shrewd salesman, who will call the shots. These, in turn, are usually playing to the lowest common denominator, and going with what has been proven to "work"—that is, what will play to the crassest appetites of the box office, and what most approximates successful films of the recent past.

The appetites of the box office, it should be remembered, are for the most part "kiss-kiss, bang-bang," the appetites of adolescent America, which has been subjected to the brain-reduction surgery and social indoctrination of public education. MTV ("Music" television) has succeeded in reducing the adolescent attention span to that of a hummingbird. Accordingly, studios dumb down the product, so the kids can understand it.

But to be fair to the Leaders of Tomorrow, adult audiences also leave much to be desired. John Simon saw Mel Brooks' *Blazing Saddles* with a sophisticated New York audience, and notes that they laughed loudest and longest at a scene in which a bunch of cowboys sit around eating beans and breaking wind. "If that is what makes audiences happy," concluded Simon, who is no fan of Brooks, "then all hope for the future of cinema is gone with the wind."[62]

As evidenced by filmmakers such as Francois Truffaut and Federico Fellini, any quality product is likely to be the result of long-term collaboration and continuity. Unfortunately Hollywood is not an ensemble operation, and few people get to work together on an extended basis. When personnel show up on location, it is likely that they have never met each other before. They sometimes discover that they don't like each other and don't work together very well. Such "collaboration" can sometimes resemble civil war.

Given the foibles of the system, it is a wonder than any decent films get made at all. In short, the commercial films viewed by countless millions worldwide reflect the hard realities of a highly competitive, inefficient, and wasteful business, which is run by a decidedly insulated and cliquish elite. As for its "factual" content, the commercial cinema also reflects the views of several hundred people in Los Angeles. Those views are the subject of the next chapter.

NINE

THE HOLLYWOOD WORLDVIEW

Hollywood people lived and still live in a world of fantasy, and they are accustomed to making things up, to fibbing and exaggerating, and to believing all their own fibs and exaggerations.

(Otto Friedrich)[1]

Partly as a result of my limited experience in the place, I do not believe it either presumptuous or inaccurate to speak of a "Hollywood worldview." This is not, of course, to contend that everyone in the film colony is exactly alike, but simply to state that there is a widely shared outlook in the film colony. One notices it immediately, and this has been confirmed by others with much more experience.

Hortense Powdermaker cites a Hollywood veteran as calling the community a "sealed chamber" whose inmates "accepted its standards and values, forgetting about others."[2] That this has not substantially changed is confirmed by the experience of Ben Stein, who in the late 1970s discovered that people in Hollywood possessed a homogeneity of views that was "almost uncanny." In addition, these views were "highly idiosyncratic and unique."[3] Moreover, there was a "marvelous uniformity" to the beliefs, with no gap between labor and management.[4]

This thesis would seem to be corroborated by the undeniable uniformity of the product, whether television or film. Hollywood movies, in particular, have a certain look, feel, and sound to them, and only the roaring lion before the titles distinguishes the films of MGM/UA from those of Fox in overall cinematic style. It is a reasonable assumption that people who operate from the same set of presuppositions will tend to produce the same result. But what are the beliefs that rule in Hollywood?

RELIGION

> I'm interested in spirituality, not religion. Religion creates barriers between people, spirituality transcends barriers between us.
>
> (Martin Sheen)[5]

There have been a large number of religious films produced in Hollywood, some of them critical and financial successes. These will be dealt with in a separate chapter. This section will examine the dominant religious beliefs of the movie community. The fact that movies have been made about religion does not indicate that religious people make them, only that filmmakers have at various times perceived a public demand for religious fare.

As might be deduced from a study of contemporary films, Hollywood is a highly secularized community. A survey of the entertainment elite found that 93 percent of them seldom or never attend religious services, and only the military ranked lower on their scale of values related to leadership.[6]

Sometimes a distinction is made between "organized religion" and a supposedly purer unorganized brand, but the distinction is largely meaningless. Even Shirley MacLaine's New Ageism, a *gazpacho* of Eastern ideas and assorted nostrums, which the *New Republic* has called "Moronic Convergence,"[7] is highly organized. For its gurus, including MacLaine, it is also highly profitable. Cults such as the Unification Church and Scientology are also highly organized and highly profitable.

In many cases, Hollywood people are simply ignorant of or indifferent to the subject of religion, as they are to, say, quantum physics. But it is not exactly the case that Hollywood is a spiritual democracy, in which all religious ideas are accorded the same value, be they the veneration of Jehovah as in Judaism and Christianity, or the veneration of former Ethiopian emperor Haile Sellassie, as in the Rastafarian faith. There is a certain preference for nontraditional, unconventional practices, anything outside the Judaic-Christian mainstream. Otto Friedrich calls the place a "city of cults" and notes the observation of Nathaniel West that in the Los Angeles area one could find everything from the crusade against salt to "the Aztec theory of brain breathing."[8] The late David Niven wrote that some Hollywood people were "Holy Rollers," by which he probably meant neither Pentecostals nor Roman Catholics, but simply those who were openly religious. He added that "quite a number" of film people "practiced black magic."[9] He provided no names in either group.

Ronald Reagan, it might be noted, is not the only actor to favor astrology. Among their patrons, local astrologers list Sylvester Stallone, Tom Smothers, and Angie Dickinson.[10]

Dreams and visions can also affect Hollywood business in unusual ways. A number of people have opposed the movie *Wired*, the story of John Belushi, including his brother and former agent. However, Michael Chiklis, the actor chosen for the lead role, reports that John Belushi appeared to him in a dream and pronounced his blessing on the project.[11] It sounds like something from the *Book of Mormon*. In the face of such events, one begins to understand that the Guru Brahmin from Waugh's *The Loved One* was no exaggeration. Indeed, Hollywood boasts a veritable who's who in gurus.

The tendency to favor unconventional religious ideas is sometimes accompanied by a marked hostility to more established faiths, along of course with the ethics and morals those faiths represent. In the Lichter-Rothman survey, only 33 percent of the entertainment elite expressed the belief that adultery is wrong, only 5 percent said that homosexual behavior was wrong, and 91 percent favored abortion.[12]

In addition, this hostility is personal and specific, and not simply a reflection of the knowledge that religious themes and people generally do not play well in drama. Some of the animus may be occupational, similar to what the butchers' union feels toward the vegetarian movement. Movie moguls cannot be expected to harbor warm feelings toward those who tell their flock to stay away from the movies; indeed, such people pose a threat. But the matter surely goes deeper.

Ben Stein describes what he calls a "frequently encountered Hollywood attitude," the belief that "the United States Army is the same as the Ku Klux Klan is the same as Protestant fundamentalism."[13]

While this might sound like overstatement, it should be noted that Stein, who is Jewish, is a sober writer with an academic and legal background who started outlining these topics for *The Wall Street Journal*, hardly a bastion of yellow journalism.

While the separate section on religious films will show examples of this view, one is particularly apposite at this point. In Mel Brooks' *Blazing Saddles*, the hero, Sheriff Bart, played by Cleavon Little, and his sidekick, the Waco Kid, played by Gene Wilder, attempt to infiltrate a group of desperadoes by masquerading as Ku Kluckers. Unfortunately, Bart's black hand gives them away, and they flee. Still wearing their robes, they stumble upon a similarly clad congregation at an outdoor baptismal service, where the fugitives fit right in. This is not overt antireligious propaganda but a subtle dig, probably intended to be an inside joke: Baptists and Ku Kluckers, one in the spirit. That's the view from Sunset Boulevard.

It is perhaps fair to point out that Ben Stein noted that some of the most "extreme animus" against religion was "directed against coreligionists," both among Protestants and Jews.[14]

There are, of course, notable exceptions, in both the production and management side of filmmaking. Some who abandoned religion in their youth are now returning to the fold.[15] Among those who protested *The Last Temptation of Christ* were sixty-one Christians in the film and television industries.[16] But it remains true that they are the exception, not the rule. A director friend who was present at an early private screening of *Chariots of Fire* recalls that when Eric Liddell began a speech with the words "Jesus said," the result was sarcastic laughter from the audience, largely composed of studio biggies and Academy members.

Hollywood has shied away from movies which might be controversial in a political sense. Among those shelved by Darryl F. Zanuck was *The Secret Crimes of Josef Stalin*.[17] Perhaps it would have required too many extras and exhausted the supply of fake blood. But there is seldom a reluctance to be controversial in a religious sense, as in the film version of *Jesus Christ Superstar*. Despite protestations to the contrary, the Monty Python troupe's *Life of Brian* ridiculed the person of Jesus Christ. The same charge has been made of *The Last Temptation of Christ*. Producers know that such controversy can help sell tickets.

On the other hand, producers would quickly flood the country with concert footage of Tammy Faye Bakker if millions could be made by so doing. The propagandist's mentality must compete with that of the mercenary. But one can't imagine a Hollywood film whose entire purpose was to ridicule, say, homosexual activists, feminists, animal rights crusaders, or environmentalists. That would be blasphemy. Hollywood understands that religious people, particularly Christians, are the last group in America besides businessmen who may be defamed with impunity.

But for the most part, Hollywood operates on the constitutional principle of separation of church and screen. In the words of Job, the film colony says to God, "Leave us alone! We have no desire to know your way."[18] Of course, it is not the only community to do so.

HOLLYWOOD POLITICS AND DRAMATIC CONVENTION

> Public virtue is a kind of ghost town into which anyone can move and delare himself sheriff.
>
> (Saul Bellow)[19]

Joan Didion is a keen observer of the American scene and has both lived and worked in Hollywood. She notes a tendency among the glitterati to reduce political ideas to simplistic, almost manichean good-versus-bad choices: equality is good; genocide is bad. This type of discourse, she found, "tends to make even the most casual political small talk resemble a small rally," and to preclude more detailed and extensive discussion.[20] The process seems natural enough for actors: you select your favorite lines, the ones most capable of stirring the audience, and repeat them.

Further, Didion noticed that Hollywood politicos displayed a "faith in dramatic convention." In movies, for example, there is a cause-and-effect relationship which makes things "happen" and pushes them forward to a resolution, quite often an upbeat resolution. To perceive the *world* in these terms, writes Didion, "is to assume an ending for every social scenario."[21] Unfortunately, neither the world nor the political process works that way. There are always compromises, failures, trade-offs, losses, and many loose ends.

One could take this line of thinking further and state that there is in Hollywood a tendency to favor messianic and utopian programs, which, historically, have been characteristic of the Left. Film people see themselves as creative people, and indeed each film creates its own world. Quite often, the lead character becomes a *deus ex machina*, a messiah figure who vanquishes the enemy and solves all problems.

In similar style, leftist utopians see themselves as building "a better world" or "transforming society," and their schemes hold strong appeal for, especially, directors, who create worlds of their own, and who are often compared to dictators. They give orders; they tell people where to stand, what to say, and when they are no longer needed. Directors transform a chaotic situation into a product. They have a time by which everything must be in the can. Hence, it should come as no surprise that, in politics, they tend to favor those, foreign and domestic, who portray themselves as transformers of society or the world. In that connection, 35 percent of the entertainment elite agree that American political institutions need a "complete overhaul."[22]

This is not to say that all directors lean in that direction, only that their craft has occupational dangers. Waugh observed a similar peril among teachers, whose prolonged struggle with order, association with the immature, obeisance to authority, and quest for uniformity gave them a taste for totalitarian government, which does all the same things on a larger scale.[23]

To gain support in Hollywood, it does not matter whether the utopian succeeds at transforming humanity, nor even whether his efforts make conditions worse. The important point is that he *intends* to make them better and says so. This fits perfectly with the Hollywood posture. "The public life of liberal Hollywood," notes Joan Didion, "comprises a kind of dictatorship of good intentions."[24]

ONLY LIBERALS NEED APPLY

Though he did not, like Ben Stein, set out to examine the beliefs of the movie world, Mark Litwak's own experience confirms that Hollywood is a decidedly liberal community.

An attorney with a Naderite group in Albany, New York, Litwak set out for Hollywood in 1979 to make movies. This was in spite of the fact that he knew nothing about the craft, seldom saw films, and had not watched television for ten years.[25]

Though this would not seem to be the pedigree for an auspicious debut, he did have other credentials of equal weight: his Naderite liberalism. Litwak's strategy was simple and audacious. He simply hit town, telephoned the heads of major studios, and told them that his experience with Nader had provided him with a backlog of stories suitable for films and television programs. Quite likely, the recurring theme was the rapacious dragon of Corporate America ravishing the "little guy," the consumer, with the noble Consumer Advocate as the rescuing knight. That melodramatic scenario would square with Naderite ideology, and it certainly struck a chord in the studios. Within several weeks, some big players were bidding for Litwak's services and before long he was in business.

As it turned out, he didn't stay in business too long, but to get as far as he did so fast, with no previous experience and no relatives in the business, was truly remarkable.

But suppose Mr. Litwak had called to say that his years as a missionary or pastor had provided a wealth of stories. Imagine that he was a small businessman who had survived against overwhelming odds and wanted to share his vision with the masses. Or what if he had been a refugee from Bulgaria, with a memory bank of gripping tales from the labor camps? Had any of these scenarios been the case, there is no doubt that his call would not have got past the receptionist. If the executives heard about such pitches, it would likely have kept them laughing for several days.

PARTISAN POLITICS

The blacklist, the Hollywood Ten, and the past political wars of Hollywood will be outlined in a separate chapter. At present, there is much evidence to back up the claim of Nina J. Easton of the *Los Angeles Times* that "most of Hollywood, and its money, leans liberal."[26]

Jeremy Larner, the screenwriter for *The Candidate*, was a speechwriter for Eugene McCarthy, and Warren Beatty and other stars were tireless promoters of George McGovern. When the entertainment elite said they didn't know anyone who voted for Nixon, they were likely telling the truth. One survey showed that they were 82 percent behind McGovern.[27] On a "Crossfire" broadcast on the Cable News Network, Ben Stein said that in thirteen years he had never met another Republican in the Writers Guild.

Before his recent political demise and fizzled comeback, Gary Hart was the politician of choice in Hollywood. He had "star quality," an oft-used phrase. Actors such as Warren Beatty (again), Debra Winger, and Steve Martin once auditioned the former divinity student for assorted parties and fund-raisers.

With Hart out of the race, Hollywood political support during the 1988 primaries was mostly divided between Michael Dukakis and Jesse Jackson. Some forty-seven entertainers, including Bill Cosby and Margot Kidder, openly endorsed Jackson. Thirty-eight came out for Dukakis, including Sally Field, Richard Gere, Woody Allen, and Lauren Bacall.

That Hollywood should opt for Jesse Jackson is entirely natural. He was clearly the best-looking, most charismatic, most telegenic candidate, and by far the best public speaker. Comedian Arsenio Hall contended that, whoever won the election, Jackson should make all the speeches. He exemplifies what Julius Lester calls the "messiah mentality." While the Reverend Martin Luther King, Jr. never offered himself as the solution to segregation and disenfranchisement, "the answer Jesse Jackson offers," says Lester, "is Jesse Jackson."[28] This is bound to attract those accustomed to having a strong central character resolve all difficulties. And Jackson is, of course, the candidate farthest to the left on the current scene.

With Jackson out of the running, Dukakis was the darling of Hollywood. Francis Ford Coppola says of his film *Tucker*: "Yeah, this is like a Dukakis movie! Not a Reagan-era movie. The public is so aware of their shrinking purchasing power."[29] That sounded like a Dukakis stump speech. Actually, at the time of the statement, the purchasing power of the American public was quite high, certainly much higher than during the inflationary reign of Jimmy Carter.[30]

By contrast, only eight actors and three executives were on record as supporting Republican candidate George Bush. They included Cheryl Ladd, Tom Selleck, Helen Hayes, and, not surprisingly, Clint Eastwood.[31] It should be added that Ronald Reagan's Hollywood lineage did not get him much support from the film community in 1980 or 1984. Indeed, the colony opposed him, for the most part. Jane Fonda is something of a spokesperson for Hollywood politics, and was on record as saying that Reagan was a lousy actor and would be a lousy President. Doubtless, the stars "don't know anyone who voted for Reagan," just as they knew no one who voted for Nixon or Ford. But even stars have only one vote, and it seems clear that Mr. Reagan didn't need them. Republicans do have support in California, but it tends to come from outside the film colony.

Los Angeles political writer Ronald Brownstein describes what he calls the "Hollywood Primary," also known as the "money primary," because Los Angeles is "the Iowa of money." In this affair, the stars get a crack at picking the President. Any serious Democratic candidate must meet the approval of influential biggies such as Jane Fonda, Ed Asner, and Norman Lear. They must also curry favor with Sidney Sheinbaum, a tireless fund-raiser for liberal and leftist causes, who is married to the daughter of movie mogul Harry Warner. They also must contend with the Hollywood Women's Political Committee, which raised $1.5 million dollars from a one-night splash at the home of Barbra Streisand. [32] Nothing similar exists on the Republican side, in spite of high-profile conservatives such as Charlton Heston and Tom Selleck.

Publicist Pat Kingsley of the PMK agency, a Dukakis supporter, is a liberal activist with considerable clout. She screens politicians for her liberal activist clients such as Sally Field, Candice Bergen, and Lily Tomlin. Francis O'Brien, a Dukakis consultant and himself a former movie publicist, considers Kingsley's endorsement "like the Good Housekeeping seal of approval," capable of unleashing a tide of contributions from fat Hollywood bank accounts. Kingsley once arranged a party for Dukakis at the home of Sally Field, but the presidential candidate's staff said he had to be in Massachusetts that day, in the Statehouse. However, after a few calls from Kingsley, Dukakis canceled his official duties and went to the party.[33]

Hollywood involvement goes beyond endorsing or opposing candidates. Judicial nominees are now fair game. By directing a media barrage that featured a (largely untrue) statement by actor Gregory Peck, film and television producer Norman Lear played a leading role in defeating the confirmation of judicial nominee Robert Bork. The nominee was effectively made into a symbol of reaction and repression. Anthony Podesta of Lear's People for the American Way calls the technique "selective reality."[34]

While the fact of so much Democratic Party activism would reveal a certain Hollywood profile on specific issues, it will serve our purpose to make further observations.

BUSINESS AND ECONOMICS

Hollywood is a place of fashion, in films, styles, and ideas. The current vogue, as exemplified by the hit movie *Wall Street*, is a kind of progressive chic featuring anticapitalism. Where could such a posture come from, in profit-conscious Hollywood? Ben Stein saw a youthful flirtation with socialism as responsible for many Hollywood attitudes. Many of the people he interviewed told him that they had been left-wingers, and that they were proud of it. Stein saw people he interviewed as being possessed of a "left-over left wing infatuation," coupled, of course, with the frustrations of working in an industry where the profit motive is so important.[35]

Thus, Oliver Stone demands big money to make a movie which attacks the perceived morals of Wall Street—greed, selfishness, unscrupulousness, faithlessness—and thoroughly demonizes the businessman and his craft. Richard Grenier calls this "leftism tempered by greed."[36] It is characteristic of the McGovernite mentality to loathe capitalism, with an important qualification. Grenier notes that:

> They are of that specialized breed of socialist ideologue which wants to destroy capitalism root and branch—except for their three-picture deal with Orion. Also their $10 million home in Bel Air, their Mercedes, Jaguar and Maserati.[37]

In an October 17, 1987 speech at the Second Thoughts Conference[38] in Washington, P. J. O'Rourke contended that some movie stars are not content with fame, money, and power. They must have more. He cited Shirley MacLaine as example. She has everything anyone could possibly desire, but must still claim to have been Cleopatra and Joan of Arc in previous lives. Such declarations, O'Rourke said, put greed in a whole new light.

The documentary film *Hollywood's Favorite Heavy* shows how the businessman has become an omnipresent villain. One producer's explanation is that the audience is for the most part composed of mindless clods who can barely operate a microwave oven, and that the businessman bad-guy is a lowest-common-denominator villain that everyone will understand. Contempt for the audience can hardly make for good drama. While the focus of that film is on television, the same mentality informs movies.

While many people struggle just to earn a living in Hollywood, those who make it can acquire great wealth instantaneously. Those who are simply handed lots of money, which they don't deserve, and know it, sometimes insist that *everyone* simply be handed money; not *their* money, that is, but other people's money. They fail to understand how wealth is created, but insist that it be "redistributed." Hollywood socialism is characterized by a desire to be generous with the earnings of others, and calls this attitude "compassion" or "sensitivity." One sometimes hears complaints about "old money," but there is plenty of that in Hollywood. Walter Huston the actor begat John Huston the director, who begat Anjelica Huston the actress. It is a fair bet that Anjelica has a rather tidy inheritance. Old money indeed.

Liberal guilt, coupled with ambivalence about the craft, is likely a key motivation for Hollywood politics. But one does not find Hollywood millionaires sharing their mansions with the homeless, nor building shelters for them out of their own money, which they possess in abundance. Rather, they lobby the government to do the work. A number of religious leaders follow a policy of making their tax returns public. If Hollywood types would do likewise, one could see just how much of that compassion actually trickles down to the needy.

INTELLECTUAL MATTERS

> Hollywood was hardly a nursery for intellectuals, it was a hot-bed of false values.
>
> (David Niven)[39]

To say that Hollywood is anticapitalist is not to say that the film community has a firm grasp of economic realities, nor even of any realities. In Hollywood, it is fantasy *uber alles*. In any case, there is very little intellectual life in Los Angeles of any sort, and the film colony is about as anti-intellectual a place as one can find. Hortense Powdermaker saw it as atavistic, "gradually emerging from the age of magic into the present."[40] But the present climate throughout the country is not particularly intellectual either. Ours is a psychological, not an intellectual, age.

Though many of the people Ben Stein interviewed had been to college, none was extensively educated. He noted that in the fare they produced, education and intellectual matters played practically no role at all, and that those who had libraries were likely to be villains.[41] "There's always been something subversive about movies," notes Oliver Stone. "They make fun of teachers, of school."[42]

One has only to hear Hollywood stars pronounce on the homeless, the minimum wage, or nuclear weapons to realize that their approach is seldom intellectually coherent or empirically informed. In Hollywood, it is forever emotion and posturing over intellect and substance.

AMERICA THE BAD

> My next movie is called *Contra* because the word symbolizes "against." It's not just about contras. It's about America being against everything that's progressive. . . . I'm beginning to think that the only solution is a war that involves Americans, because it's the only way this country is going to wake up to what is really going on down there. I think America has to bleed. I think the corpses have to pile up. I think American boys have to die again. Let the mothers weep and mourn.
>
> (Oliver Stone)[43]

The above quote summarizes a prevailing attitude in Hollywood since the mid-1960s, when the adversarial culture took over. In 1968 Pauline Kael wrote of the "mythical America of message movies," which was "evil."[44]

Conspiracy theories are rampant in Hollywood, as a startled Ben Stein discovered when he moved there in the mid-1970s. When prominent producers found out that he had worked for Nixon, they pumped him for information about the international conspiracy for which Nixon was merely a pawn. In the producers' view, a few powerful industrialists ran the world, along with American politicians such as Alexander Haig and Henry Kissinger, who were in turn manipulated by octogenarian Nazis. Every year this group met and decided the results of each election, whether wars should be started, what the inflation rate should be, and so on. Stein was amazed at the ideas, more so because the producers believed them to be common knowledge, and that if you didn't know about the conspiracy, you were either a fool or a collaborator.[45]

More recently, there has been much Hollywood support for a lawsuit filed by the Washington-based Christic Institute, which alleges a long-standing and labyrinthine conspiracy involving U.S. foreign policy, the CIA, terrorism, and drug smuggling. This demonology is reflected in the movie *Lethal Weapon.* [46] A number of Hollywood stars, such as Jane Fonda, Mike Farrell, Daryl Hannah, and Ed Asner, have supported the institute financially.[47] A Miami judge dismissed the suit in June of 1988.[48] And Christics have ever been criticized in leftist publications such as *The Nation* and *Mother Jones.*

In the trendy Hollywood outlook, America is "Fascist," a generic term for anything and anyone the Hollywood Left doesn't like, or, more often, for anyone who criticizes the Left. In this view, corporations are Fascist (with the possible exception of the one with which you have that three-picture deal); nuclear power is Fascist; hunting is Fascist; *Rambo* is Fascist; and so on.

Hollywood's most high-profile activist, Jane Fonda, and her New Left veteran husband, Tom Hayden, have established what they call a "Network." The organization conducts what amounts to political indoctrination sessions for "brat pack" actors such as Rob Lowe and Daphne Zuniga at the Fondas' Santa Monica mansion. Actress Ally Sheedy said that Fonda and Hayden are "incredibly effective at motivating and opening up your mind."[49]

The manifestation of these concepts in specific movies will be dealt with later, but suffice it to say that the Hollywood elite is living quite comfortably in "Fascist" America.

There are, of course, more than a few who do not share these views, but what Lenin called infantile leftism is the ideological fashion in Hollywood, and in popular culture it is always dangerous to go against the trends. I once did some work on a script for a best-selling novel that was strongly conservative and anti-Communist. The producer was enthusiastic about my work, but added, "You realize of course that this will offend every leftist in Hollywood." He had in mind the very real possibility that if he went ahead with the project, some key people might be unwilling to work with him in future, and he was probably right. When you think about it, it's kind of like a blacklist.

It is perhaps worth recalling the generally bipartisan and pro-American Hollywood stand of the past, especially in wartime. The Hollywood Canteen opened on October 3, 1942 and remained open every day for three years. The volunteers included Betty Grable, Olivia de Havilland, and Greer Garson. Fred MacMurray, Basil Rathbone, and John Garfield served as busboys, while other stars washed dishes. Bing Crosby and Bob Hope sold war bonds, as did Al Jolson. Movie theatres stressed direct sales of war bonds to patrons and held free-movie days for bond purchasers. Theatres also cooperated in salvage drives.[50]

It is safe to say that such phenomena would be unthinkable today, and were certainly not in evidence during the Vietnam War. At that time, it should be remembered, Jane Fonda traveled to North Vietnam and broadcast anti-American propaganda over Radio Hanoi. Fifteen years later, she attempted a feeble and ultimately fraudulent attempt at an apology on ABC Television's "20/20."[51]

One does not expect a "my country right or wrong" attitude from film stars or anyone else. However, movie stars, while not politicians, are public figures and as such wield considerable power. Such power should be exercised responsibly. Unqualified enmity, or even support for the opposition on the part of some, can hardly be called responsible. But recent experience strongly suggests that that is precisely what may be expected.

DOUBLE STANDARDS

Catholic priest and UCLA professor Blase Bonpane has introduced Daniel Ortega and other members of the Nicaraguan Dictatorship of the Proletariat to the Hollywood elite, where they were very well received. In Hollywood, one can easily organize a benefit for Nelson Mandela of the Communist-dominated African National Congress, but dissidents from the Eastern Bloc go begging.

In its distribution deal for the independent film *Red Scorpion*, starring Dolph Lundgren, Warner Brothers stipulated that any contact with South Africa would cancel the deal, and in fact did kill the agreement.[52] But while any contact with South Africa makes one an international pariah, there is a spirit of willing cooperation with the Soviet Union, a far more oppressive regime with its own "national homelands" policy. Fres Film, an American company, has signed an agreement with the Soviet Mosfilm to produce a feature movie.[53]

Actor Robert Redford travels often to Moscow and has praised the Soviet film industry.[54] Redford has also been feted by Cuba's Latin American Film Institute and has sponsored a script-writing workshop in Havana.[55] The Cuban and Soviet film industries, it should be noted, are both entirely controlled by their respective Communist regimes, and required, as Nestor Almendros notes, "to make propaganda films *ad infinitum*."[56]

Thus, in the Hollywood outlook, opposition to foreign regimes bears no relation to the degree of internal repression or external aggression of those regimes, nor to any threat they might pose to the United States and its allies. It is entirely a matter of political fashion, along, of course, with careful attention to one's career. The selective indignation of Hollywood politicos is a self-serving emotional luxury that enables those who are fabulously wealthy to feign solidarity with the poor. It also enables them to appear to be bravely speaking out against injustice while actually taking no risk at all. Moreover, it simultaneously provides free and favorable publicity, and even furthers one's financial prospects. Not many deals offer such multiple benefits. John Gunther was right that in Hollywood, money was the final arbiter of behavior.

SUMMARY

While there are notable exceptions, the dominant Hollywood worldview is, politically, that of McGovernite liberal-leftism, with occasional forays into what the British call the "loony left." This view sees the United States as a bully and exploiter, at home and abroad. It advocates isolationism, appeasement, and unilateral disarmament, and becomes positively hysterical whenever the United States acts, such as in the case of Grenada. Though it is generally sympathetic to leftist experiments, it does not, like the leftism of the 1930s and 1940s, spend a lot of time praising the Soviet Union, though with *glasnost* things may well revert to the old pattern. Its central certainty is that the United States is bad, an outlook entirely negative and destructive.

Socially, the views are those of the adversarial culture, particularly indulgent toward the homosexual and feminist lobbies. The neanderthal idea that violent criminals are victims of society also finds favor in these regions. It is from a preponderant, ever-encroaching government that all good things flow.

The religious outlook is a kind of secular fundamentalism, or in some cases an inclination toward Eastern mysticism and New Age nostrums. This is coupled with a marked hostility to the Judaic-Christian tradition in general and any sort of conservative Christianity in particular.

If one may judge by recent presidential elections, these are not the views of the majority of Americans. But this is the *Weltanshauung* that informs the commercial cinema, especially its message movies.

TEN

RELIGION AND THE MOVIES

WE AMERICANS DEMAND BETTER MOVIES!
PRODUCERS REPENT! THOU SHALT NOT KILL—
WHY BUTCHER?
(Protest signs carried by two demonstrators at the opening of *The Greatest Story Ever Told* in Los Angeles)[1]

BIBLICAL EPICS

In the world of the commercial cinema, the Bible has been a handy sourcebook for attempts at the spectacular, which frequently emerged as rather tawdry costume epics. In addition to earning money, the vaguely religious themes gave the studios additional prestige.

The Italians led the way with the original *Quo Vadis?* and *Cabiria*, which drew record crowds and demanded the highest admission prices. American filmmakers showed their staunch adherence to the primary law of their trade: whatever makes money will be imitated. D. W. Griffith, fresh from making *Birth of a Nation*, was up to the task.

He launched a new epic called *Intolerance*, which focused on the destruction of Babylon in the sixth century B.C., the ministry of Jesus Christ, and the massacre of the Huguenots in France in 1572. A more ambitious and expensive project could hardly be imagined. Several seasons of "Masterpiece Theatre" would barely be up to the task, and it is doubtful whether Alistair Cooke would still be around at the end.

Griffith's financial backers were concerned that the project did not include "enough sex" to attract audiences. Griffith obliged his bag-men by spending $200,000 on one massive orgy sequence, more than the entire cost of *Birth of a Nation*, which had been the most expensive film made in its time. As if the sex, along with the varied themes, was not enough, the new film included a pacifist parable in which modern soldiers laid down their guns and gazed skyward to a band of angels. The final tally for the picture was nearly two million dollars, but the public showed little tolerance. It became the first big-scale box office bomb in history.[2]

Cecil B. De Mille, on the other hand, enjoyed great success with his 1929 version of *The Ten Commandments*, which he remade in 1956. The picture earned $14 million on an investment of $1.5 million.[3] His other works in this genre include *King of Kings, The Sign of the Cross,* and *Samson and Delilah*. De Mille was serious about his work, and sometimes held devotional services on location, much to the consternation of the cast and crew. He evidently believed that audiences would be automatically attracted to religious fare.

His rival Darryl Zanuck contended that the enormous box-office success of *Samson and Delilah* did not indicate that the public wanted Biblical pictures. Rather, "It indicates that they will accept a biblical picture providing it is loaded with box-office ingredients and showmanship." He added that "*Samson and Delilah* is basically a sex story and when you can get one in biblical garb apparently you can open your own mint."[4]

Zanuck's 1929 production of *Noah's Ark*, however, bore more resemblance to the work of D. W. Griffith. It cut back and forth between ancient and modern scenes and used a veritable army of extras and animals. In one scene, crews released thousands of tons of water which rushed downward through chutes and finally crashed onto the set of a pagan temple. During the filming of the sequence, three extras died and a number suffered crippling injuries. For their part, audiences fled the picture, which critics consider among the worst ever made.[5]

Films such as *David and Bathsheba, The Robe, Ben Hur, Barabbas, Sodom and Gomorrah*, and *The Silver Chalice* enjoyed considerable success, and, amidst the glitz, provided the occasional flash of authenticity. Others were flops and embarrassments, such as *The*

Greatest Story Ever Told, which sought to avoid sensationalism and strove for verisimilitude. In preparation for his shoot, director George Stevens showed himself quite ecumenical. He read over thirty different translations of the New Testament, consulted with thirty-six Protestant ministers, held a consultation with Pope John XXIII, and even discussed the script with David Ben-Gurion. To elicit expressions of wonder and awe, Stevens told his actors to imagine that John Glenn had landed in front of them in a space capsule.

In spite of a number of stars, including Charlton Heston, who had previous Biblical movie experience, and a budget of some $20 million, the picture was a disaster. It ran nearly four hours, which prompted critics to dub it "The Longest Story Ever Told." It earned only $8 million in the twenty years following its release in 1965. However, the picture lives on in the lore of cinema primarily because of one sentence delivered by a Roman centurion played by none other than John Wayne and spoken in his best accent: "Truly, this man wuz the son of Gawd." It was his only line.[6]

In spite of this failure, Biblical epics did not disappear from the scene. The following year, John Huston tried his hand with *The Bible,* which title was more than a slight exaggeration since he didn't even get out of the book of Genesis. The film was quite authentic in places, but abysmally slow. Huston doubtless counted on a number of sequels to finish out the canon, but none has come to pass.

Probably the ultimate in Biblical epics was Franco Zeffirelli's six-hour *Jesus of Nazareth*. This made-for-television movie was critically acclaimed and achieved record viewing figures.

In a sense, Biblical epics reveal the worst of Hollywood: sentimentality, sensationalism, wastefulness, and just plain fraud. But they may also indicate that the industry does have (had?) something of a conscience. And in the cinematic culture of an illiterate age, it can't hurt to have films that at least attempt to deal with the Bible. Someone may see one and later pick up the genuine article. And even if the reader is John Wayne, Biblical epics have made Scriptural texts a part of film history.

In addition, it may be said of these films that, while they are exploitative and far short of being authentic, they were not made in a spirit of malice and did not intend to slander the Jewish or Christian religions and their followers. And although they often failed to provide an accurate portrait of the time, they were not deliberately revisionist attempts to falsify history. As will be seen, that is one of the latest cinematic trends, something for which film is well suited.

TRADITIONAL THEMES

As the proverb has it, there are no atheists in foxholes, and wars have sparked renewed interest in religious films. Griffith made his epic *Intolerance* during World War I, the "war to end all wars," when religious themes were common. The World War II era saw such efforts as *Going My Way, Song of Bernadette, The Keys of the Kingdom,* and *The Bells of St. Mary's.* Bombed-out churches were the most common metaphor of the decade. After the war, interest waned, and an expensive production of *Joan of Arc* bombed at the box office, as did a religious picture called *The Next Voice You Hear.*

Around the end of the 1950s there was *A Man Called Peter, A Nun's Story, Inn of the Sixth Happiness, Saint Joan,* and *The Cardinal.* Some of these experienced modest success, in some cases critically, in other cases at the box office. But from a dramatic standpoint, all were subject to the limitations of the medium. None was a "smash," even though the religious theme was sometimes a cover for something else. Peter Ustinov calls *A Nun's Story* "one of the sexiest films ever," in which "abstinence became an erotic barometer and the unrequited longings of the protagonists kept hovering on the brink of obscenity."[7]

Specifically Catholic films such as *The Miracle of Fatima* have found favor with their target audience regardless of prevailing conditions. And there always seems to be a market for fantasy films which deal with life and death. *Heaven Can Wait,* for example, appeared in different manifestations some forty years apart.

HORROR, MYSTERY, AND RELIGION

Reformed theologian R. C. Sproul makes a case that dramatic presentations of horror are inherently religious in nature. He draws heavily on Mircea Eliade, an historian of religion, and Rudolf Otto, who adopted the term *mysterium tremendum* as practically synonymous with "the holy." This, in turn, derives support from Biblical characters expressing fear and dread in the presence of God. The same idea finds expression in lyrics such as, "sometimes it causes me to tremble," from the old spiritual "Were You There When They Crucified My Lord?"[8] Sproul also notes that a popular radio drama from the 1940s was called "Inner *Sanctum*."

This is not to say that the Hollywood horror films express or cultivate the same reverential awe or "fear" of God characteristic of Abraham or Moses, only that horrific themes do evoke a sense of the mysterious, something that modern culture has largely lost. Thus, when the powerful medium of film raises the specter of the mysterious, and then fails to explain it away, the effect is often profoundly disturbing. Bill Cosby is to be believed when he describes the craven terror he and his boyhood chums experienced at the Saturday horror flicks. R. C. Sproul notes that his wife is fond of these movies, but refuses to watch them alone.

Unfortunately, just as Biblical epics have been a cover for rather squalid soap operas, horror films are currently a cover for what Jay Leno calls "slice and dice movies," such as *The Texas Chainsaw Massacre*. Those who patronize this type of gore deserve everything they get.

But the fact that people do like to be scared shows a need for what are essentially religious themes. The commercial cinema will likely continue to fill that need, subject to all the limitations of the medium and the outlook of the business.

THE MANUFACTURE OF MYTH

> The true field of the movies is not *art* but *myth*.
>
> (Parker Tyler)[9]

From this writer's point of view, there is little artistic reason why such films as *E.T., Star Wars,* and *Close Encounters of the Third Kind* should be among the most successful cinematic ventures of all time. For the most part, they are infantile, noisy, sentimental, often nonsensical, and substitute technical gimmickry for genuine human feeling. Their most compelling characters are robots, and their musical scores are weak. *Return of the Jedi* was perhaps the most expensive muppet movie ever made, and broke new ground in merchandising hucksterism.

For all their defects, however, these movies show great breadth of imagination. George Lucas apparently intended *Star Wars* to be a Disney-style science-fiction movie, appealing to a rather limited audience. But unlike most science fiction, he placed the story not far into the future, but in the distant *past*, in a galaxy far away. This struck a chord with a society whose Judaic-Christian founding beliefs have been thoroughly discredited in the public mind, and whose substitutes—scientistic, materialistic, sensual, pseudo-religious—have been tried and found wanting. The *Star Wars* genre stepped into this void, as a *Newsweek* writer put it in 1979:

> People can croak, "Entertainment! Entertainment!" until they're blue in the face. The fact remains that films like "Close Encounters of the Third Kind," "Superman," and even "Star Wars" have become jerry-built substitutes for the great myths and rituals of belief, hope and redemption that cultures used to shape before mass secular society took over.[10]

These films evoke preexisting worlds and cultures, unravel myths of knights and empires, and portray something called "The Force." They feature a clearly delineated good-versus-evil struggle, which is sorely lacking in modern drama. This lacuna has even been offered as an explanation for the popularity of televised wrestling, where such a struggle isn't lacking, but where good taste is.

Consider the fearful symmetry of Stephen Spielberg's *E.T.* In this film, a being with special powers comes to earth, lives in humble circumstances, shows compassion, is loved and followed by many, but, feared and misunderstood by the authorities, dies, and then is resurrected from the dead. During the filming of the picture, the many parallels between the extraterrestrial and Christ suddenly dawned on the cinematographer and the screenwriter, a Catholic. They pointed them out to Spielberg, who responded, "I'm Jewish and I don't want to hear anything about this."[11]

In short, one could say that people need to believe in *something*, and that the long lines outside theatres confirm that a few astute filmmakers gave them something to believe in. Their films assure people that they are not alone in the universe. That may not be much, but one should never expect much from film.

On the other hand, there are films which seem to say that we *are* alone in the universe. *Altered States* was a kind of existential howl. Robert Short, a keen student of popular culture, calls *2001: A Space Odyssey* a parable of hopelessness, and bad philosophy masquerading as good entertainment.[12]

POSITIVE PORTRAYALS

Some commercial films, while not overtly religious, feature heavy Christian symbolism. The young priest played by Gene Hackman in *The Poseidon Adventure* sacrifices himself that others might escape with their lives. A similar incident takes place in *Grey Lady Down.*

In *The Omega Man*, Charlton Heston is the only man left in the world whose blood is not contaminated. Everyone else is affected by a plague that causes them to thrive in the darkness and hate the light. Mathias, the leader of the malevolent hordes, strikes Heston down with a spear, and he dies in a Christ-like pose. A quantity of his blood survives, however, leaving a ray of hope.

Some have seen a Christ figure in Alec Guinness's Ben Kenobi, who tells Darth Vader, "If you strike me down, I shall become more powerful than you can imagine."

The Mosquito Coast, though heavily flawed, does a good job of showing man's predicament. It is made clear that Allie, the central character, rejects religion and believes in himself. He is a man trying to get back to the Garden. However, civilization, technology, politics, and even nature are all shown to have their evil side. He discovers that it is not possible to set up a utopia on earth.

Alfred Hitchcock's *The Birds* similiarly debunked scientism and raised the possibility of a malevolent nature. Whether such symbolism goes over the top is anybody's guess, but one should not write it off. In any case there are always writers such as Robert Short who are willing to use it as a parable.

Others eschew symbolism for verisimilitude, and some succeed. Paddy Chayevsky's *Marty* is a simple story of an aging bachelor, played to perfection by Ernest Borgnine. The characters are truly human. They have morals, consciences, and freely discuss matters such as going to church. In short, they are allowed to be themselves, and the religious and moral dimension makes for deep characterization and a moving story. These are true "ordinary people," not the cloying sybarites and neurotics played by Donald Sutherland and Mary Tyler Moore in the film of the same name.

As noted, *Chariots of Fire* was not preachy, but simply allowed Eric Liddell, the missionary candidate, to be himself. He is the "muscular Christian" who makes people stand up and take notice. But he is also a gentleman, as is every major character in the film. Even the rather jaded aristocrats are likable in their own way.

In *The Verdict*, the lawyer played by Paul Newman is something of a down-and-out character. But at least he is unafraid to discuss his religious beliefs in a public forum. One gets some idea that his faith inspires him, and that is to be appreciated. It would have been no trouble at all to leave religion completely out of the picture.

Places in the Heart was a more nostalgic treatment, and evoked a strong sense of religion's place in the life of that time. There is one rather hard-hearted deacon, but on the whole the picture is positive. The movie opens to the strains of "Blessed Assurance," which was certainly a surprise. There is some typical Hollywood fakery and nonsense, but the major characters gather together in a mystical Lord's Supper at the end. This is much more than one normally expects.

Likewise, *Hoosiers* does not banish religion from its portrayal of small-town Indiana. The minister is a little overbearing when the new coach comes to town, but he is not caricatured. One of the players is fond of getting on his knees and praying before games, and staying in prayer long after the others have departed for the court. But there is no attempt to mock his beliefs or practices. At one point the coach, played by Gene Hackman, tells him, "God wants you on the court," and the player agrees.

In Horton Foote's *Tender Mercies*, country singer Mac Sledge attempts to put his shattered life back together. He works for a woman who sings in a Baptist choir and eventually finds faith himself. Fortunately, Mr. Foote understands both drama and cinema. He handles these themes with delicacy and elegance. The director takes advantage of the dramatic qualities of the baptismal act itself. In a medium shot, we see Mac in the baptistery; we hear the words of Scripture; we see him go under and come up. Then we cut to a close shot of Mac in the truck, with his smiling face fairly aglow. It is a complete transformation from the dark and gloomy countenance he wore at the beginning of the story. Had a "Christian" company that wanted to be sure to "get the gospel in" made this movie, there would have been a full sermon coupled with some testimonies. It would not have played, and that is where the story would likely have ended.

Unlike the conventional Billy Graham films, a good part of *Tender Mercies* takes place *after* the conversion. It is far from the case that every day in Mac's new life is "sweeter than the day before," as the revivalist hymn so fraudulently puts it. Every day is *not* sweeter than the day before. Mac still suffers heartache and loss, but now he is not alone. Most important, we *see* the change in Mac; he doesn't just *talk* about it. He stops getting drunk and spends a lot of time throwing the football with his new son, a parable of Mac's new relation with his heavenly Father. I thought that this film was about as good as the cinema gets with religious themes until Foote released *The Trip to Bountiful.*

As this film opens, two children run across a field, to the strains of Cynthia Clawson's rendition of "Softly and Tenderly, Jesus Is Calling." It is a flashback. The story deals with Carrie Watts, an elderly lady living in Houston with her stoical son Ludie and his insufferable wife Jessy May. Carrie is unhappy in this cramped environment and wants to visit her hometown of Bountiful before she dies.

Carrie is an openly Christian woman, given to hymn singing, which torments Jessy May. The film shows how childhood and old age are similar, the bookends of life. At both stages we are utterly dependent and in need of love. Carrie finds out that you can't go home again, that the direction of life is forward, not backward. In the background, the score gently adds, "Come home, come home, ye who are weary come home." If anyone is not moved by this film, I don't want to hear their problems.

Say Amen Somebody was a documentary about black gospel music. Roger Ebert called it the most joyous movie he had ever seen, and it was generally well received. As Stanley Crouch has noted, the "molten nobility of Negro religious emotion" is a "legacy that speaks to all Americans," regardless of color. It is the "spiritual tuning fork that has always brought the orchestra of domestic morality up to pitch."[13] There would seem to be room for more films of this type. Unfortunately, black gospel singers and nostalgic old ladies are not most producers' idea of good box office.

Christian minister and journalist Will Eisenhower pointed out a startlingly theological bit of dialogue in *Broadcast News*. In this film, Aaron Altman (Albert Brooks) refers to a slick professional rival by saying that if the Devil appeared in human form, he would be like that. He would not have horns and a tail but would be "attractive, nice and helpful," and would "lower our standards where they're really important."[14] That is pretty much the way it is.

The reader can surely come up with other examples of films that offer a positive portrayal of religion in general, or offer the occasional insight. But for the most part, the pickings are slim in the commercial cinema. Most of the action is on the other side.

ATTACKS ON RELIGION

> The Christian, in the pure and absolute meaning of the word, has no place on earth.
>
> (Spanish filmmaker Luis Buñuel)[15]

It has already been noted that religious experience usually does not play, and one cannot blame filmmakers for preferring themes better suited to their craft. However, the laws of drama do not sanction the deliberate misrepresentation of religion, much less direct attacks on religious people. But attacks are not always the problem.

As Paul Johnson has noted, "The outstanding non-event of modern times was the failure of religious belief to disappear."[16] Seventy years of atheistic propaganda and vicious persecution have failed to extinguish religion in the Soviet Union, where it is on the increase. And in spite of the many diversions, a highly secularized educational system, a general spirit of hedonism, and the ACLU, religion continues to thrive in the West.

The United States is the most openly religious nation in the Western world. High percentages of Americans believe in God and attend church or synagogue regularly. But one could easily deduce from the commercial cinema that religion scarcely exists in America. Religion in American cinema is as rare as Trotsky in Soviet cinema, or Huber Matos and Carlos Franqui in Cuban cinema.

The easiest way to stack the deck in film is simple elimination. Whatever you don't like, you simply keep out of sight. To be sure, it is not possible to ignore it completely; but in film religion often plays little if any role in the lives of major characters, just as it plays little if any role in the lives of those who produce, direct, and write movies. The all-too-apparent result is that a major dimension of American life is effectively banished from the screen, resulting in a highly distorted picture.

The Hollywood doctrine of separation of church and screen is a major reason why commercial movies cannot represent America, only an elite whose mores and beliefs do not parallel those of mainstream society. Can anyone seriously contend that *Porky's, Caligula,* and *Cruising* represent America?

Casting decisions sometimes place Christian characters in an unfavorable light. In *Norma Rae* the minister is disturbingly odd-looking and comes across as unintelligent and seedy. The missionary lady in *Murder on the Orient Express*, played by Ingrid Bergman, is dim and drab, most unlike the other characters. Actually missionaries who have spent years in places like Africa, which is where Bergman's character had lived, are usually interesting people, often with enormous erudition from translating the Bible into obscure dialects.

The minister in *Fanny and Alexander* is handsome and articulate, but he is a man of fathomless evil. That is to be expected, since anti-Christian themes are both common and well-developed in Bergman's films. Others take a different route—for example, the quick putdown.

When Diane Keaton is interviewing baby-sitters in *Baby Boom*, one prospective couple says that they believe "the Lord" wanted them to accept the job. Upon hearing this easy reference to Deity, Keaton dismisses them immediately. The impression is that anyone who refers to God in that fashion is a fanatic.

Richard Grenier dealt with this attitude in his novel *The Marrakesh One-Two*. In one scene, a woman who views herself as progressive offers "property is theft" as the most profound statement she can think of. She challenges her lover to offer his. He thinks for a moment and responds: "I am the resurrection and the life." She then gasps in horror that she has been involved with a "religious maniac."[17]

It might be remembered that a prevailing attitude in Hollywood is that the Christian religion is roughly equivalent to the Ku Klux Klan or American Nazi Party. Accordingly, a number of films have been openly hostile to religion, particularly Christianity. *Elmer Gantry*, currently appearing on stage, attacked hypocrisy, but one senses that the real target is Christianity. The same might be said about *Inherit the Wind*, about the Scopes Trial, which is also being revived.

The films of Luis Buñuel attacked the Roman Catholic Church and flaunted atheism. But according to some who are thoroughly familiar with Buñuel, which I am not, he at least treats the Church as a worthy adversary.[18] That is certainly not true of a film like *Monsignor*, which shows the Church as a crypto-Fascist organization secretly allied with the Mafia. This is one of the oldest anti-Catholic canards, roughly equivalent to the portrayal of Jews in *The Protocols of the Elders of Zion*. It is bigotry. *Monsignor* also portrays the Pope as a kind of senile, decrepit "E.T." character. On the other hand, Christopher Reeve, the hero, is a handsome, dashing chap. With his red cape, one almost expects him to take off, as he did in *Superman*. Even that desperate act, however, would not have saved the film.

Closer to home, *Malone*, with Burt Reynolds, spins a tale about a Christian paramilitary cult which, with widespread support, is attempting to overthrow the United States government. This theme has been used in films and television to the point of redundancy.

The opening scene of *Taps* shows marching military cadets, backdropped with a loud and heavily editorializing rendition of "Onward Christian Soldiers." The audience is clearly supposed to disapprove, and the implication is that this is what Christianity is about: militarism, violence, hypocrisy, etc.

Pass the Ammo lampooned television evangelism, as did *The Mosquito Coast*, much more severely than Paul Theroux's novel on which the film is based. *Dragnet* shows a pompous and moralistic television preacher (Christopher Plummer, hopelessly miscast) in league with a pornography tycoon. To be sure, television evangelists are often self-satirizing, and are surely the most battered bull's-eye around. But could any other kind of religious figure be so regularly ridiculed in the same way? One doubts it.

Films of this type rarely have much dramatic or artistic merit. When a movie sets out to attack something, there is seldom any sense of mystery for the audience as to whose side they are to be on. Who is going to pull for a TV preacher in league with a porn king? The filmmaker simply sticks pins in his favorite voodoo doll and expects the audience to cheer their approval or disapproval. In addition, a true work of art is normally a work of love, but this type of film is inspired by contempt, or even hatred. It is bound to show in the final cut.

It would require a separate work to catalogue the antireligious and anti-Christian content of contemporary film. The examples are endless: the Scripture-spouting homicidal maniac and Southern racist played by Telly Savalas in *The Dirty Dozen* is by now a stock character. Then there are the duplicitous missionaries in *Papillon*, the two-faced padre in *Blazing Saddles*, and the lisping prelate in *The Princess Bride*.

In Stanley Kubrick's *Dr. Strangelove*, the two wackiest characters, General Turgidson (George C. Scott) and General Ripper (Sterling Hayden), are the only ones who express religious beliefs. Scott's character even prays. To be sure the scenes are funny, but there can be little doubt that we are supposed to be laughing *at* religion. Ridicule is a lethal weapon, as Norman Lear knows all too well.

Overall, the negative or hostile portrayals of religion in general and Christianity in particular far outnumber the positive, but some changes may be on the way. Since the arrival of liberation theology, positive portrayal of radicalized priests are allowed, or even encouraged. Traditional priests continue to be ignored. One notes that Daniel Berrigan served as advisor to *The Mission*. There were also allusions to liberation theology in *Man Facing Southeast*, a highly original film from Argentina.

In the days of the Code, studio bosses deleted the phrase "rattling a tambourine" from a script because they thought it might offend the Salvation Army.[19] The present code encourages offenses to Christianity. The code is unwritten, of course, but understood, and to some degree enforced, if only by peer pressure.

In the final analysis, the portrayal of religion in contemporary films runs from ignorance to ridicule to outright hostility. Little wonder that viewers are so constantly disappointed. But it is not only Hollywood fare that fails to deliver the goods.

FILMS BY CHRISTIANS

It may be that the movies produced by companies such as Gospel Films and World Wide Pictures would be better served not by a general book on film such as this, but by a discussion of audiovisual aids for Christian ministry. For the most part, that is what they are and how they are advertised. Certainly the general public has little knowledge of them because, with the exception of movies by World Wide Pictures, these films may not be found in commercial theatres. They are usually screened in churches for a largely Christian audience, a kind of home movie for the Christian family.

Such films tend to repeat certain themes: the narrow escape, the sob story involving a disease or injury, and especially the dramatic conversion, usually from a life of drugs or alcohol, with the story focusing on the preconversion life. And whenever possible, it seems, Christian filmmakers focus on a converted celebrity or athlete.

In some cases I recall such films to have been amateurish and quite heavy-handed. I remember a documentary on the subject of cults in which the narrator sounded like *Dragnet's* Sergeant Friday reading some criminal his rights. However, a friend who regularly reviews Christian films tells me that the production values of some are approaching the level of commercial films.

Those who pay the bills have every right to make a film according to their own vision and purposes; and as didactic or evangelistic tools, these surely have their uses. In most cases the producers, cast, and crew do not pretend that they are involved in anything more than ministry. But even within these confines there are some points that should be made, or perhaps reviewed.

As noted, a didactic purpose often makes for poor drama. In addition, spiritual experience is difficult to convey. Communion is not the same as communication, and is not always verbal, let alone visual. I believe it has been forgotten that God can, and does, speak through silence. Film quite often fails when it attempts to evoke the mysterious, in a religious sense.

The use of film as an evangelistic tool must be tempered with the knowledge that, as Virginia Owens points out, Jesus' ministry shows a complete lack of technique. He never handed out tracts and used none of the modern salesmanship and marketing approaches so characteristic of television evangelism. Christ's approach with each seeker was different. He told some to follow Him and others to stay put. To be sure, there were "mass" gatherings, but on these occasions the people showed up for food or to see miracles, not for the teaching, which, when they heard, they did not always understand.[20]

In Malcolm Muggeridge's "Fourth Temptation," Jesus turns down Satan's offer of a television network because the Savior was "concerned with truth and reality," whereas what Satan's emissary had in mind was "fantasy and images."[21] It might be added that Muggeridge himself has made a number of documentaries, some on religious subjects. But his parable, I believe, has great validity and must be heeded.

Virginia Owens is surely on target when she writes that "we are poor imitators of the cultural productions of our society," and that we should be concerned about a Christian lifestyle which "parasitically lives off whatever is technologically mediated to the entire populace."[22] Christian television chat shows ape mainstream chat shows, and sometimes Christian films imitate Hollywood fare. For example, not long after *Heaven Can Wait* was released, a Christian film called *Kevin Can Wait* made an appearance. And I believe there is a Christian awards ceremony to parallel the Oscars. Such developments raise the question: is the Christian film industry perhaps not "ministry" after all, but merely sanitized entertainment for a ghettoized Christian subculture?

In summary, I believe it is a fair judgment that, with some exceptions, the Christian use of the cinematic medium reflects three prevailing attitudes. First, an arbitrary and un-Biblical division of the world into spiritual and secular spheres. (The word *secular* does not appear in the Bible.) Second, pietism, the belief that only certain overtly religious themes are legitimate for the Christian, with the others being "worldly." Third, utilitarianism, that any artistic endeavor must be in the service of propaganda, or, if you like, ministry.

The results are evident: redundancy, timidity, imitation, mediocrity, along with the same faults which characterize much religious writing: unctuousness and spiritual exhibitionism.

At least one Christian filmmaker has turned his attention to the mainstream. In 1986 Franky Schaeffer, who had produced a series of documentaries with his father, released a commercial film called *Wired to Kill* (an earlier title was *Booby Trap*). The picture was certainly not unheralded. There were full-page ads in the *Los Angeles Times* and on area television. Mr. Schaeffer went so far as to rent the Academy for a premiere screening and invited a veritable who's-who of the film community. But while the promotional campaign rates a "10," the picture was something else.

Having carefully examined this movie twice, I am confident that there is barely an original idea in it. In a massive, prescreening handout, Mr. Schaeffer admitted that *Wired to Kill* was "influenced" by *A Clockwork Orange, Blade Runner*, and *Road Warrior*, and that is certainly apparent. He adds that his film is "laced with what I would call small Fellini tributes,"[23] but these got by me, as did some of the dialogue, barely audible in places. As in *Airplane*, one hears jokes and messages over an intercom. As in many a recent film, the hero is a teen-age electronic whiz who depends on a gadget to defeat the Bad Guys. In this case, the gadget is a converted wheelchair named Winston, who serves as a *deus ex machina*. The difference here is that neither the character nor the electronic contrivance are believable.

The movie wallows in gruesome violence but was not at all exciting. Moreover, it exuded despair and hopelessness. More could be said, but suffice it to say that many people walked out of the premiere. The film lives on in video, however, and if readers think my judgment harsh, let them rent the film and judge for themselves.

It might be recalled that in 1981 Mr. Schaeffer wrote a book called *Addicted to Mediocrity*, which was sharply critical of the films produced by Christians. Many of his judgments were all too true, but in view of his first feature, it appears he might have waited before expressing them. One hopes Mr. Schaeffer can do better next time, if there is a next time.

ELEVEN

POLITICS AND DRAMATIC FILM

From its inception, the new government showed a complete mastery of vocabulary. A new art was born, the art of propaganda, of changing the meaning of things by changing their name.
(Mikhail Heller and Aleksandr Nekrich, *Utopia in Power*)[1]

WHAT IS POLITICAL?

Conservatives believe that human beings are flawed—sinful, as the Judaic-Christian tradition has expressed it—and not perfectible. Hence, they distrust utopian schemes. They look to the past for wisdom and oppose change for the sake of change. They stress personal redemption over systemic alteration. The center of their lives is usually religious, with politics a secondary concern. In many cases, they look for another world beyond this one, and are at pains not to make the present one into a utopia, but to keep it from becoming worse than it already is.

For the Left, and for many liberals, however, politics *is* a religion, which is why they take it with such deadly seriousness. In general, they do not look for a divinely established world to come, but have, as Eric Voegelin put it, immanentized the eschaton. In other words, their Kingdom of God is on earth. The Left considers the past a dark chronicle of oppression and talks incessantly of a Bright New Day just around the corner, if only the evil "structures" of a free market, a democratic polity, and in some cases religious belief could be removed. The Left believes that human nature is malleable and human beings are perfectible through the alteration of their environment. Hence the Left is constantly agitating for a Better World, which could be accomplished if only people like themselves could be in power, and everyone else forced to do what they say.

Given these fundamental differences, it is entirely natural that the Left should dominate the message business. The leftist axiom that everything is political applies particularly in the arts. And one should add that, for the Left, everything that is not specifically political is considered to be political by default.

For example, a Soviet *cinéaste* once told Irvin Kershner, director of *The Empire Strikes Back,* that American films were highly political. He based this judgment on the fact that in ordinary American movies there are usually several telephones and a well-stocked refrigerator in one house. In addition, the supermarkets are full of food and teenagers drive their own cars. These are simple and accurate depictions of American life, but for the Soviet filmmaker, this was pure propaganda.[2] It was for similar reasons that Stalin would not let *The Grapes of Wrath* be shown in the Soviet Union. In spite of its dreary picture of American life, it nevertheless showed that in the United States the poor had trucks and could go wherever they wanted. That too was "political," even though the intention of the filmmakers was to show the downside of American life.

TECHNIQUES OF PROPAGANDA

When American leftists marched off to fight on the Republican side in the Spanish Civil War, they did not call their battalion the Karl Marx Brigade or Josef Stalin Brigade, but the "Abraham Lincoln Brigade." This is in keeping with the basic dishonesty of the Left in misrepresenting what it stands for by adopting linguistic camouflage, terms such as "peace" and "democracy," and by hiding behind symbols of freedom.

Thus it is rather silly to search films looking for mention of the Communist Party, class struggle, Leninist hagiography, or the labor theory of value. In the films of the old Hollywood Left, as Andrew Sarris of the *Village Voice* has noted, "Revolutionary language has been sanitized into populist puerilities," such as "the people." The writers disguised class hatred as egalitarianism and smuggled in nationalism as populism. The battle consisted of "The People" versus "Them." The enemy could be openly identified as "fascism" or "Nazism," but the alternative could not openly be communism or socialism.[3]

As noted, film is not comfortable with ideas or philosophizing. It is better at symbolism and reductionism, taking complex situations and issues and turning them into a simplistic standoff between good guys and bad guys. And it is always easier to identify the bad guys than to flesh out the good. For the last generation, one bad guy has predominated.

IMAGES OF EVIL

Fascism is not, as is often erroneously supposed, a variant of capitalism but national *socialism*. The full name of the Nazi Party is the National Socialist German Workers Party. Communism purports to be *international* socialism, but, practically speaking, amounts to loyalty to the Soviet state. Both Hitler and Mussolini considered themselves Socialists and revolutionaries, and both loathed capitalism. They saw their revolutions as the triumph of labor over money.

Hitler's National Socialist regime is an important subject for films and lends itself to film treatment with its flaunted symbols of hatred and violence. And although not all films about the National Socialists and their genocidal work are good, they nonetheless leave, in film critic Annette Insdorf's words, "indelible shadows" for posterity.

Although the National Socialist regime ceased to exist nearly half a century ago, it continues to occupy a major place in cinematic demonology. According to Insdorf, there are at least eighty films dealing specifically with the Holocaust.[4] To these one must add the many combat movies of the postwar period. In a way, the preoccupation is understandable.

Movies are made for Everyman, and Hitler's malevolence is something everyone understands and opposes. Moreover, the National Socialist regime is a safe subject, and may be deplored at no risk whatsoever. Communism, on the other hand, is by nearly every standard worse than National Socialism, particularly in the area of mass murder. Official Soviet publications such as *Novy Mir* and *Nedelya* now freely admit that the forced collectivization of agriculture killed some ten million people, and that Stalin's policies were responsible for *fifty million deaths,* more than twice the number of Soviets killed in World War II,[5] and close to Solzhenitsyn's estimate of sixty million killed by Stalin. *Risk-2,* a documentary film shown on Soviet television, compares Stalin and Hitler, with Stalin apparently the loser.[6] But in spite of this superior malevolence, there are few films about communism, which is still very much in business and may not be deplored without risk.

Hollywood still prefers to play it safe, and this is part of the legacy of show business Stalinism, which will be taken up in detail in the chapter on the blacklist. Show business Stalinism is, as Pauline Kael has noted, "basically not political but psychological; it's a fashionable form of hysteria and guilt that is by now not so much pro-Soviet as just abusively anti-American."[7] Hollywood is still "fighting fascism," but identifies fascism's heirs as the United States. As Andrew Sarris notes, "The idiot left likes nothing better than to brand its current enemies exact replicas of Hitler."[8]

THE EVIL EMPIRE

In *Marathon Man,* for example, renegade American officials are shown cooperating with an old Nazi, with strong parallels drawn between Nazi activity and that of the CIA. *The Formula,* with George C. Scott, links the Nazi regime to American oil companies. In *The Big Fix,* a piece of 1960s nostalgia, a character fumes that "Fascists" are now running the government.

The House on Carroll Street dredges up the ever-present "McCarthy Era" and alleges a conspiracy to smuggle Nazi war criminals into the United States. This kind of ghost story is a staple of the Hollywood Left. These shadowy Nazis are held to be the secret source of American anticommunism, as though Stalin's genocide and expansionism, the Korean War, the Berlin blockade, and Khrushchev's "We will bury you" had nothing to do with it. As is often the case with the Left, the theory has scant factual support.[9]

In contemporary film, the CIA has become a three-letter code for evil. In *Three Days of the Condor,* the bad guys are a faction within the CIA, but one gets the impression that the rot goes very deep, and all the way to the top. Robert Redford plays an agency reader who uncovers a plot and then must be eliminated. It is for this role that Redford is best-known in the Soviet Union, which continues to show the movie to this day.[10] But the anti-CIA demonology may not play as well at home. The lesson John Simon derived from the film was that Americans should be grateful to the CIA because it does what the schools no longer do: hire people to read books.[11]

The aforementioned *Malone* links the CIA with dozens of foreign assassinations, and with domestic crazies like the Aryan Nations. *Lethal Weapon* portrays the CIA as a shadowy, drug-dealing mafia, led by robot-like thugs. There is a CIA buffoon in *Ishtar,* in which the good guys are left-wing Arab revolutionaries. In the spy thriller *Hopscotch,* the CIA man even wears a black hat, as do strike-breaking goons in *Reds.*

From these tactics it seems clear that it is only in technique that Hollywood films have become more "realistic." The nefarious CIA man is now a stock character, along with the Religious Fanatic, the Small Town Bigot, the Whore with a Heart of Gold, and the Crazed Vietnam Veteran.

Constantine Costa-Gavras' *Missing,* advertised as a "true story," is another work of anti-American demonology, alleging CIA conspiracy not just in the coup d'etat that brought down Allende in Chile, but in the death of an American, Charles Horman. Actually, Horman's relatives dropped the suit they had brought against the government for lack of evidence. The film plays fast and loose with the facts, keeping some actual names of characters and changing others, which resulted in a number of lawsuits.

Costa-Gavras' *State of Siege* showed the U.S. acting hand-in-glove with an odious foreign regime in Uruguay, and portrays the Marxist-Leninist Tupamaros as benevolent Robin Hood types. In reality, they were more like the Weather Underground or the Red Brigades. The director takes great care not to show them killing anybody.

The impression left by these pictures, which are well-crafted, is that if there is evil anywhere in the world, the United States is responsible. And the domestic situation is just as bad.

The China Syndrome, another dramatically effective film, is of course largely anti-nuke agit-prop. At the end, however, there is a montage of television commercials for various electric appliances.

Thus, it is American consumerism, with its demand for electricity, that is the "root problem." The message is that everyone should feel guilty, not just the executives of utility companies. Do the stars of *The China Syndrome* have any electrical gadgets in *their* homes? One would tend to think so.

The American political system has been treated roughly in films such as *The Candidate,* but never so cynically as in *Being There.* Though a thoroughly enjoyable movie on many levels, particularly as a satire of television, the story contains a parable of absolutely pristine Marxism. In Marxist theory, the government of a capitalist state has no power in itself, but is simply a tool of private industry, the bourgeoisie. The film makes the point in several ways. The President seems completely vacuous and must abjectly seek advice from a multimillionaire industrialist. He winds up taking advice not from the industrialist but from a disinherited gardener with the mind of a ten-year-old. Moreover, to press the point of the President's helplessness, he is shown as sexually impotent. Finally, at the funeral of the industrialist, the deceased's advisers whisper that the demented gardener is "their man" and will enable them to "hold on to the presidency."

Films such as *Roller Ball* and *Running Man* are anticorporate agit-prop masquerading as futurism. In *Roller Ball* people sing a "corporate anthem," and in *Running Man* one hears announcements of airline flights to "Anaconda, Chile." In *Robo-Cop* there are some heavy-handed anti-SDI messages.

MILITARY BUFFOONS

Stanley Kubrick's *Dr. Stangelove* contains some marvelous comic moments, but also perpetrates a favorite screen stereotype: the American military wacko. Sterling Hayden is General Jack Ripper (a subtle touch, that) in one famous scene shot closely and from below, giving him an air of larger-than-life dementia. He chomps a cigar and rambles on about bodily fluids and wild flouridation conspiracies, which lead him to launch a nuclear attack on the Soviet Union. The raving general Turgidson urges a further preemptive strike, and another buffoonish military man, Colonel Bat-Guano, places the interest of the Coca-Cola company above the cause of peace. The eponymous Dr. Strangelove, adviser to the U.S. President, is an old Nazi. It's all here, every shibboleth. It is implied that the Soviets are wacko as well, but the audience does not *see* any Soviet military buffoons, only American ones. General Ripper and Colonel Bat-Guano are what Hollywood politicos believe all U.S. military men are like.

Dr. Strangelove was ostensibly intended to show the dangers of nuclear war. But as Pauline Kael notes in a perceptive review, it failed to tell us how we are to gain control, intensified feelings of powerlessness and hopelessness, and left the impression that the nuclear threat meant that *everything* was a joke, that our leaders were clownish monsters. "It is not war that has been laughed to scorn," Kael writes, "but the possibility of sane action."[12]

Spies Like Us is probably the most elaborate piece of anti-SDI propaganda ever made, and is full of General Rippers. Costa-Gavras has a most apporpriate bit part as a Soviet border guard, and the evil CIA makes its compulsory appearance. *Deal of the Century* blames the American military and arms suppliers for wars around the world, one of the oldest and most thoroughly discredited clichés of the Left, but one adopted by Hollywood with all the joy of Archimedes.

THE VALE OF TEARS

The Grapes of Wrath, a fine film on many counts, is the precursor of a genre that sets out to portray the United States in the worst possible light. It was widely considered a leftist tract. At one point, a rather dim Henry Fonda wonders, "Who are these 'reds' anyway?" It should be noted that Ma Joad's manifesto at the end, "We'll go on forever because we're *the people,*" was added by producer Darryl Zanuck, who was no leftist, because he thought the movie was too depressing and wanted it to end on an upbeat.[13] Ironically, the California Okies depicted in the film later constituted some of Ronald Reagan's strongest supporters.

The Chase uses the South as a metaphor for the whole country. Everybody is racist, and even the kids are wicked. The director resorts to a device often used by those who wanted to vilify blacks: the portrayal of characters as sexually obsessed and prone to irrational violence. The picture also contains a parable of the Kennedy assassination. The writer was Lillian Hellman.[14]

In the Heat of the Night, on the other hand, written by Sterling

Silliphant, dealt with the South and racism in a more intelligent way, without being preachy. Here the characters are actual human beings, and show themselves capable of change. But this fine film has not been the pattern. The negative stereotypes of *The Chase* linger on in such pictures as *Easy Rider, Lords of Discipline, Fort Apache the Bronx,* and a host of others. They show an America of trigger-happy bigots, racists, religious hypocrites, and predatory capitalists, a nation that preys together.

VIETNAM

> We were destined to lose because this war had no moral purpose and it was fought without any moral integrity.
>
> (Oliver Stone)[15]

Films such as *Rambo, Missing in Action,* and *Uncommon Valor* focus not at all on the political questions of U.S. involvement, strategy, and historical background. They deal largely with the issue of POWs still in Southeast Asia, and they amount to rather cartoonish rescue stories. They are tales of the brave individual against the compliant bureaucrat, and as such have been popular with audiences. But one learns nothing about Vietnam from them, and they are only "political" by default. The Left hates them for what they lack: flagellation over American involvement.

One of the latest and most popular efforts, *Good Morning Vietnam,* backdrops scenes of bombing and napalming with popular songs. This is a cinematic expression of Susan Sontag's notion that there was a direct link between Lawrence Welk and napalming. The war itself comes across as essentially meaningless and without context; myriads of American soldiers simply showed up and began fighting. As Martha Bayles comments, the bad military men are made to contrast the good guy, "The Rockin' American."[16] The pro-American Vietnamese are shown as seedy and even depraved. One, a man, asks the Americans for a nude picture of Walter Brennan. But those Vietnamese sympathetic to the Viet Cong are charming and noble.

Platoon, Apocalypse Now, and *Full Metal Jacket* deal with small groups of Americans in battle and compress the larger sweep of the war into a small frame. For the most part, these films portray the war as futile and unwinnable. As critic George Szamuely has remarked, it is as if one made a film about British soldiers in World War II based solely on their defeat at Dunkirk.[17]

In these films Hollywood has added another stereotype to its already impressive collection. As Vietnam veteran William K. Lane puts it:

> The other image is created by the cultural termites in Hollywood: The American soldier in Vietnam as racist, neurotic, drug crazed, feral, a hopeless pawn of a rotten society sent to fight an unjust war. Even the cartoonish Rambo character is a societal misfit, a mumbling killer exorcising his demons in a revenge ritual.[18]

The image bears about as much verisimilitude as other Hollywood staples, such as the eyeball-rolling darkie or sinister Oriental. The vast majority of American soldiers in Vietnam were not racists, nor murderers, nor drug addicts. Lane is surely right that such people "deserve better than to be caricatured by Hollywood as a legion of losers."[19]

One profound difference between these films and those dealing with World War II is screen time allotted the enemy. In World War II films, viewers could eavesdrop on Nazi plotters and see their nefarious deeds. That dimension is either missing or distorted in most Vietnam movies.

The Green Berets shows the Viet Cong attacking in formation, as though they got their strategy from Napoleon. In *Good Morning Vietnam,* they come across as a kind of street gang at worst, misguided kids with legitimate grievances at best. In the second *Rambo* picture, they appear to be World War II Japanese. In all cases, they are one-dimensional stick figures.

Platoon and *Apocalypse Now* are supposedly more realistic treatments and contain some vignettes that are authentic depictions of combat. (A veteran acquaintance gives the nod to *Apocalypse Now.*) The filmmakers appear to believe that they are making a profound statement simply by showing that modern warfare is not a day at the beach. But their realism has limits. No Hollywood movie shows the true face of North Vietnamese communism in the same way that World War II movies showed the face of Nazism. None provides information about Ho Chi Minh's long career as a Soviet cadre. None attempts to show North Vietnamese atrocities, such as the massacres at Hue.

As noted, *The Killing Fields* never mentions the word "communism," and attempts to blame the Cambodian genocide on the United States. The bloodiest scenes are the result of an accidental American bombing. The Khmer Rouge atrocities are conveyed by a pile of skeletons, which don't cry or bleed. There is no clue as to *why* the Khmer Rouge slaughtered people. Director Roland Joffe was not up to the task of showing class hatred in action.

What became of Vietnam *after* the departure of American forces is a subject the Hollywood Left prefers to ignore. Only hard-core leftists such as William Sloan Coffin, Jim Wallis, and Cora Weiss now praise the present Communist regime. With the exception of Noam Chomsky and some of his imitators, no one denies Communist atrocities. And few dispute that the Diem and Thieu regimes, with all their faults, were preferable to what the Vietnamese people must now endure.

An Asian production called *Boat People* attempted to show what life under the "liberators" was like. Though it contained some gruesome scenes, it was likely understated. Unfortunately, the film did not receive wide distribution.

The Hanoi Hilton's treatment of American prisoners was accurate, but episodic and poorly acted. The story included a Jane Fonda type, and implied, accurately, that the activism of such people on the part of the North made the captives' plight worse. This was too much for most critics, who hated the film. Audiences never took to it, and it made a quick exit from the theatres. The earlier *Deer Hunter* showed the horrors of captivity but avoided other, larger evils.

Many have hoped for a Vietnam film that would address the mind, not just the emotions, that would not caricature the American soldier, and that would deal seriously with the facts. Many would like to see a sensitive, responsible handling of the moral tragedies involved in that conflict, as well as its aftermath. The much-heralded *Platoon* is not that film, and given the realities of Hollywood, such a picture is not likely to emerge.

OFFICIAL HAGIOGRAPHY, OFFICIAL DEMONOLOGY

One would like to launch into a lengthy study of the bum-numbing three-and-a-half-hour epic *Gandhi,* with the purpose of showing it to be almost entirely fraudulent. But, alas, that has already been masterfully done by Richard Grenier in *The Gandhi Nobody Knows.*

I agree with Grenier that the performance by Ben Kingsley was certainly superb, the cinematography provided an effective travelogue, and the costumes and accents were accurate; but that is about all that can be said for *Gandhi* on the positive side. The cinematic Gandhi was largely a fictitious character, a kind of "Asian E.T." deprived of his orthodox Hinduism. Neither he nor anyone else in the movie uses the word "caste," India's peculiar and long-standing system of apartheid which consigns hundreds of millions of people to permanent inferiority.[20]

The cinematic Gandhi appears sanitized from some of his more intriguing habits, such as a preoccupation with scatology. He received guests while relieving himself, enjoyed giving and receiving enemas, and liked sleeping with nude girls. Moreover, Gandhi refused to allow his wife to accept medicine, but willingly accepted quinine for himself when he was in distress. He also appealed to the European Jews that they yield to Hitler's genocidal designs and urged Churchill to surrender on the grounds that a Nazi regime would not be all that bad.

The movie implies that the British caused Indian poverty, which had existed from times immemorial and was actually considered virtuous, even holy. It stacks the deck by showing the British needlessly killing several hundred Indians, but fails to show the Indians butchering each other after independence, which they freely did, simply because their fellow-citizen happened to be of a different religion.

Gandhi amounts to a pacifist tract, paid for largely, perhaps entirely, by the Indian government, which scrupulously controlled the project from start to finish. It was likely intended to influence the nuclear freeze campaign.[21]

The same filmmaker, Sir Richard Attenborough, took considerable liberties in *Cry Freedom.* He compresses the events of many years into one vignette and, most glaringly, substitutes white police for black. The government of Zimbabwe helped finance the film, which did poorly at the box office. Attenborough allowed the Communist-dominated African National Congress full censorship privileges.[22]

William Walker was a Confederate adventurer hired by the Nicaraguan Liberal Party to fight their domestic political rivals, the Conservatives. *Walker* tried to portray this man as the forerunner of the *contras*. The ruling Marxist-Leninist Sandinistas bankrolled the film. Though promoted as a "true story," it featured scores of factual errors. Some of the gaffes had Nicaraguan audiences laughing. Roberto Fonseca of Managua'a *Ventana* magazine called *Walker* "a joke in bad taste."[23]

Nicaragua, it might be noted, has given asylum to screenwriter Bill Norton (*Branigan, Big Bad Momma*). Norton and his wife were jailed in France for smuggling arms to the Irish Republican Army (IRA). They were wanted throughout Western Europe and in the United States, where they originally procured the weapons.[24]

The Communist government of Peking paid for *The Last Emperor,* which was directed by Bernardo Bertolucci (who also made *Last Tango in Paris* and is a member of the Italian Communist Party). The film, which won many awards, gives the official version of Chinese history, conveniently leaving out the millions slain by Mao Tse-tung, the persecution of intellectuals and writers, the invasion of India, the annexation of Tibet, and other minor details. The Red Guards make a cameo appearance as a kind of traveling accordion troupe. One nearly expects them to break into "We Are the World."

There are no private film companies in Cuba or the Eastern Bloc, and everything must bear the imprimatur of the Party. This was evident in *Moscow Does Not Believe in Tears,* a tedious film in which characters pause to deliver long rhapsodies about the workers. There have been, however, some recent films such as *Repentance,* which attempted to grapple with Stalin. The future of such efforts may well depend on the life span of *glasnost.* And even under this supposed openness, one should not expect a realistic treatment of Lenin, the true "root cause" of Soviet problems.

In summary, the expensive propaganda films outlined above were all sponsored by governments on the left, and there will likely be more of them in future. Nothing similar exists from either the Western democracies or the various authoritarian regimes on the right.

PRIVATE POLEMICS

With Vietnam safely in the hands of their kind of people, Hollywood politicos have turned their attention to Central America. *Under Fire* dealt with American journalists in Nicaragua and is generally sympathetic to the Sandinistas. Oliver Stone's *Salvador* features a left-wing photographer who is fond of the Marxist-Leninist insurgents. The film's musical score effectively editorializes. As Michael Medved has noted, when the government troops are shown, the music sounds like that of 1950s monster films. But when the guerrillas come into view, it sounds like the Vienna Boys Choir singing the "Internationale."

Cinematographer Haskell Wexler (*American Graffiti*) produced *Latino,* which portrayed the Sandinistas as harmless agrarian reformers and innocent guitar-strummers. Those who opposed the Sandinistas, on the other hand, were all pathological killers and torturers who had been taught their craft by American Green Berets. One of them, an hispanic, sees the light and learns to love the revolution. Charles Krauthammer comments that, compared with *Latino,* "*Rambo* takes on the subtlety and depth of *War and Peace.*"[25]

The Archdiocese of Los Angeles, along with other Catholic organizations, is financing *Romero,* which examines the assassination of Salvadoran Archbishop Oscar Romero by unknown gunmen on March 24, 1980. The film takes a number of liberties with the facts and provides a pulpit for the neo-Marxist catechism of liberation theologians. There is also another treatment of Romero in the offing, *The Devil's Bishop* by leftist director Gillo Pontecorvo.[26]

Marlon Brando has chosen to return to the screen in a Central American setting. He will write the political thriller *Jericho,* in which he will also play a CIA agent. The film purportedly deals with "the U.S. role in Central America."[27]

Also in the works as of this writing is *Covert Action,* dealing with the assassination of a Central American diplomat and featuring the usual CIA assassins and wicked American businessmen.

At present, the latest film on South Africa is *A World Apart,* written by Shawn Slovo, daughter of Joseph Slovo, the General Secretary of the South African Communist Party, and the only white member of the African National Congress' military wing.[28] Film critic

Stanley Kauffmann, who is no conservative, states that the film's treatment of communism is disturbing. The story implies that anyone who brings up the issue of communism is a red-baiter and witch-hunter.[29] It is all quite dishonest.

A number of other South Africa films are in the works, including *A Dry White Season,* filmed in Zimbabwe, and starring Donald Sutherland and Marlon Brando. During the shooting of the picture, black extras complained that a dog was paid twice as much as they were.[30]

It has been a long time since *Mission to Moscow* was packing them in, and one is hard pressed to think of a film that openly praises the Soviet Union. *Reds* was a glorification of American fellow-traveling journalist John Reed, author of *Ten Days That Shook the World* (foreword by Lenin) and one of only three Americans to be buried in the Kremlin. The others are Bill Haywood and C. E. Ruthenberg, but Warren Beatty has yet to produce a film on them. But even in *Reds,* Emma Goldman (Maureen Stapleton) says of the Soviets that they "violate human rights," a miniature U.N. speech. At times Beatty, who plays Reed, appears to have wandered in off the set of *Shampoo,* and Diane Keaton, as Reed's lover Louise Bryant, looks like an outtake from Woody Allen's *Sleeper,* in which she played a revolutionary who promotes "government by the workers and the downtrodden masses."

In *Letter to Brezhnev* two British girls fall in love with two Russian merchant seamen, who argue that the ladies would be much better off in the Soviet Union than that awful Great Britain. Why, they say, all this business about Soviet food shortages, repression, and military aggression is nothing but lies spread by the reactionary bourgeois press. One of the girls decides to emigrate, and none other than Mr. Brezhnev himself sends her an airline ticket in response to her letter. As she boards the plane she says, "One must simply believe in Russia," and her friend says, "You're right." There the story ends, with no portrayal of the Happy New Socialist Life allowed. This is craven, goose-stepping propaganda.

There is a movie in the works about the Soviet downing of KAL Flight 007, which reportedly follows the Soviet version of that incident.

None of these films openly calls for Marxism-Leninism and totalitarian government. But all too often, the Marxists are the good guys and equated with "the people." Whatever the setting, the enemy is always to the right. Among the myths these films perpetrate are:

communism either does not exist or constitutes no threat; individual Communists, in the rare event that they are identified, are really only compassionate idealists; anti-Communists are all vile witch-hunters; Communist governments do not commit atrocities, and if they do, those of the West are just as bad, or worse.

Who and what are these pictures for? As agit-prop, they are surely intended to sway opinion, and in a highly cinematic and deeply anti-intellectual culture they have doubtless had some success. But that is not their sole function. Costa-Gavras once told Andrew Sarris that "the purpose of the ideological cinema is not necessarily to convert the enemy, but to enrich the consciousness of one's supporters."[31] Sarris adds, "Why shouldn't the Left have its own John Wayne type entertainments?"[32] In both cases, the patrons are manipulated by heavy-handed symbolism and juggling of the facts, which can always be excused on the grounds that it is "only a movie." The image-bank of these films provides a prefabricated memory.

In response to such films, one notes a pronounced strain of triumphalism, the notion that if the politics of a filmmaker are "correct," then his films must necessarily be good from an asthetic and dramatic standpoint, however much evidence exists to the contrary.

MISSING IN ACTION

Surveying the present scene, one is struck by how few films may be found on the other side. When has there been a dramatic film of: the Soviet invasion of Finland in 1939, the Soviet invasion of Hungary in 1956, the Soviet massacre of Polish officers in the Katyn Forest, the Soviet invasion of Czechoslovakia in 1968, the Soviet detention of Raoul Wallenberg, the Bulgarian oppression of its Turkish minority, the Patriotic Front's downing of an airliner in Rhodesia and slaughtering all the survivors, the murderous regime of Idi Amin, the *Achille Lauro* hijacking, the attempted assassination of Pope John Paul II, the kidnaping and assassination of Italian Prime Minister Aldo Moro, the kidnaping of Nicholas Daniloff, the Cuban occupation of Angola, the Biafra conflict, the Ukrainian sailor deported to the Soviet Union against his will, the persecution of Andrei Sakharof, Sweden's relationship with the Third Reich during World War II (they were the Nazis' main supplier of iron ore), India's invasion and annexation of Goa,

Indira Gandhi's campaign of forced sterilization, China's invasion and annexation of Tibet, China's policy of forced abortions, massive forced resettlement in Tanzania, a man-made famine in Ethiopia, Vietnamese aggression against the Hmong people, the Sandinista treatment of the Miskito Indians, the persecution of the Church in Romania, the Solidarity union in Poland? And what about Operation Keelhaul, in which untold thousands of Russians were repatriated against their will, to be executed or sent to the Gulag? None of these subjects lacks dramatic potential. Most pit the "little guy" against overwhelming odds.

Why have no films been made of William F. Buckley's popular spy thrillers, or the science-fiction novels of C. S. Lewis? What about the fascinating accounts of defectors such as Arkady Shevchenko or formerly imprisoned Christian writer Irina Ratushinskaya? Will Tom Clancy's *The Hunt for Red October* make it to the screen? *All the President's Men* named names and involved many people still alive. Why then can we not have a dramatic film about Chappaquiddick? The FBI and CIA have been done over, but when will it be the turn of the IRS?

Films have been made of the Solzhenitsyn novels *One Day in the Life of Ivan Denisovich* and *The First Circle,* but they have not been given wide release. *The Unbearable Lightness of Being,* based on a novel by Milan Kundera, showed Russian tanks in the streets of Prague, but the invasion is not the central theme of the film.

It is curious that there have been countless daring escapes from Cuba and the Eastern Bloc, but few have been made into films. The only one in memory is *Night Crossing,* an effective and not at all preachy treatment of a family's escape from East Germany in a makeshift hot-air balloon.

There are, of course, such cartoons as *Red Dawn* and *Rambo III,* hardly the conservative equivalent of Costa-Gavras. The *mujahedeen* shoot up a Soviet base in *The Living Daylights,* but one does not see the Soviets bombing civilians. One does not see Afghan children being mutilated by mines disguised as toys. One does not see journalists kidnaped and assassinated. One does not see four million refugees—the largest refugee population in the world—in neighboring Pakistan.

The upcoming *To Kill a Priest* deals with the murder of Polish priest Jerzy Popieluszko by government cadres. But I will be quite surprised if a way is not found to either exonerate the Polish government or blame the United States for that too. I hope I am wrong, but I predict that the writer will draw a parallel between the priest's murder and death squads in El Salvador, for which the U.S. will be held responsible by implication.

I have heard and read reports that film producers have bought the rights to Robert Conquest's *The Great Terror,* the definitive study of Stalinist genocide. William Friedkin, director of *The French Connection,* has reportedly optioned Armando Valladares prison memoir, *Against All Hope.* But the purchase of rights is no guarantee of a movie. Overall, the commercial cinema is decidedly imbalanced in favor of the Left, and that is not likely to change.

TWELVE

POLITICS AND THE DOCUMENTARY

I was very interested in this question of putting the working class on the screen, bringing the working class thing alive in another form than we were getting on the soapboxes of Glasgow Green. . . . I was on to it by 1924, that film could be turned into an instrument of the working class.

(Scottish-Canadian documentary filmmaker John Grierson)[1]

CINÉMA VÉRITÉ?

The earliest films were of "real" events and subjects, what the French called *cinéma vérité* or "cinema of truth." In like manner, the documentary form is usually considered a cinematic but "factual" treatment of a subject that has an existence outside the mind of the filmmaker. But can films be neatly divided into fiction and nonfiction?

Russian poet and playwright Sergey Tretyakov makes no such distinction, and states that in a documentary it is only "a question of the greater or lesser falsification of the material being filmed. There is an arbitrary element in any film."[2] Historian Arthur Schlesinger, Jr. adds that the documentary is a "dubious" enterprise, and, like dramatic film, a "contrivance" because the process of editing and selection of material involve a subjective viewpoint.[3] John Grierson's comment that the documentary is "the creative interpretation of reality" confirms these judgments.[4] One should add that it is the creative interpretation of reality by one person.

A LEFTIST PEDIGREE

All sorts of documentaries have been made for all sorts of purposes: educational films, missionary chronicles, training films, industrial films, promotional trailers, and commercials. Robert Flaherty made his classic of the genre, *Nanook of the North*, as advertising for a fur-trading company. The Third Reich staged their massive Nazi Party convention with Leni Riefenstahl's *Triumph of Will* in mind, as part of a film production. Riefenstahl described the operation in her book.[5] In spite of its odious subject, it is still considered one of the best documentaries ever made. When *Triumph* was shown in New York in the early 1960s, the lines stretched around the block.[6]

Frank Capra, who had churned out what critics dubbed "Capra-corn," produced an uneven series of documentaries on World War II called *Why We Fight*. At the government's behest, Darryl F. Zanuck produced a documentary on the Korean War.[7] But outside of governments, no one has made more use of the documentary than the political Left.

As Leo T. Horowitz wrote in 1934, "The synthetic documentary has become an important form for film workers in the revolutionary movement."[8] There were early cinematic pamphleteers such as the Film and Photo League, which produced *Taxi*, about a cab drivers' strike, and *Sheriff*, about landlords and evictions. A company called Frontier Films produced *Heart of Spain*, about the Spanish Civil War, and such pictures as *China Strikes Back*.

In a more modern setting, Tore Sjoberg's *The Face of War* failed to mention or show anything related to the Nazi-Soviet Pact, the Soviet invasion of Finland, and Communist militancy in Spain. Emile de Antonio's high-concept *In the Year of the Pig* was similarly one-sided.

For contemporary leftists and some liberals, Marcel Ophuls' *The Sorrow and the Pity* has taken the place of *Potemkin* as the definitive political film. Ophuls sets out to chronicle the Nazi occupation of France from 1940-1944, but as Andrew Sarris has pointed out, the film never pursues the rivalries between Communist and non-Communist resistance factions from 1939-1941, when the Nazi-Soviet pact was in operation. The behavior of the French Communist Party during that time is also conveniently left out. Most of the accounts come from the town of Clermont-Ferrand, near Vichy, with the rest of the country largely ignored. Such omissions led Sarris to conclude that, in spite of its nearly five-hour length, *The Sorrow and the Pity* was, intellectually and morally, "one of the shortest pictures of the year."[9] Veterans of the period agree.

As a liaison officer with Gaullist Intelligence who spent the last year of the war in Paris, Malcolm Muggeridge has a wealth of first-hand experience on this subject. He writes that "Ophuls' film is distorted and slanted to an almost incredible degree."[10] Further, it contains little intimation of any help from the Allies, a crucial element in the resistance struggle. In Ophuls' creative reinterpretation of reality, all the heroes are Communists, who, as Muggeridge reminds the reader, "did everything in their power to procure the defeat of France and a Nazi victory" during the period 1939-1941. "If collaboration is a crime," says Muggeridge, "then of all the collaborators, the Communists bore the heaviest guilt."[11] Unfortunately, Ophuls' work is the only memory of the period that many people have.

THE QUESTION OF BALANCE

The Left does not quite have the field all to itself. Werner Herzog's *Ballad of the Little Soldier* is the only cinematic treatment of the Sandinista campaign against the Miskito Indians. Nestor Almendros' *Improper Conduct* deals with repression by the Castro regime, as does Orlando Jimenez-Leal's *The Other Cuba. Harvest of Despair*, produced in conjunction with the National Film Board of Canada, was the first film of any kind to deal with Stalin's terror famine in the Ukraine, and won a number of awards. *Candle in the Wind* examined religious persecution in the Soviet Union. Outside of these, there is not much material, and not enough people have seen what does exist.

All the above films were high-quality productions by veteran filmmakers, but none received more than token distribution. Almendros' *Improper Conduct* has also won awards and was broadcast on French television. But the only film of the above five to be aired on the major outlet for documentaries in the United States, the Public Broadcasting Service (PBS), was *Harvest of Despair*. Moreover, PBS would not air the film alone, on the fraudulent excuse that its artistic standards were not high enough. Indeed, they were much higher than most PBS fare, particularly the works of Bill Moyers. William F. Buckley eventually made *Harvest of Despair* part of a special "Firing Line" program.

But PBS never hesitates to broadcast documentary material with a leftist point of view. Among the examples: *From the Ashes—Nicaragua Today*, a piece of pro-Sandinista puffery; *Cuba—In the Shadow of Doubt*, considered by many to be pure Castroite propaganda; *The Secret Government—The Constitution in Crisis*, a video version of Bob Woodward's *Veil* with a conspiratorial Christic Institute view of politics; *The Africans*, which vilified the West and praised Moamar Qaddafi; *El Salvador: Another Vietnam*, which came down strongly on the side of the Marxist-Leninist guerrillas; *Sanctuary*, a promotional piece for the sanctuary movement; *Legacy of the Hollywood Blacklist,* which practically denies that there was any Communist activity in Hollywood; *Witness to Revolution: The Story of Anna Louise Strong*, a hagiographical portrayal of probably the most shameless propagandist for Stalin, with the possible exception of the *New York Times'* Walter Duranty; *The Secret War*, a version of conflicts in the Baltic States from the Soviet view; *Seeing Reds*, another "Communist as victim" treatment; *On Company Business*, a forum for CIA defector Philip Agee; and many others of similar themes.

The Corporation for Public Broadcasting dropped plans to investigate the imbalance. No change in their approach is likely. In addition to the problem with outlets, the organizations which sponsor and give awards to documentaries are strongly slanted toward the Left.

SUMMARY

The documentary form can be as subjective or fanciful as the wildest science fiction. Since it purports to be a calm "factual" treatment, a documentary can for that very reason be more deceiving. Most of the documentaries tend to follow the agenda of the liberal Left, which is very much in the tradition of the genre. The Left consider the documentary, like the agit-prop theatre, a political weapon.

What many documentary filmmakers produce actually amounts to melodrama, with easily identifiable good guys and bad guys, and the data, pictures, and sound arranged to reinforce the director's scenario. In case some PBS viewers miss the point while out making a sandwich during pledge week, there is sometimes an authority figure such as Bill Moyers to summarize. On the other hand, dramatic films such as those of Costa-Gavras are becoming documentaries in that they purport to tell "a true story." The didactic is becoming dramatic, and vice versa. Film already blurs the line between truth and fantasy enough without this added confusion.

THIRTEEN

THE HOLLYWOOD BLACKLIST

We can't expect to put any propaganda in the films, but we can try to keep anti-Soviet agit-prop out.

(Communist Party USA Chairman William Z. Foster)[1]

As for them, the more innocent they are, the more they deserve to be shot.

(Dramatist and screenwriter Bertolt Brecht, referring to the victims of Stalin's terror)[2]

The political struggles of the film colony reach far beyond the flickering shadows on the screen. They involve some of the major people, conflicts, and events of this century, and are not only a matter of history but also of news, since they continue to the present day and are likely to flare up again.

For example, in the late 1940s, the House Committee on Un-American Activities held hearings on Communist influence in the film industry. One group of uncooperative witnesses became known as the "Hollywood Ten." As a result of those hearings, a number of people were blacklisted during the 1950s.

Many people's knowledge of the subject comes from brief reminiscences by veterans of the 1950s who, in spite of the fact that they have long been fully restored to Hollywood clover, appear to believe that the dark days of the blacklist have never ended. Impassioned statements from worshipful relatives are all the data some people have.[3] Still others rely on the film *Julia*, about Lillian Hellman, Woody Allen's *The Front*, or documentaries such as *Hollywood on Trial* or *Legacy of the Hollywood Blacklist*. Some may have ventured into books such as Lillian Hellman's *Scoundrel Time* or Victor Navasky's *Naming Names*. All these are to varying degree revisionist and tendentious treatments largely designed to promote a general amnesia on the period they cover. Such works have perpetuated loaded descriptions such as "McCarthy Era," "Cold War," "anti-Communist hysteria," "witch-hunt," and so on—slogans that serve as incantations, a substitute for thought and research.

One would never understand from the above works, with the exception of *Naming Names*, that the relevant issues are quite complicated. They would have us believe that everything is marvelously simple, a political melodrama of good guys versus bad guys, in which the only villain was the government. That is far from the case. It is more accurate to say that it involved a tide of half-truths met with half-lies, or perhaps the other way around. On this subject one should follow the advice of Albert Camus and "see nuances and understand; never dogmatize and confuse."[4]

Some Hollywood liberals and leftists are perhaps right that the blacklist should be remembered, to keep such a thing from happening again. But William O'Neill is surely more correct, and fair, in his contention that the *causes* of the blacklist should also be remembered, for the same reason.[5] The period of the blacklist may be regarded as a political drama, and no drama can be understood without an examination of its major character. That is precisely who is largely missing from the revisionist accounts.

THE STALIN ERA

> It was my impression that the best hope for mankind lay with the Soviets. Only in Russia were massive construction and planning for the future going on at a time when the West was either locked

in stagnant depression or, like Germany, headed resolutely back to barbarism.

(Ring Lardner, Jr., member of the Hollywood Ten and author of the screenplay for *M*A*S*H*)

Many Western liberals and even Socialists were dubious about the Soviet Union in the days after the Bolsheviks seized power. Ironically, it was after the ascension of Josef Stalin, when it became a full-blown totalitarian and genocidal power, that they began to admire, praise, and even defend the regime. With the Western world collapsing and fascism on the rise in Germany, it was an easy and popular position to take. The new Soviet regime had no past, only a Glorious Future, and a ruler, Stalin, who was described as "the greatest leader of all time and of all peoples." In the 1930s, Stalin's admirers, many clergymen among them, carried their adulation to ridiculous excesses which have been thoroughly chronicled in Paul Hollander's *Political Pilgrims*. American journalist Anna Louise Strong, who wrote for *Harpers* and the *Atlantic*, said that one should not call Stalin a "god" because "he was too important for that."[6] Eugene Lyons was not exaggerating when he titled his study of the 1930s *The Red Decade*.

It was during that period when the American Communist Party grew by leaps and bounds, and the American academic and intellectual classes were thoroughly radicalized, a condition from which they have never fully recovered. It was the era of the popular "front" in which Communist organizations made common cause with liberals. The influence of these fronts may be gauged by the fact that one of them, the League of American Writers, succeeded in enrolling Franklin Roosevelt, the President of the United States.[7]

SHOW BUSINESS STALINISM

Show business people are both giddy and desperately, sincerely intense. When Stalinism was fashionable, movie people became Stalinists, the way they later became witches and warlocks.

(Pauline Kael)[8]

The rise of the Soviet regime and its Great Leader also met some of the deeper needs of people in the movie community. Because of the competitive and uncertain nature of the business, film people are often unsettled. Stalinism held out the appeal of solidarity and certainty. Screenwriter Richard Collins explains that when he joined the Party, he was "handed ready-made friends, a cause, and a viewpoint on all phenomena."[9]

Former Communist Party member Elia Kazan describes how at secret meetings, a Leading Comrade would lay down the law and everyone else would think about it, nod their head, and say, "I agree." They would then go home and do what they were told. This was called "democratic centralism." "Only people as full of self doubt as actors," says Kazan, could go to such extremes.[10]

As indicated above, Pauline Kael believes that Hollywood Stalinism was a question of following a political fashion, which was surely true. But Kael also believes that movie writers lacked self-respect because of the kitsch they were required to produce, and attempted to pursue self-respect through political channels. They became "naively, hysterically pro-Soviet," and "ignored Stalin's actual policies," she believes, "because they so badly needed to believe in something."[11]

Much Communist activity in Hollywood, as elsewhere, was secret. Nancy Schwartz contends that the business of clandestine meetings, secret names, and so on held a romantic appeal for the show business community.[12] For the Hollywood Left, secrecy was their mysticism and Stalinist politics was their religion. And even in that bleak creed, faith without works is dead.

DRAMA IS A WEAPON

American Communists believed that the theatre could help them foment revolution. Armed with the slogan "Drama Is a Weapon," they attempted to infiltrate and control the New York stage.[13] As far as political content was concerned, the Left had the field to itself. Morgan Himelstein, author of a lengthy study of the radical stage, notes that there were "virtually no plays advocating a right-wing revolution."[14]

It was in this environment that future Hollywood writers and directors such as John Howard Lawson, Elia Kazan, Lillian Hellman, Alvah Bessie, and others learned their craft, and in some cases, their politics. John Howard Lawson, who would later become the first president of the Screen Writers Guild, wrote, "I do not hesitate to say that it is my aim to present the Communist position and to do so in the most specific manner."[15]

In 1936, Communist officials V. J. Jerome and Stanley Lawrence began setting up a Party branch in Hollywood. According to Victor Navasky, their reasons were threefold: to use the prestige of the business to their advantage, to gain a new source of financial support, and to influence "the weapon of mass culture."[16] John Howard Lawson became known as the "commissar" of the Party's Hollywood branch.

Hollywood was a generally apolitical place until semi-Socialist Upton Sinclair ran for governor in 1934. The studio heads opposed him, and even assessed some of their employees a day's pay for the cause. The confiscation of their money for political purposes outraged the workers, particularly the writers, and helped to both unify and politicize them.

So did the rise of Nazism in Germany, and fascism in Italy and Spain. The Spanish Civil War, in which Alvah Bessie fought, was a favorite cause. Books like Sinclair Lewis' *It Can't Happen Here* envisioned a Fascist America, and many concluded that membership in or association with the Communist Party was the best way to "fight fascism." Many popular front organizations arose in the entertainment industry.

Prominent among them was the Hollywood Anti-Nazi League, started in 1936, and which once boasted over five thousand members.[17] One of its committees included John Ford, Myrna Loy, Joan Crawford, Melvin Douglas, Claude Rains, Spencer Tracy, and Burgess Meredith.[18] The leaders of the League, however, were mostly Communists and fellow-travelers who unswervingly followed the Soviet line.

John Cogley notes that the Communists held a "virtual monopoly" on activist organizations and viciously suppressed their enemies, particularly those they dubbed "Trotskyites." He writes that there was never any effective opposition to the Communists, even from groups on the Left. Cogley, it should be noted, was hardly an apologist for the government, the studios, or the anti-Communists. His 1956 study of movie blacklisting earned him a subpoena from the House Committee on Un-American Activities, which harassed him as it did many of those in the film community.[19]

The Communist influence may be demonstrated by the actions of another organization, the Motion Picture Democratic Committee

(MPDC), which was organized to help political candidates. The position of the Communist Party was that the 1939 Soviet invasion of Finland was a just "defense" against Finish imperialist "attack," which was inspired by the United States, France, and Britain, along with Wall Street financiers eager for gain.[20]

But while the conflict still raged, the MPDC refused to hear a motion calling for a condemnation of Stalin's aggression, which included the bombing of Helsinki. Thereafter liberal members such as Melvin Douglas walked out, and the committee collapsed. But the Hollywood Anti-Nazi League stayed in business, under a new name.

THE NAZI-SOVIET PACT

In the late 1930s, defectors from Soviet intelligence such as Walter Krivitsky predicted that Stalin and Hitler were about to come to terms, but American Communists denounced the rumors as Fascist lies. They were to regret such words.

On August 23, 1939, Hitler and Stalin signed a nonaggression pact which provided for the division of Poland and conceded the Baltic States to the Soviet Union. The Pact, which effectively precipitated World War II, caused a panic among American Communists, who had to reverse their entire line overnight. They had been vociferous anti-Nazis, but now would have to calm that rhetoric. They had been ardent interventionists, but now had to be just as zealous in the promotion of isolationism, the dominant mood in the country. Indeed, the federal government, fearful that Hollywood might be too "prowar," launched an investigation of the movies in 1941.[21]

During the time of the Pact, the foreign Communist parties under Moscow's control opposed all Western efforts at rearmament, leaving Hitler free to swallow up Europe. French Communist leader Maurice Thorez made anti-Western broadcasts from Moscow. For his part, Stalin handed over many German-Jewish Communists to the Gestapo, at whose hands they perished.[22] Such events confirm that Stalin did not use the Pact simply to protect himself, but actively cooperated with the Third Reich against the West.

Elia Kazan writes that "we all knew" that such things were going on, "and some even thought it justified."[23] Some later spoke out, but others remained silent. Being in the Party, it should be remembered, required one to defend the Nazi-Soviet Pact, along with the show trials of the old Bolsheviks, the vast purges, and the forced famine in the Ukraine, even if one knew that millions were being slaughtered. Many were not up to the task and left the Party. It goes without saying that anyone who would *join* the Party in those circumstances was a special kind of person.

Dalton Trumbo was probably the most talented, questionably the most famous, and certainly the wealthiest member of the Hollywood Ten. He admits joining the Communist Party in 1943, but colleague Paul Jarrico claims he recruited Trumbo to the Party during the time of the Pact. Nancy Schwartz, a writer on the Left who is sympathetic to Trumbo, notes that it would have been characteristic of him to "fight on the side with two strikes against it."[24]

While Trumbo's anti-war novel *Johnny Got His Gun* was finished before the Pact was signed, Schwartz admits that it "coincided with the anti-war activities of the CP during the period of the Pact."[25] That judgment is confirmed by the fact that the Communist Party newspaper, the *Daily Worker*, serialized Trumbo's book.[26]

Meanwhile, it was no longer politically correct to be anti-Nazi. The Party line was that the fight against Hitler was an "imperialist war" that the United States should avoid at all costs. Alvah Bessie sent petitions to writers such as John Steinbeck and Ernest Hemingway, urging them to collaborate on anti-interventionist plays, but none of the authors responded.[27] A popular slogan was "The Yanks Are Not Coming." The Hollywood Anti-Nazi League suddenly became the Hollywood League for Democratic Action, and later the Hollywood Democratic Committee.

THE WAR YEARS

On June 22, 1941, Hitler turned his guns on the Soviet Union, thereby ending the Nazi-Soviet Pact. On December 7, 1941, Japan attacked Pearl Harbor, and four days later Germany declared war on the United States. The Western powers and the Soviet Union had a common enemy in Hitler. In Hollywood, the Stalinist screenwriters again performed the about-face required by the Party line.

They quickly scrapped all talk of appeasement, pacifism, isolationism, and neutrality. The "imperialist war" suddenly became the "people's struggle," the noblest of all causes. "The Yanks Are Not Coming" became "The Yanks Are Not Coming Too Late."

As John Cogley notes, "The most blatantly jingoistic organizations in the motion picture industry were those in which the Party had influence."[28] Ted Enright observed that the films of the Hollywood Stalinists contained "a ton of chauvinism, jingoism," and "hatred incitement."[29]

The Hollywood Left labored tirelessly on war films which cultivated hatred for the enemy, the subhuman "Krauts" and "Japs," and glorified the American soldier. Sometimes they even put American soldiers in places where they weren't, as in Alvah Bessie's *Objective Burma.*

From 1941-1945, the period of Soviet-America collaboration, one or more of the Hollywood Ten received credit on forty-nine feature films. More than half of these were war films, and as Dorothy Jones' study of film content notes, the proportion of war films made by the Hollywood Ten as a group "was almost twice as high as that made by the industry as a whole during the war years."[30] John Howard Lawson scripted *Action in the North Atlantic* and *Sahara.* Dalton Trumbo wrote *Thirty Seconds Over Tokyo* and *Tender Comrade.* Other products of the Ten included *The Pride of the Marines, Hitler's Children, Destination Tokyo, Counter-Attack*, and *Pacific Blackout.*

It is sometimes contended that there was no specifically Communist or Stalinist propaganda in the movies of this period, but that is far from the case. The 1943 *Mission to Moscow* was based on the book by former American Ambassador to the U.S.S.R. Joseph Davies, whom Sidney Hook describes as a "political illiterate" who owed his post entirely to campaign contributions.[31] It has been argued that the picture was made at the behest of Roosevelt himself, who urged the producers to "make a case for Stalin."[32] The film, like the book, certainly did that.

Mission to Moscow contended that Stalin's purges were justified, that the defendants of the Moscow Trials were all guilty as charged, and that Stalin's terror campaign was the *cause* of Uncle Joe's victories over Hitler. It was produced by Warner Brothers and advertised as "One American's Journey into Truth." American Stalinists helped promote it. Two other films which glorified Stalin's regime were *Song of Russia*, written by Richard Collins, and *The North Star* by Lillian Hellman, a doctrinaire Stalinist. She once attacked a theatrical relief committee attempting to help Finnish victims of Stalinist aggression. The relief, she said, was a form of intervention.[33] So much for compassion.

For any anti-Communists, be they conservative, liberal, or Socialist, these were dark days. It was implied that to be critical of the Soviet Union was to be pro-Nazi. Some fourteen publishers rejected George Orwell's brilliant anti-Stalinist satire *Animal Farm*, and at one point he considered publishing it himself.[34] In 1942, Random House founder Bennett Cerf proposed that the industry withdraw from the market all books that were critical of the Soviet Union.[35] William Phillips of *Partisan Review* magazine was one of those who had broken with communism. He recalls that the Stalinists did their best to keep people like himself from being published in various journals, and from getting jobs at universities.

In Hollywood, the Stalinists did everything in their power to keep anti-Communists from working. Communist story editors quashed projects by anti-Communist writers. In a letter to the *Daily Worker*, Dalton Trumbo bragged that the Hollywood Communists had been able to keep Arthur Koestler's *The Yogi and the Commissar* and other anti-Communist works from reaching the screen.[36] In general, the Left maintained an informal blacklist, largely by circulating rumors and innuendoes. Director Edward Dmytryk, one of the Ten, has written of a list of anti-Communists who were denied work at the height of Stalinist influence.[37]

THE POST-WAR PERIOD

After World War II, the Allied armies demobilized and began the reconstruction of Europe, aided by such provisions as the Marshall Plan. Stalin, however, proceeded to take over country after country: Latvia, Lithuania, Estonia, Czechoslovakia, Hungary, and the rest of Eastern Europe. In a July 1988 conference, a Soviet delegation officially recognized that Stalin had imposed Communist hegemony over the region, violating the Yalta Agreement's promise of free elections.[38] This is the origin of the "Cold War," and hence revisionist accounts are now at odds with the official position of the U.S.S.R.

As Hilton Kramer writes, the revisionist version of the post-war period takes the view that the Cold War was "launched" by Truman, or

Churchill, and was somehow "a malevolent conspiracy of the Western democracies to undermine the benign intentions of the Soviet Union."[39] As is so often the case with the Left, the exact opposite was true.

The Hollywood Stalinists continued to follow the Party line, which had dropped collaboration with the West and resumed its former hostile posture, particularly toward the United States. They were also Stalinists with their own.

Screenwriter Albert Maltz once complained in *The New Masses*, a Party organ, that the concept of art as a weapon was a "strait-jacket." He also praised anti-Stalinist writer James T. Farrell, author of *Studs Lonigan*. The faithful were outraged; they hauled Maltz into a meeting and charged him with heresy. When he rose to defend himself, the others shouted him down. The Party press attacked him, and Maltz was eventually forced to publish a humiliating retraction.[40]

Richard Collins, Jules Dassin, Ring Lardner, Jr., and others attempted to quash production of *Tennessee Johnson*, a film that did not share their politics. They did this openly, circulating a petition at MGM.[41] They were not entirely successful at keeping anti-Soviet and anti-Communist content out of movies, but this was sometimes to their advantage.

Films such as *The Red Menace* and *I Was a Communist for the FBI* were oversimplified, lurid, and ultimately misleading. Like Senator Joe McCarthy, they probably helped the Communists more than harmed them. Other films such as *Guilty of Treason, The Iron Curtain*, and Elia Kazan's *Man on a Tightrope* were more realistic, but none of the anti-Communist films did well at the box office.

As noted earlier, the Stalinist writers knew the difficulties of injecting blatant Communist propaganda into a collaborative medium over which the studio bosses held sway. It could, however, be done subltly, on occasion. Elia Kazan recalls leftist writers boasting about the "good things" they had smuggled into their scripts, which the studio heads were "too stupid and too unpolitical to notice."[42] But what did get by the moguls probably got by the audience as well.

Union leader Roy M. Brewer, who fought Stalinists on the labor front, contends that the Communists were content to write films emphasizing the downside of American life, attempting to show the United States as a decadent and moribund society. He also believes the discrediting of religion was a definite priority.[43] Former movie censor

Jack Vizzard contends that the Left was definitely activist after the war, and the "the campaign to downgrade all departments of democratic-capitalist life was both highly organized and completely saturationist."[44]

THE HUAC INVESTIGATION AND THE STUDIO BLACKLIST

The House Committee on Un-American Activities came to Hollywood not so much because of specific misdeeds, but because the Party was there. The Communists had not been able to turn the film business into a propaganda machine. And certainly they were not in a position to betray military secrets. Indeed, a former Party functionary, Elizabeth Glenn, admits, "We weren't keeping secrets from the enemy." Rather, Communist secrecy amounted to "keeping your political beliefs from the people you wanted to influence."[45] It should be noted that it was not, and is not, a crime to be a member of the Communist Party.

Without doubt, the government investigators intended to use the glamour of the movie business for purposes of publicity, much as the Communist Party itself had done. Chairman John Rankin of Mississippi was an open anti-Semite and was doubtless motivated by the fact that Jews held so much influence in Hollywood. Six of the Hollywood Ten were Jews. Rankin, Jack Tenny, and J. Parnell Thomas likely saw the hearings as a passport to popularity and long, successful careers. Joe McCarthy was not involved in Hollywood.

Walt Disney and Jack Warner were concerned about Communist influence, and still held bitter feelings about the massive 1945 Hollywood strikes, for which the Communists were largely responsible. It was entirely possible that the hearings could aversely affect the studios. As Hilton Kramer notes, the industry reacted the same way it always does whenever there is a threat to its profits, with "whatever mixture of caution, cowardice, prudence, hypocrisy, dissembling and emergency planning was necessary to its prosperity and survival."[46]

Some actors, directors, and screenwriters chose to cooperate with the hearings. Some provided the names of other Party members, some did not. Still others testified but did not cooperate, and were thus designated "unfriendly." The Hollywood Ten, originally nineteen, were the most famous of these.

The hearings themselves were raucous and disorderly, for which the Ten were largely to blame. As Orson Welles noted, some witnesses informed on others not to save their lives but their swimming pools.[47] But the Ten contributed to the confusion by following the Party line, which was for them to lie, to deny their Party membership. This blurred important distinctions between the Communists and anti-Communist liberals, and ultimately caused suspicion to fall on the truly innocent.

As a result of the hearings, some three hundred people were blacklisted in Hollywood and one hundred and fifty in television and radio. There was no blacklist on Broadway or in publishing. That many suffered severely and unduly cannot be doubted. Some served time in prison for contempt of Congress. In a highly dramatic sequel, Lester Cole and Ring Lardner, Jr. were joined in jail by J. Parnell Thomas, convicted of accepting kickbacks in 1948. Some of the dialogue must have been riveting.

Some writers such as Bertolt Brecht fled the country. Many were later rehabilitated, and some continued to write under pseudonyms, earning substantial fees. Performers were at a disadvantage, since no one could "front" for them. Dalton Trumbo won an Oscar for *The Brave One*, written under the name Robert Rich. This showed that the blacklist could be beaten, and it eventually collapsed.

SUMMARY: THE MYTH OF INNOCENCE

The HUAC leaders such as Rankin and Thomas were rather unsavory people, and the studio bosses were for the most part their willing collaborators. Many people suffered, their careers and reputations ruined. Some may have committed suicide as a result of the blacklist.

Given all this, however, it does not follow that all the accusations were false, nor that the government was completely wrong in its belief that there was a threat to its security. Neither does it follow that people have a right to lie, and that others have an obligation to defend their right to lie. It does not follow that Communists or any other group have a divine right to a job in Hollywood. Above all, the perfidies of HUAC do not mean that those accused were heroes. Even Dalton Trumbo, in a 1970 speech, contended that it was futile to look for heroes of that time, "because there were none."[48]

The Hollywood Stalinists made life miserable for both their

friends and enemies, and in positions of power would surely have made life miserable for everyone. But it is precisely the myth of innocence—specifically Communist innocence—that revisionist treatments of the period aim to perpetuate.

In Woody Allen's *The Front*, a blacklisted writer tells the man who is fronting for him that he is a Communist. That's as far as it goes, the reluctant and fleeting admission that, yes, there were Communists in the media after all. (The frequent use of the term "witch-hunt" implies that there were none.) Woody Allen's character, Howard Prince, does not ask the man how he could defend the Moscow Trials, the Nazi-Soviet Pact, the Katyn Forest massacre, and other Stalinist atrocities. That would have upset Allen's morality play by creating another villain.

The documentary *Hollywood on Trial* omitted, along with other disquieting details, Dalton Trumbo's own admission that he had twice been a member of the Communist Party. According to Elia Kazan, Lillian Hellman "spent her last fifteen years canonizing herself."[49] Others did it for her in the film *Julia*. In the book *Scoundrel Time*, she glossed over her abject defense of Stalinist atrocities, which she continued to defend even *after* Khrushchev had denounced them. She projected Richard Nixon, still fresh in Watergate memories, and a symbol of reaction, backwards onto the earlier era, in which he also played a role. It was a form of guilt by association, as well as an attempt to unite the Old and New Left. Hellman believed that she and her comrades had not done harm, that Nixon was responsible for the Vietnam War, etc.

Hilton Kramer believes that the flurry of revisionist works are a defense of 1960s radicalism, the consequences of which were all too apparent by the mid-1970s. In Kramer's view, the revisionists sought to acquit sixties radicalism by falsely portraying thirties radicalism as benign and altruistic. William O'Neill believes that works such as *Scoundrel Time* and *Naming Names* are basically "acts of vengeance," written for the sake of the authors' political ancestors.[50] That is why they are so selective and one-sided.

One point is beyond dispute: had there been no Hollywood Stalinism, there would have been no HUAC investigation, and no blacklists. The Hollywood Communists, to use Orwell's phrase, wanted to be anti-Fascist without being antitotalitarian. They put the interests of another country above those of their own. They were obedient followers of Josef Stalin, the greatest mass murderer of this century, perhaps of all time. The Hollywood Stalinists faithfully denied or defended his genocidal policies, under which millions of innocent people lost their freedom and under which their fellow-writers and artists were being tortured, imprisoned, and executed.

Worst of all, they were trying to extend Stalin's influence to this country, and the fact that they failed in that miserable quest does not excuse them any more than it excuses members of the German Bund or those Americans who were pro-Japanese or pro-Mussolini, such as Ezra Pound. They did this while taking advantage of the liberties of American democracy, and, courtesy of capitalism and the American people, enjoying great wealth. Those who believe that these people were innocent victims, whose actions were of no consequence, say a great deal about themselves.

Though both Stalin and high-profile Hollywood communism are gone, the legacy of those times lives on. As Pauline Kael has noted, the show business Left is now not so much pro-Soviet as just abusively anti-American. The Hollywood Stalinists are forgotten but not gone.

PART FOUR

WHAT CAN BE DONE?

FOURTEEN

THE CHRISTIAN FILMMAKER

That the Christian community should respond to the undeniable influence of the movies is obvious. What form that response should take is not quite as clear.

Far be it from me to choose a career for someone else, but I am aware of nothing that prohibits a Christian from being a film actor, director, writer, or, more important, a film producer. But before considering what Christians can do within the industry, we should examine some attempts at reform.

An official of World Wide Pictures once told me that it was their purpose to "bring some light" into the film business, doubtless one reason why they set up shop in Burbank. Some of their films, notably *The Hiding Place,* have received good notices, but their effect on the business as a whole is negligible. As of this writing, their Burbank studio is for sale and they are moving to Minneapolis.

Of greater interest is the case of David Puttnam.

GOLIATH AND DAVID: A FAILED REFORMER

David Puttnam began his career in advertising and was briefly an agent for photographers David Bailey and Richard Avedon. He went on to produce "little" movies such as *Bugsy Malone.* His first effort for the big time was *Midnight Express,* about American hashish smuggler Billy Hayes and his stint in a Turkish prison. Oliver Stone wrote the script. The movie was, to put it mildly, hard-core stuff, with enough violence and sadism to touch off a dozen "studies" at universities in Stockholm and the northeastern United States. Hayes calls the Turks all sorts of nasty names, and in one scene bites out the tongue of an informer.

Puttnam expected crowds to cringe when this happened, but instead they cheered. And while the movie became a great success, to the delight of the director and writer, it had the opposite effect with Puttnam, who felt that he had betrayed his country's image and his own values. He felt that he had descended to pandering through the powerful medium of film, and his distress was such that he sought out religious counseling. A Jesuit priest suggested that he redeem himself by making films that would elevate, not downgrade, the moral sensibilities of the audience. That, indeed, is a tall order, but Puttnam decided to give it a try.

While thumbing through a book of Olympic records, he came across accounts of British runners Eric Liddell and Harold Abrahams. The wheels started turning and the movie that eventually emerged was *Chariots of Fire,* a low-budget, wildly anglophile feature which broke all the rules: the heroes were foreigners, there were no big stars, no sex, no violence. The script was literate, and Hugh Hudson was a first-time director. Most shocking of all, religious characters were actually portrayed not only as human beings, but in a positive light. The film beat out Warren Beatty's pretentious and expensive *Reds* for Best Picture in the 1982 Academy Awards.

Chariots of Fire proved a favorite with religious viewers, and was widely praised in the religious press; later it was shown in many churches, a rather unusual fate for a movie neither made nor financed by outgoing Christians. Screenwriter Colin Welland is by all indications an agnostic, and the money for *Chariots* was largely supplied by Dodi Fayed, an Egyptian shipping magnate and a Muslim.[1]

In any case, after this rousing success, Puttnam vowed to stay clear of Hollywood. He made *The Killing Fields* and *The Mission* from a home base in his native England. But Francis T. Vincent of Columbia and the brass at the Coca-Cola company (which owns Columbia) lured him back. Puttnam wanted to prove that Columbia could make films with first-time directors, without big stars who bloated the budgets, and without the packaging parasitism of high-powered agents. He told them that neither the box office nor public taste could be the sole arbiters of film content.

The Coca-Cola people liked the ideas and did not balk at his demand for a hefty salary (some $3 million a year) and essentially total control of the studio. They wanted to sign him for five years, but he insisted on three. He was the first foreigner to head a studio since World War II.

Puttnam brought in so much talent from the old country that his studio got dubbed "British Columbia." He also purged staff and brought down film budgets. He went through the inventory of projects and junked many of them. But then he began to run into the system. As it were, the stars came out.

He clashed with Bill Murray and Dan Aykroyd of *Ghostbusters*. He inherited clunkers such as *Ishtar*, which embodied everything he detested. It was some $15 million over budget, a "vehicle" for "stars," and was produced by Warren Beatty, whose *Reds* Puttnam had previously thrashed in the race for the Oscars.

Puttnam did not see eye to eye with Bill Cosby over *Leonard Part 6*, the name of which is apparently designed to satirize the *Rambo* films. In short, he made enemies among the powerful. In a town full of people who view themselves as very special indeed, he proclaimed that "there are no special people."[2] It was blasphemy. He began to be perceived as an outsider, a cultural colonist. His ways were not the ways of tinsel town, whose chief beatitude is: "but the greatest of these is money."

Puttnam quickly grasped the ethos of the place and spoke his mind to anyone who would listen. "Hollywood plays to your weakness," he said. "Whatever you are, it makes you more than you want to be. If you're a bit aggressive, it makes you very aggressive. If you're a bit deceitful, it makes you into a liar. It's literally a godless place."[3]

Though he resigned shortly after a year on the job, Puttnam's good judgment carried on after him. Two of his projects, *Hope and Glory* and *The Last Emperor*, were nominated for Academy Awards. Puttnam has succeeded as a film producer but failed as a reformer. The "system" remains intact.

That someone in such a powerful position failed to effect meaningful and lasting change at even one studio should sober those who enter the business with high expectations for change. But Puttnam's failure does not mean that change is impossible. Nor does it mean that Christians should not enter the business, only that there are hazards involved.

BREAKING AWAY, BREAKING IN

The Christian filmmaker must first decide who he or she wants to talk to. If it is only other Christians, there is little reason to enter the commercial film business. If, however, one wants to address the larger public, then one must enter the mainstream.

From an artistic standpoint, the Christian who hopes to break in will have to abandon the strictly didactic and utilitarian approach to the craft—the belief that film and drama are only valid inasmuch as they promote the gospel. This is essentially the same attitude as that of the old Hollywood Left, which placed art at the service of propaganda and criticized "bourgeois art." The philosophical basis for that practice is materialism, which the Christian must reject.

If someone breaks out of that cocoon, and abandons the three or four "safe" themes characteristic of religious films, he can likely expect some heat from his fellow-Christians. They may wonder why he is not making "Christian films" or not "getting the gospel in."

Also like the Left, Christians in film are sometimes guilty of triumphalism, the notion that as long as the ideas of the film are "correct"—in this case "orthodox"—then the product must of necessity have artistic merit. Unfortunately, it does not work that way.

Some Christians do not wish to have their works judged on the quality of their dramaturgy, cinematography, editing, lighting, music, etc. Rather, they seem to assume that their *intention* to serve a religious purpose is enough to merit the automatic support of their fellow-Christians or even the populace. In other cases, they believe that their faith and intentions are enough to shield them from any criticism, even that which is constructive.

I also know of a Christian producer who constantly received calls from co-religionists who had little experience, but who thought they deserved acting jobs simply because they were Christians. They were infuriated by the producer's practice of turning them down in favor of superior talent from the Screen Actors Guild. The reader who objects to that decision should ask herself: Would I hire an inexperienced surgeon or plumber simply because he happened to be a Christian? And if they did a poor job, would I accept a word of prayer and a Bible verse as compensation? Again, the practice of hiring on a sectarian basis has been characteristic of the Left.

None of this will do. Christians must understand that doctrinal orthodoxy, spirituality, and good intentions do not confer dramatic talent. Faithful church attendance does not equip one to conceive compelling stories with a beginning, middle and conclusion; with living, breathing characters; with a sense of surprise and pacing, and dialogue that crackles; with an abiding sense of mystery that hints at the transcendent, as in Peter Weir's *Picnic at Hanging Rock;* and with a satisfying payoff which lingers in the audience's mind for more than half an hour.

To be sure, artistic talent is God-given. Consider Bezalel, the son of Hur, of the tribe of Judah, to whom God had given "skill, ability and knowledge" to "engage in all kinds of artistic craftsmanship."[4] But even this man's talent had to be developed. He could have wasted it.

Modern technological society stresses efficiency, quick solutions, and instantaneous success. The Christian filmmaker cannot afford to indulge such worldliness. He or she must serve an apprenticeship. This means realizing how little one knows, along with a willingness to work on projects not dear to one's heart in order to acquire experience. The person dedicated to one story, like the one who enters the trade as a moralist, intent on "cleaning it up," is virtually guaranteed to fail. Film school can help, but it will not ensure success or even a job. It could even be ruinous.

Nestor Almendros, probably the premier cinematographer in the world today, occasionally works on commercials. Indeed, this is where many directors and cinematographers have learned their craft. Ridley Scott *(The Duellists)* and Jean-Jacques Beineix *(Diva)* are two examples of many. In a commercial, one has thirty seconds, or less, to tell the story, and only the finest camera work will do.

It was only after years in the trade that Elia Kazan realized how little he knew about directing, and Maugham is surely correct that "a masterpiece is more likely to come as the culminating point of a laborious career than as the lucky fluke of untaught genius."[5] And as anyone who has seen *Terms of Endearment* knows, the fact that a film gets an award does not mean it is a masterpiece. And as films as diverse as *Howard the Duck* and *Wired to Kill* showed, advertising hype cannot create a "hit." Dramaturgy and marketing are not the same thing.

That Christians have something to say is unquestionable. That they could make the film industry better is certainly possible. That there are Christians with a God-given talent for drama and storytelling is evident. But most efforts to date have been disappointing. Before they can gain a wider hearing in the film community, and with the populace, Christians must first earn the right to be heard. That will not be easy.

THE RIGORS OF THE BUSINESS

Film writer and lecturer Molly Gregory describes filmmakers as survivors, people able to take brutal criticism and punishment and who show an ability to bounce back. They must possess "the organizing abilities of Bismarck, the financial acumen of J. P. Morgan, the spiritual tolerance of St. Francis, all of which they are called upon to exhibit regularly." In addition, the filmmaker is a "masochist, warrior, scientist, artisan, market analyst, storyteller, athlete, magician."[6] French filmmaker Eric Rohmer *(Pauline at the Beach)* performs many tasks himself, including running errands and even sweeping the floor.[7] No pampered Hollywood softy, he. If a prospective filmmaker does not have such qualities, he should seek a partner who does.

The filmmaker should understand that there are a host of things that can go wrong and usually do. Things will always cost more and take longer than one expects. Though the chances of failure are great, the filmmaker must never give up.

One should understand that chances of success are not good. Hundreds arrive daily with the same quest. Many leave, daily, broken and destitute. Mark Litwak admits that if he had been aware of the nature of the business, he might not have made the attempt.[8]

On the other hand, every month there are new names in the rolls of the screen guilds and new faces on the screen. A producer friend told me about a script he described as the worst he had ever seen. That writer now has a three-picture deal with a major studio. One can find people who rise from mailroom to great heights, but these are the exception. As Ben Stein put it, the door is not exactly open, only slightly ajar. But the business is crazy enough that anything is possible. Consider Pee Wee Herman, for example.

It should also be understood that in the roles of writer, actor, and even producer, one is largely limited to commercial fare, and subject to the rules of the game. In one form or another, you are an employee, without a great deal of "creative freedom."

In that connection, the business of the "casting couch" should be dismissed. In spite of many sensational stories, there is no more illicit sex in Hollywood than anywhere else, and it is entirely possible for an actor or actress to advance without moral compromise. Most actors and directors live entirely normal family lives. That is not to say that there are no perils in the trade. Many have been outlined already. But there are also perils in being an ironworker in Chicago.

This author would hope that, in addition to smaller roles, Christians would approach film as filmmakers, cinematic dramatists in charge of their own projects. As George Lucas points out, film is becoming more diversified, more regional, a development he welcomes. The technology of making movies is also more accessible. Lucas contends that you can make a professional film for *under* a million dollars, and that the distribution system—Hollywood, in a word—is dead and destined to fade away. He contends that you can sell your picture to cable by making five telephone calls.[9] Not all of this is certain. One may be sure that George Lucas could sell *his* film to cable with five calls; others, maybe not. But the trends are encouraging. The market has expanded, and some of the foibles of Hollywood may now be avoided.

Just as anything is possible for individuals in Hollywood, the sky is the limit for smaller independent productions. *The Gods Must Be Crazy*, produced in South Africa on a low budget, ran for months in California. Even an amateurish, goofball comedy like *Attack of the Killer Tomatoes* has become something of a cult classic, and even been picked up by an airline. A sequel is in the works.

MONEY

Talent, business sense, endurance, opportunity: these are all essential, but are not enough. Films are made because there is money to make them. The Christian community has as much money as any other, but here we run into a problem.

Historically, Christians have been most generous when giving to church and philanthropic concerns—in short, the Lord's work. They will shell out millions for television time, much of which is taken up with pleading for money so they can stay on television. But when it comes to popular culture, particularly drama, they tend to slam the vault shut. A producer I once worked for went to a Christian billionaire—yes, *billionaire*—for help in financing a movie with conservative political themes. He had an impressive list of credits, a script, an excellent director, and two major stars, but didn't get a nickel. The project is dead.

Christians tend to be wary of anything that is not a "Christian film." They fail to understand that liberals and leftists dominate popular culture because they are willing, for whatever reasons, to spend what it takes to do the job. Unless there is a new attitude on the part of Christians, there is not likely to be any change.

Compounding the problem is the false pietism referred to earlier, which considers the whole realm of popular culture off-limits, yet constantly refuses to do anything about that content other than complain. That is a vicious circle indeed.

On July 15, 1988, Bill Bright of Campus Crusade for Christ offered to pay *$10 million* to purchase and *destroy* all copies of *The Last Temptation of Christ.*[10] For those, myself included, who have failed to gain support for film projects, this type of action is most depressing. I can think of much better uses for $10 million. Instead of raising and spending millions to destroy a picture one doesn't like, why not use the money to finance some low-budget films by Christian filmmakers? With ten million dollars one could make at least ten low-budget films, or maybe two features. I realize that the proverb, "it is better to light a candle than to curse the darkness," is not in the Bible, but I believe it has a lot of merit.

SUMMARY

Assuming that all is in place, including financing, one must still bear in mind the limitations of the cinematic medium as outlined earlier. If these limitations are violated, failure is certain.

The Christian filmmaker must have realistic goals. Film is not going to be an evangelist or Bible teacher. Christian *cinéastes* should be content to make strong dramatic films to the best of their ability. These films should acknowledge, not in a heavy-handed sort of way, the existence of religious life, and avoid the caricatures and distortions of religious people so typical of commercial fare. Indeed, as *Marty* shows, the lack of such omission and distortion will make them stronger dramatically. When Christian characters appear, they should be allowed to be themselves. They must be human beings, like Eric Liddell or Mac Sledge. Like the kind sheriff in *The Trip to Bountiful,* they must be people whom the audience will recognize and care about. In short, the Christian filmmaker should aim for truth without descending to propaganda.

As is evident in the work of Peter Weir, Paddy Chayevsky, Horton Foote, and others, the cinema, with all its difficulties and limitations, is still capable of great things. And as John Simon puts it, "Once a form has been shown capable of greater things, why settle for lesser ones?"[11] There is a creed for the Christian filmmaker.

FIFTEEN

THE CHRISTIAN FILM VIEWER

As among the general populace, the tastes of Christians vary. Francis Schaeffer was fond of Fellini, whose works are quite frank about sex and even feature sporadic nudity. The Reverend Donald Wildmon would surely disapprove. In addition, there are a number of specifically Christian publications telling people what they should see.

I will leave this to the general viewer, except to say that, as in so many areas, common sense should be a guide. It hardly takes a genius to understand what *Revenge of the Nerds* or *Friday the 13th Part VI* are going to involve. Sequels are generally bad news. Slapped-together exploitation flicks or "laff riots" released during holidays are generally easy to spot, and usually disappointing.

The ads say a great deal, and they too can be reviewed. One can generally tell from the imagery whether the film is "kiss kiss" or "bang bang," or both. Ads also tell as much about the deal as the picture. The character pictured to the left is always the one given prominence. The same applies for the names of the actors. If the name of an actor or director appears above the title, then that person's fingerprints will be all over the property. These details are all finalized in the deal stage.

One should pay attention to the director, the *auteur,* since directors tend to be repetitive. If it is a Brian de Palma film, then there is likely to be a lot of slow-motion butchery; if Mel Brooks, a lot of bathroom humor; if Roger Vadim, a lot of naked bodies; if Stephen Spielberg, lots of gosh-golly characters and gadgetry; if Peter Weir, a lot of attention to detail and a penchant for the stunning visual.

Ads often make a big deal about awards the film has won. These should not be the determining factor. Neither should the star system of critics, who give pictures two stars, three stars, etc.

REVIEWS

One can, however, learn the taste of critics, both local and national. Some love and praise trash, others are more discerning. With attention, one can discover who may be trusted. Television reviewers on local stations are notorious for liking everything, and the trailers they run are provided by the studio and constitute a commercial.

The state of film criticism is almost as bad as that of film. Too many critics think they've done their homework if they read the publicity pack. Very few can deal with the background and ideas of a film. Nothing gets past John Simon, and Richard Grenier has a built-in propaganda detector. Grenier is about the only truly "investigative" journalist dealing with film. As John Simon has noted, criticism at best is "an invitation to thinking," but criticism that thinks *for* the reader is "perfectly worthless."[1] The most important critic, however, is the viewer.

HOW TO WATCH A MOVIE: THE CRITICAL FACULTY

The actor Ralph Richardson wrote that a member of the audience, "if he's worth anything at all," will criticize the entertainment he has seen at home. It is only natural that he should, "and it hasn't done him any good if he does not."[2] The critical reaction is usually delayed, since, as noted, the primary response to a film is emotional. The intellectual process kicks in later. But there are advance preparations which are not only helpful but necessary.

One can be prepared to evaluate the film on several basic categories. Is it original? Is it plausible? Is the theme clear? Does the dialogue ring true, or is it contrived? Has it been done before? If so, has it been done *better* before? Does the director's style respect the viewer, or is it manipulative? Do the actors act, or, as is so often the case, do they simply posture? What is the "look" of the film? Does the action drag, or is it well-paced? Has the editor removed the fat, or do his cuts merely confuse? Does the musical score enhance the action and dialogue, or does it editorialize? Does the film rely on music and effect for emotion, or does that come from the tale itself? These questions deal with style and dramaturgy, but the heart of the matter is content.

A film patron should be like a good customs officer, asking the film what it has to declare. What view of life comes through. (And there must be one.) What distortions are apparent? What has been left out?

"We build excitement . . . Pontiac!" "The heartbeat of America, that's today's Chevrolet." Those slogans are not objective statements about the automobile industry, but commercials paid for by General Motors and designed to sell its products. Similarly, in the case of propagandistic films such as *Gandhi* and *A World Apart,* one should ask some basic questions.

First, who pays? If a film is financed by a government or political party, that says a great deal in itself. Second, *cui bono?*, or, who benefits as a result of the presentation in question? The second is often easier to discern than the first. A related question is, "who loses?"

A propagandistic film likely means something is being covered up, or that history is being altered. This should encourage the intelligent viewer to get the real story. Half an hour's research will reveal more about Pol Pot than *The Killing Fields.* The briefest survey of Chinese history will reveal the lacunae in *The Last Emperor.* In fact, the real character was much kinkier than the one in the film.

On all points, discussion is valuable, particularly with younger people. What about the decisions made by the characters in the film? Did they do the right thing?

THE VCR

While movies lose a great deal on the small screen, they also afford the viewer more control. They give parents a chance to preview films for their children. They allow flexibility of schedule, and save money on baby-sitters, gasoline, and popcorn. They offer liberation from boorish morons who talk during movies. They allow the viewer to stop the action and make a sandwich, or discuss some crucial point. If one misses something, you can back up, something impossible in the theatre.

More important, the VCR broadens choice. In addition to the

many local outlets, including public libraries, there are mail order houses offering a wide variety of films. Some specialize in documentaries, but practically everything is available. Hence, one may resist the pressure to cave in to hype and see a film *right now!* It will be on cassette, by and by. One may avoid the herd, always good policy in any case.

THE QUESTION OF PROTEST

This writer finds most protests of films embarrassing and quixotic, and believes that they are usually counterproductive. Kurt Vonnegut noted that those outraged over popular novels come across as people who don a suite of armor and attack an ice cream sundae. The same is true of many film protests. Almighty God is not menaced by Hollywood fakery. In this writer's opinion, the persecution of religious believers in the Eastern Bloc and the death by abortion of millions of preborn children are more worthy causes for public protest. This is not to say, however, that one should never speak out.

In a democratic society that respects free speech, anyone has the right to protest a film that he or she feels defames his or her race, national background, sex, self, or religion. It might be recalled that the 1964 Civil Rights Act includes the word "creed." Filmmakers have the right to make films as it pleases them, and the populace has a right to protest and even conduct boycotts if it pleases them.

Homosexuals took to the streets over *Cruising*, and the pacifists and war-toy opponents are up in arms over *Rambo*. Arabs protested *Victory at Entebbe*, and animal rights groups whipped themselves into a lather over *Blazing Saddles* and *Apocalypse Now*, in which a man chops up a cow on screen.

These protests are respected, but journalists seem to have a double standard for Christians. Christians who protest are depicted as obscurantist neanderthals, out to censor the screen. The impression is often given that their protests are illegitimate, and that they are wrong even to dislike the film in question.

It is true, regettably, that some Christians denounce films before they see them, but they are far from alone on that score. I recall a San Diego protest of *The Border* with Jack Nicholson. On a television news broadcast, an official of a Chicano rights organization attacked the movie as border patrol propaganda that slandered Hispanics. The reporter asked him if he had seen the film. He had not.

During the filming of *Alamo: The Price of Freedom* in San Antonio, no less than *thirty* Latino organizations demanded to see a rough cut of the movie and denounced it as insulting to Hispanics. Moreover, San Antonio City Councilman Walter Martinez, not one for originality, said the picture "has no redeeming social value." The Latino groups demanded "deletions as well as additions," and threatened a boycott if the producers did not give in. Further, they demanded to see a final version of the film within thirty days.[3]

Speaking of censorship, many American blacks object to the depiction of themselves in "Amos 'n' Andy," and have succeeded in banishing that portrayal from screens large and small.

It bears repeating that Christians are the last group in America who may be publicly defamed with impunity, and even attacked for their protests. The situation clearly constitutes an injustice. Without endorsing or criticizing any particular protest, this author maintains that Christians have every right to publicly object to material that defames their religion. Such protest, however, should be responsible, civil, and above all informed. If these conditions are not present, and if someone exploits the protest for publicity, then it will only be counterproductive. Christians who have a legitimate grievance should avoid and denounce those protesters whose motivations are anti-Semitic.

SUMMARY

Every movie ticket or rental is a kind of ballot that will eventually register with the industry. Film viewers should keep their expectations of Hollywood realistic. They should cultivate high standards, keep their propaganda detectors in good working order, and take a hard look at how they spend their time and money. They should reward what little good exists and avoid the junk. Good films require good audiences.

SIXTEEN

CONCLUSIONS

If Adolf Eichmann arrived at a studio with a good script and Robert Redford committed to star, they'd park the Mercedes for him and say, "What six million?"

(Screenwriter Steve Shagan
on the expediency of Hollywood)[1]

The hard reality is that present audiences are not very demanding. Accordingly, Hollywood's creed continues to be whatever the traffic will bear. Putting bums in seats is the name of the game.

In the early days of film, directors adapted novels and stage plays. The present tendency is to adapt other films, to scrounge bits and pieces from the great celluloid slag heap. The practice often makes watching movies a game of, "spot that reference."

For a natural hydraulic system to work, there must be a source above the outlet. That is precisely what is lacking in Hollywood, from both an artistic and spiritual standpoint. The commercial cinema is insulated and isolated, weak at showing the deeper side of life, afraid of mystery, drawn in upon itself. The trends are not promising.

I believe that comedy films are becoming variety shows, with *Ishtar* and *Good Morning Vietnam* as prime examples. The stars perform some sight gags, tell some jokes, and maybe sing a few songs, with a threadbare "story" serving as host. It is "what else?" instead of "what next?," practically a return to Vaudeville.

Action and adventure shows are becoming protracted music videos. They tend to feature weak or ludicrous story lines, skin-deep characters, frantic action, assorted visual tricks, and sound tracks which, to use Bill Cosby's description, sound like an airplane crash with drum accompaniment. No one hates this kind of thing more than screenwriters, who are always pressing to do material they can be proud of, but who seldom get the chance.

In current parlance, "serious" films are those which deal with political and social themes from a liberal-left perspective. This is ostensibly in the cause of "justice" and therefore quite in line with the spirit of the age. From Managua to Luanda, there is hardly a violent confrontation in the world today that does not have "justice" (usually undefined) as its rallying cry. Justice easily puts on a false face, unlike truth. But the commercial cinema is not interested in truth. Sometimes a "serious" film is one that sets out to debunk some aspect of traditional religion or morality, or to demonize some public figure. It is a depressing situation indeed.

To be sure, as far as sheer craft is concerned, commercial films are better than ever, and the American product still dominates the world market. In pure technique, certainly, everything is state-of-the-art. But it is surely one of the great ironies of our age that, at the very time when the technology is the finest, the people who command it have so little to say.

A metaphor Pauline Kael used in a review of *The Professionals* might serve for the entire industry. Kael said the film "had the expertise of a cold old whore with practiced hands and no thoughts of love."[2] It is not the gentlest of comparisons, but it fits. A work of art must be a work of love.

Longevity is the toughest test for anything that purports to be art, and rare is the work that endures more than a generation. One may be confident that *The Competition* or *Manhattan* will not be occupying serious minds a century from now. In fact, there is some question as to whether, in a physical sense, films can be permanently preserved at all. To fade away is a fate many deserve.

I agree with Mark Litwak and other observers that contemporary cinema reflects poorly on America, with the judgment not limited to any particular genre of film. This is doubtless because the commercial cinema does not represent the people of America, only the mind-set of a small group of people in Los Angeles, some of whom hate America.

A more serious problem is the cumulative effect of the commercial cinema, which, along with television, has made our century the age of show business. It has inundated our society with dramatic communication and turned us into a nation of passive *voyeurs.* A cinematic culture, practically speaking, amounts to no true culture at all. Virginia Owens has a point when she says the counterculture failed because there was no culture to counter.[3] Where the public educational system is filling minds with narrow, prefabricated ideas, the commercial cinema provides narrow, prefabricated emotion and mass-produced fantasies. As Hortense Powdermaker noted, its premise is that everyone's dreams should be equal.

The United States is a society with a highly decentralized political system and many centers of political power. But the commercial cinema is a highly centralized business. At this moment, in cities across the country from New York to Albuquerque, the same handful of feature films are playing. The medium needs to be democratized and decentralized. But deeper problems remain.

Allan Bloom writes that the omnipresent Walkman earphones prevent his students from hearing "what the great tradition has to say." When they take them off, which they eventually must, "they find that they are deaf."[4] John Fowles' character Daniel Martin sees a similar process happening with film. "Somewhere the cinema, like television," he muses, "was atrophying a vital psychic function: the ability to imagine for oneself."[5] This is true, and a tragic business indeed. Just as in Orwell's *1984,* in which the language Newspeak narrowed the range of thought by eliminating words, the language of cinema narrows our imagination by substituting its images and memory for our own. Perhaps that is why Christians have historically been people of the word more than people of the image.

NOTES

INTRODUCTION *Apologia Pro Liber Suo*

1. See Lloyd Billingsley, "The Gospel from Outer Space," *Christianity Today*, March 16, 1984.
2. Lloyd Billingsley, "Fanny and Alexander," *Christianity Today*, August 5, 1983.
3. Lloyd Billingsley, "Footloose," *Christianity Today*, May 20, 1984.
4. Martin Esslin, *An Anatomy of Drama* (New York: Hill and Wang, 1976), p. 13.
5. Parker Tyler, *Magic and Myth of the Movies* (New York: Simon and Schuster, 1947), p. xvii.
6. See Malcolm Muggeridge's appraisal of Peter Sellers in *My Life in Pictures* (New York: Morrow, 1987), p. 84.

CHAPTER ONE *Christians and Movies*

1. Stephen W. Paine, *The Christian and the Movies* (Grand Rapids: Eerdmans, 1957), p. 70.
2. *Ibid.*, p. 5.
3. Carl McClain, *Morals and the Movies* (Kansas City: Beacon Hill Press, 1970), p. 17.
4. Stephen Paine, *The Christian and the Movies*, pp. 6, 7, 79.
5. *Ibid.*, p. 62.
6. *Ibid.*, p. 70.
7. See "Top MCA Figure a Focus of Probe into Mafia Dealings," *Los Angeles Times*, June 29, 1988. Part I, p. 1.
8. See the section "Some Rejoinders Considered," in Stephen W. Paine, *The Christian and the Movies*, pp. 60-71.
9. Hortense Powdermaker, *Hollywood, The Dream Factory* (Boston: Little, Brown, 1950), p. 78.
10. *Ibid.*
11. See Jerry Z. Mulder, "Communism, Anti-Semitism, and the Jews," *Commentary*, August 1988.
12. See Neil Gabler, "Sound and Fury," *Los Angeles Times Magazine*, July 31, 1988, p. 20. The article is an excerpt from Gabler's book *Empire of Their*

Own: How the Jews Invented Hollywood* (New York: Crown Publishers, 1988).

13. See John Dart, "2 Step Back From 'Temptation' Protest Over Anti-Jewish Tone," *Los Angeles Times*, July 23, 1988, Part I, p. 27. See also Marita Hernandez, "Christian, Jewish Critics of Film on Christ Quarrel," *Los Angeles Times*, July 25, 1988, Part II, p. 4.
14. Pauline Kael, *Kiss Kiss Bang Bang* (Boston: Little, Brown, 1968), p. 5.
15. Quoted in Carl S. McClain, *Morals and the Movies*, p. 7.
16. J. D. Salinger, *The Catcher in the Rye* (New York: Bantam, 1981), p. 29.
17. Romans 12:2, emphasis added.
18. Romans 12:3.
19. 1 Corinthians 5:9-11.
20. See "Piety Versus Pietism," in Herbert Schlossberg and Marvin Olasky, *Turning Point: A Christian Worldview Declaration* (Westchester, IL: Crossway Books, 1987), pp. 25-42.
21. See Francis Schaeffer, *Art and the Bible* (Downers Grove, IL: InterVarsity Press, 1970).
22. See Romans 14.
23. *Ibid.*
24. Carl McClain, *Morals and the Movies*, p. 25.

CHAPTER TWO *What Is Drama?*

1. Short for agitation and propaganda, a designation for a play or film consisting largely of rhetorical questions and Marxist answers. Marxist governments have a "Minister of Agitation and Propaganda."
2. Roger Ebert, *Roger Ebert's Movie Home Companion* (Kansas City: Andrews, McMeel and Parker, 1985), p. 1.
3. *Ibid*, pp. 176, 177.
4. Quoted in Bryce J. Christensen, "Shadows in Light," *Chronicles*, April 1988, p. 45.
5. W. Somerset Maughan, *The Summing Up* (New York: Signet, 1964), p. 89.
6. Interview in *Film Comment*, April 1988, p. 26.
7. Quoted in Mark Litwak, *Real Power: The Struggle for Influence and Success in the New Hollywood* (New York: Morrow, 1986), p. 102.

CHAPTER THREE *Christianity and Drama*

1. Quoted in Diana Rigg, *No Turn Unstoned* (New York: Doubleday, 1983), p. 10.
2. See *The Republic of Plato*, Francis Macdonald Cornford, trans. (New York: Oxford, 1964), pp. 85, 337-340.
3. Quoted in Carl S. McClain, *Morals and the Movies* (Kansas City: Beacon Hill Press, 1970), p. 18.
4. Percy Scholes, *The Puritans and Music* (London: Oxford University Press, 1934), p. 198.
5. See Francis Schaeffer, *Art and the Bible* (Downers Grove, IL: InterVarsity Press, 1973).

6. *Ibid.*, p. 28. See Ezekiel 4:1-3.
7. Paul Johnson, *Modern Times: The World from the Twenties to the Eighties* (New York: Harper and Row, 1983), p. 697.
8. Acts 17:28
9. Quoted in Percy Scholes, *The Puritans and Music*, p. 199.
10. Luke 13:4.
11. Quoted in Scholes, *Puritans and Music*, p. 201.
12. See "Opera in England," in Percy Scholes, *The Puritans and Music*, pp. 195-213.
13. See Leland Ryken, *Worldly Saints: The Puritans as They Really Were* (Grand Rapids, MI: Zondervan, 1986).
14. Quoted in John Wenham, *The Goodness of God* (London: Inter-Varsity Press, 1974), pp. 7, 8. This neglected volume is an excellent discussion of the moral problems raised by the Bible.
15. *Ibid.*, p. 201.
16. Quoted in Bill Hendersen, *Rotten Reviews* (Stamford: Pushcart Press, 1986), p. 72.
17. *Ibid.*, p. 81.
18. Quoted in "Lear, Tolstoy and the Fool," in George Orwell, *Inside the Whale and Other Essays* (London: Penguin Books, 1957), pp. 101, 103.
19. Quoted in Percy Scholes, *The Puritans and Music*, p. 201.
20. Otto Friedrich, *City of Nets* (New York: Harper and Row, 1986), p. 6.
21. Dorothy Sayers, "The Greatest Drama Ever Staged," in *Creed or Chaos* (New York: Harcourt Brace and Company, 1949), pp. 3-7.
22. See Lloyd Billingsley, "General Booth Was a Woman," *Christianity Today*, January 13, 1984, p. 68.
23. Malcolm Muggeridge, *The End of Christendom* (Grand Rapids: Eerdmans, 1980), p. 13.
24. Lloyd Billingsley, "T.V. Where the Girls Are Good-looking and the Good Guys Win," *Christianity Today*, October 4, 1985.
25. Quoted in Percy Scholes, *The Puritans and Music*, p. 200.

CHAPTER FOUR *Pictures That Move, Pictures That Talk*

1. David Shipman, *The Story of Cinema: A Complete History form the Beginnings to the Present* (New York: St. Martins, 1982), p. 294.
2. Profile of Dennis Hopper in *Seventeen Interviews Film Stars and Superstars*, Edwin Miller, ed. (New York: Macmillan, 1970), p. 382.
3. Richard Grenier, "Treason Chic," *Commentary*, January 1985, p. 65.
4. Malcolm Muggeridge, *Chronicles of Wasted Time: The Green Stick* (New York: Morrow, 1973), p. 252.
5. Siegfried Kracauer, *From Caligari to Hitler: A Psychological Study of the German Film* (Princeton, NJ: Princeton University Press, 1947), p. 289.
6. Quoted in Tina Brown, "Hollywood Knives," *Vanity Fair*, April 1988.
7. See the account of Otto Friedrich, *City of Nets: Hollywood in the 1940s* (New York: Harper and Row, 1986), p. 5.
8. See Judith Thurman and Jonathan David, *The Magic Lantern: How Movies Got to Move* (New York: Atheneum, 1978).

9. See Lewis Jacobs, *The Documentary Tradition* (New York: Hopkins and Blake, 1971), p. 3.
10. Nestor Almendros, *A Man With A Camera* (New York: Farrar, Straus and Giroux, 1984), p. 41.
11. David Shipman, *The Story of Cinema*, p. 19.
12. Richard Meran Barsan, *In the Dark: A Primer for the Movies* (New York: Viking, 1977), p. 24.
13. Bruce Torrence, *Hollywood: The First Hundred Years* (Hollywood: Hollywood Chamber of Commerce, 1979), p. 72.
14. See David Niven, *Bring on the Empty Horses* (New York: Putnams, 1975), p. 21.
15. See Otto Friedrich, *City of Nets: A Portrait of Hollywood in the 1940s*, p. xi.
16. Cited in Bruce Torrence, *Hollywood: The First 100 Years,* p. 88.
17. Quoted in Thomas W. Bohn and Richard L. Stromgren, *Light and Shadows: A History of Motion Pictures* (Palo Alto, CA: Mayfield, 1987), p. 367.
18. Jack Vizzard, *See No Evil: Life Inside a Hollywood Censor* (New York: Simon and Schuster, 1970), p. 36.
19. *Ibid.*, p. 354.
20. Hortense Powdermaker, *Hollywood, the Dream Factory: An Anthropologist Looks at the Movie Makers* (Boston: Little, Brown, 1950), p. 39.
21. See Richard Martin, "Boffo Box Office from Vidcassettes," *Insight*, November 23, 1987, pp. 8-15.
22. Quoted in Otto Friedrich, *City of Nets*, p. 24.
23. Elia Kazan *Elia Kazan: A Life* (New York: Knopf, 1988), p. 381.
24. New York: Viking, 1985.

CHAPTER FIVE *The Limitations of Film*

1. Virginia Stem Owens, *Total Image: Or Selling Jesus in the Modern Age* (Grand Rapids: Eerdmans, 1980), p. 40.
2. See Hebrews 12:26, 27.
3. Quoted in Harry Medved and Michael Medved, *The Hollywood Hall of Shame* (New York: Perigree Books, 1984), p. 138.
4. Matthew 6:16-18.
5. See profile of Bauer in Peter Brimelow, "Let Them Work Out Their Own Problems," *Forbes*, February 22, 1988, p. 81.
6. T. S. Eliot, "Religion and Literature," from *Selected Essays, T. S. Eliot* (New York: Harcourt, Brace and World, 1960), p. 347.
7. Malcolm Lowry, *Under the Volcano* (London, Penguin Books, 1973), p. 122.
8. Quoted in Theodore Taylor, *People Who Make Movies* (New York: Doubleday, 1967), p. 15.
9. See Elia Kazan, *Elia Kazan: A Life* (New York: Knopf, 1988), p. 256.
10. *Ibid.*, pp. 380, 382.
11. Quoted in Diana Rigg, *No Turn Unstoned* (New York: Doubleday, 1983), p. 154.
12. Quoted in Mark Litwak, *Reel Power: The Struggle for Influence and Success in the New Hollywood* (New York: Morrow, 1986), p. 115.

13. W. Somerset Maugham, *The Summing Up* (New York: Penguin, 1978), p. 83.
14. Nestor Almendros, "Spots of Art: How Commercials Are Changing the Movies," *The New Republic*, May 23, 1988, p. 30.
15. Oliver Snote, interview with Alexander Cockburn in *American Film*, December 1987, p. 26.
16. Quoted in Carl S. McClain, *Morals and the Movies* (Kansas City: Beacon Hill Press, 1970), p. 24.
17. Ben Stein, *The View From Sunset Boulevard* (New York: Basic Books, 1979), p. 106.
18. Quoted in Malcolm Muggeridge, *The Infernal Grove: Chronicles of Wasted Time, Volume Two* (New York: William Morrow, 1974), pp. 133, 134.
19. David Shipman, *The Story of Cinema* (New York: St. Martins, 1982), p. 1196.

CHAPTER SIX *What Film Does Well*

1. Richard Meran Barsan, *In The Dark: A Primer for the Movies* (New York: Viking, 1977), p. 8.
2. Evelyn Waugh, "Why Hollywood Is a Term of Disparagement," *The Essays, Articles, and Reviews of Evelyn Waugh*, Donat Gallagher, ed. (Boston: Little, Brown, 1985), p. 326.
3. Another example of cinematic culture: An ad for one of George Orwell's books identified him as the author of *Animal House*.
4. Quoted in Carl S. McClain, *Morals and the Movies* (Kansas City: Beacon Hill Press, 1970), p. 7.
5. Literally "god from a machine." In Greek drama, a god was brought to the stage in a mechanical contrivance to resolve a difficult situation. The phrase also means any improbable character or event used to untangle the plot.
6. See "Justice Restored," *San Diego Union*, October 16, 1987.
7. Malcolm Muggeridge, "Another King," in *Jesus Rediscovered* (London: Collins, 1969), p. 94.
8. Pauline Kael, *Kiss Kiss Bang Bang* (Boston: Little, Brown, 1968), title page.
9. Hortense Powdermaker, *Hollywood: The Dream Factory* (Boston: Little, Brown, 1950), p. 14.
10. Nestor Almendros, *A Man With a Camera* (New York: Farrar, Straus and Giroux, 1984), p. 10.

CHAPTER SEVEN *Basic Questions About Movies*

1. Quoted in John Cogley, *Report on Blacklisting: Movies* (New York: Fund for the Republic, 1956), p. 14.
2. See Evelyn Waugh, "Why Hollywood Is a Term of Disparagement," *The Essays, Articles, and Reviews of Evelyn Waugh*, Donat Gallagher, ed. (Boston: Little, Brown, 1985), p. 326.
3. Hortense Powdermaker, *Hollywood: The Dream Factory* (Boston: Little, Brown, 1950), p. 311.
4. Bob Pool, "Picketing Writers Provide Action and a Plot Twist," *Los Angeles Times*, April 4, 1988.

5. See Mark Litwak's chapter on marketing in *Reel Power* (New York: Morrow, 1986), pp. 232-253.
6. See Harry M. Cheney, "The Life of Oscar," *Eternity*, March 1985, p. 33.
7. Aljean Harmetz, "More Adults See Attending Movies," *San Diego Union*, March 3, 1988.
8. *Ibid.*
9. See Mark Litwak, *Reel Power*, p. 68.
10. Roger Ebert, *Roger Ebert's Movie Home Companion* (New York: Andrews, McMeel & Parker, 1985), p. 395.
11. See Steven Bach, *Final Cut: Dreams and Disaster in the Making of Heaven's Gate* (New York: Morrow, 1985), p. 139.
12. See Tina Brown, "How Cosby Cooked His Own Turkey," *Vanity Fair*, April 1988, p. 101.
13. See Steven Bach, *Final Cut*, p. 379.
14. See Deborah Caulfield and Steve Weinstein, "Morning Report," *Los Angeles Times*, May 30, 1988, Part VI, p. 2.
15. See Lloyd Billingsley, "Does Disney Productions Have the Next 'Chariots of Fire'?," *Christianity Today*, May 20, 1983.
16. See John Dart, "Church Leaders Upset at Delay of Film Screening," *Los Angeles Times*, June 18, 1988, Part I, p. 27.
17. David Niven, *Bring on the Empty Horses* (New York: Putnams, 1975), p. 104.
18. Elia Kazan, *Elia Kazan: A Life* (New York: Knopf, 1988), p. 380.
19. See Mark Litwak, *Reel Power*, p. 24
20. Many screenwriters make a good living without ever seeing their work on the screen.
21. Quoted in Mark Litwak, *Reel Power*, p. 223.
22. Evelyn Waugh, *The Loved One* (London: Penguin Books, 1969), p. 22.
23. *Ibid.*
24. Quoted in Richard Barsan, *In the Dark* (New York: Viking, 1977), p. 100.
25. Quoted in Mark Litwak, *Reel Power*, p. 69.
26. Quoted in Pauline Kael, *Kiss Kiss Bang Bang* (Boston: Little, Brown, 1968), p. 153.
27. Ben Stein, *The View From Sunset Boulevard* (New York: Basic Books, 1979), p. xiii.

CHAPTER EIGHT *The Film Community, the Film Business*

1. Evelyn Waugh, "Why Hollywood Is a Term of Disparagement," *The Essays, Articles and Reviews of Evelyn Waugh*, Donat Gallagher, ed. (Boston: Little, Brown, 1985), p. 325.
2. *Ibid.*
3. See George Stein, "Soviet Chic," *Los Angeles Times Magazine*, June 5, 1988, p. 14.
4. Malcolm Muggeridge, *Like It Was: The Diaries of Malcolm Muggeridge* (New York: William Morrow, 1982), p. 515.
5. Quoted in Hortense Powdermaker, *Hollywood: The Dream Factory* (Boston: Little, Brown, 1985), p. 20.

6. Mark Litwak, *Reel Power* (New York: Morrow, 1986), p. 8.
7. Quoted in Mel Gussow, *Darryl F. Zanuck: Don't Say Yes Until I've Finished Talking* (New York: Da Capo, 1971), p. 47.
8. Hortense Powdermaker, *Hollywood: The Dream Factory*, p. 305.
9. Peter Ustinov, *Dear Me* (London: Penguin Books, 1978), p. 234.
10. See Daniel Akst and Laura Landro, "Preying for Gain," *Wall Street Journal*, June 20, 1988, p. 1.
11. See Mark Litwak, *Reel Power*, p. 47.
12. Michael Cieply, "Hollywood's High-Powered Image Machine, *Los Angeles Times Magazine*, July 10, 1988, p. 16.
13. Joan Didion, *The White Album* (New York: Simon and Schuster, 1979), p. 156.
14. "A Fable (Sort of)," *Los Angeles Times Calendar*, May 8, 1988.
15. Quoted in Mark Litwak, *Reel Power*, p. 311.
16. See Joshua Hammer, "Rocky Road," *Los Angeles Times Magazine*, June 26, 1988, p. 37. The article examines the independent studios, with a focus on Stephen Friedman's Kings Road Entertainment.
17. Quoted in Otto Friedrich, *City of Nets: Hollywood in the 1940s* (New York: Harper and Row, 1986), p. 15.
18. Quoted in Steven Bach, *Final Cut: Dreams and Disaster in the Making of Heaven's Gate* (New York: Morrow, 1985), p. 78.
19. See Mark Litwak, *Reel Power*, p. 66.
20. Evelyn Waugh, "Why Hollywood Is a Term of Disparagement," p. 328.
21. Hortense Powdermaker, *Hollywood: The Dream Factory*, p. 30.
22. *Ibid.*, p. 282.
23. *Ibid.*, p. 303.
24. See Mark Litwak, *Reel Power*, pp. 72-76.
25. See Otto Friedrich, *City of Nets*, pp. 16, 17.
26. Tina Brown, "Hollywood Knives," *Vanity Fair*, April 1988, p. 155.
27. Tina Brown, "How Cosby Cooked His Own Turkey," *Vanity Fair*, April 1988, pp. 100, 101.
28. See Richard Grenier, "The World's Favorite Movie Star," *Commentary*, April 1984, pp. 61-67.
29. The entire debacle is chronicled in Steven Bach, *Final Cut*.
30. F. Scott Fitzgerald, *The Last Tycoon* (New York: Scribners, 1941), p. 19.
31. J. D. Salinger, *The Catcher in the Rye* (New York: Bantam, 1951), p. 2.
32. See Mel Gussow, *Darryl F. Zanuck*, pp. 77, 78.
33. Ben Stein, *The View From Sunset Boulevard* (New York: Basic Books, 1979), p. 27.
34. Hortense Powdermaker, *Hollywood: The Dream Factory*, p. 149.
35. See John Cogley, *Report On Blacklisting: Movies* (New York: The Fund for the Republic, 1956), p. 160.
36. Nestor Almendros, *A Man With a Camera* (New York: Farrar, Straus, and Giroux, 1982), p. 173.
37. See *ibid.*, p. 175.
38. F. Scott Fitzgerald, *The Last Tycoon*, p. 18.
39. Nestor Almendros, *A Man With a Camera*, p. 41.

40. Mel Gussow, *Darryl F. Zanuck*, p. xiii.
41. Theodore Taylor, *People Who Make Movies* (New York: Doubleday, 1967), p. 9.
42. Quoted in Otto Friedrich, *City of Nets*, p. 5.
43. See Mark Litwak, *Reel Power*, p. 226.
44. John Fowles, *Daniel Martin* (Toronto: Collins, 1977), p. 136.
45. *Ibid.*
46. *Ibid.*
47. Evelyn Waugh, *The Loved One* (London: Penguin, 1969), p. 29.
48. Michael Cieply, "Labor Strife Reads Like Stale Script," *Los Angeles Times*, May 10, 1988, Part I, p. 17.
49. *Ibid.*
50. Hortense Powdermaker, *Hollywood: The Dream Factory*, p. 30.
51. See Harry M. Cheney, "The Life of Oscar," *Eternity*, March 1985, p. 33.
52. Lewis Carroll, *Alice in Wonderland* (New York: Doubleday), p. 42.
53. From "Kid Stuff," in John Simon, *Reverse Angle: A Decade of American Films* (New York: Clarkson Potter, 1982), p. 99.
54. Quoted in Mel Gussow, *Darryl F. Zanuck*, p. 172.
55. Evelyn Waugh, "Why Hollywood Is a Term of Disparagement," p. 325.
56. See Stanley Kauffmann, "Spots Before Our Eyes," *The New Republic*, June 13, 1988, p. 22.
57. Hortense Powdermaker, *Hollywood: The Dream Factory*, p. 320.
58. *Ibid.*
59. *Ibid.*, p. 327.
60. *Ibid.*, p. 332.
61. John Fowles, *Daniel Martin*, p. 274.
62. John Simon, *Reverse Angle*, p. 145.

CHAPTER NINE *The Hollywood Worldview*

1. Otto Friedrich, *City of Nets* (New York: Harper and Row, 1986), p. xiii.
2. Hortense Powdermaker, *Hollywood: The Dream Factory* (Boston: Little, Brown, 1985), p. 22.
3. Ben Stein, *The View From Sunset Boulevard* (New York: Basic Books, 1979), p. xiii.
4. *Ibid.*, p. 129.
5. Lewis Beale, "Martin Sheen Spurns Star's Glitter," *San Diego Union*, July 3, 1988, Part D, p. 2.
6. Linda S. Lichter, S. Robert Lichter, and Stanley Rothman, "Hollywood and America: The Odd Couple," *Public Opinion*, December/January 1983, p. 55. This survey dealt largely with television, but, like Ben Stein's book, approximates the ideas in the film community as well.
7. See Richard Blow, "Moronic Convergence: The Moral and Spiritual Emptiness of the New Age," *The New Republic*, January 25, 1988, pp. 24-27.
8. See Otto Friedrich, *City of Nets*, p. 223.
9. David Niven, *Bring on the Empty Horses* (New York: Putnams, 1975), p. 106.
10. See "Stars of the Stars," *Between the Lines*, June 1988.

11. "Belushi's Ex-Manager Unhappy Over 'Wired,'" *San Diego Union*, July 4, 1988.
12. Lichter and Rothman, "Hollywood and America: The Odd Couple," p. 56.
13. Ben Stein, *The View From Sunset Boulevard*, p. 49.
14. *Ibid.*, p. 129.
15. See Ann Japenga, "Dropping Back In: A Growing Number of Baby Boomers Are Discovering That There's No Place Like Church," *Los Angeles Times*, March 27, 1988, Part VI, pp. 1, 2.
16. John Dart, "Evangelicals Intensify Struggle to Stop Film," *Los Angeles Times*, July 12, 1988, Part VI, p. 1.
17. Mel Gussow, *Darryl F. Zanuck* (New York: Da Capo, 1971), p. 190.
18. Job 21:14.
19. Quoted in Allan Bloom, *The Closing of the American Mind* (New York: Simon and Schuster, 1987), p. 85.
20. Joan Didion, *The White Album* (New York: Simon and Schuster, 1979), pp. 86, 87.
21. *Ibid.*, p. 88.
22. Lichter and Rothman, "Hollywood and America: The Odd Couple," p. 56.
23. See Evelyn Waugh, "For Schoolboys Only," in *The Essays, Articles and Reviews of Evelyn Waugh*, Donat Gallagher, ed. (Boston: Little, Brown, 1985), p. 198.
24. Joan Didion, *The White Album*, p. 86.
25. See Mark Litwak, *Reel Power* (New York: Morrow, 1986), pp. 7, 8.
26. Nina J. Easton, "Campaign '88 Gets The Star Treatment," *Los Angeles Times*, June 7, 1988, Part VI, p. 1.
27. Lichter and Rothman, "Hollywood and America: The Odd Couple," p. 56.
28. Julius Lester, "Man in the Mirror," *The New Republic*, May 23, 1988, p. 20.
29. Quoted in David Elliot, "Lucas and Coppola at the Wheel," *San Diego Union*, August 7, 1988, p. E-4.
30. Warren T. Brookes, "Myths Mask Reality of a Robust Economy," *San Diego Union*, August 7, 1988, p. C-1.
31. For the complete lists, Nina J. Easton, "Campaign '88 Gets the Star Treatment."
32. Ronald Brownstein, "The Hollywood Primary," *The New Republic*, November 23, 1987, pp. 19-23.
33. Michael Cieply, "Hollywood's High-Powered Image Machine," *Los Angeles Times Magazine*, July 10, 1988, pp. 45, 46.
34. Allan Dodds Frank, "Campaign '88: Get Ready for 'Selective Reality,'" *Forbes*, January 1985, pp. 77-80.
35. Ben Stein, *The View From Sunset Boulevard*, pp. 129, 131.
36. Richard Grenier, "The Capitalism of Wall Street," *Washington Times*, January 5, 1988.
37. Richard Grenier, "Leftist Chic and the 1987 Oscars," *The Washington Times*, February 18, 1987.
38. A gathering of ex-leftists, which I was privileged to attend.
39. David Niven, *Bring on the Empty Horses*, p. 25.
40. Hortense Powdermaker, *Hollywood: The Dream Factory*, p. 306.

41. Ben Stein, *The View From Sunset Boulevard*, pp. 12, 127.
42. Interview with Oliver Stone, *American Film*, December 1987, p. 25.
43. *Ibid.*, pp. 24, 25.
44. Pauline Kael, *Kiss Kiss Bang Bang* (Boston: Little, Brown, 1968), p. 151. Emphasis hers.
45. Ben Stein, *The View From Sunset Boulevard*, pp. 131-133.
46. See David Brock, "Christic Myths and Their Drug-running Theories," *The American Spectator*, May 1988, p. 24.
47. Robert Caldwell, "Put to the Test, the Christic Case Collapses," *San Diego Union*, July 3, 1988, p. C-5. See also Deborah Caulfield, "Morning Report," *Los Angeles Times*, May 26, 1988, Part VI, p. 2.
48. "Suite Alleging Plot by Contras, CIA Dismissed," *Los Angeles Times*, June 24, 1988, Part I, p. 4.
49. "Hayden, Fonda Court the Brat Pack," *Between the Lines*, April 1988, p. 11.
50. See Bruce Torrence, *Hollywood: The First 100 Years* (Hollywood: Hollywood Chamber of Commerce, 1979), pp. 201-204.
51. June 17, 1988.
52. See "Morning Report," *Los Angeles Times*, January 20, 1988, Part VI, p. 2.
53. Michael Parks, "Soviet and U.S. Film Firms Join in 1st Venture," *Los Angeles Times*, June 9, 1988, Part VI, p. 1.
54. See "Morning Report," *Los Angeles Times*, May 12, 1988, Part VI, p. 2.
55. See "Morning Report," *Los Angeles Times*, May 2, 1988, Part VI, p. 2.
56. Nestor Almendros, *A Man With a Camera* (New York; Farrar, Straus, and Giroux, 1982), p. 36.

CHAPTER TEN *Religion and the Movies*

1. See Harry and Michael Medved, *The Hollywood Hall of Shame* (New York: Perigree Books, 1984), p. 141.
2. *Ibid.*, pp. 19-24.
3. Otto Friedrich, *City of Nets* (New York: Harper and Row, 1986), p. 433.
4. Mel Gussow, *Darryl F. Zanuck* (New York: Da Capo, 1971), p. 81.
5. See Harry and Michael Medved, *The Hollywood Hall of Shame*, pp. 29-33.
6. *Ibid.*, pp. 134-142.
7. Peter Ustinov, *Dear Me* (London: Penguin, 1978), p. 284.
8. R. C. Sproul, *The Psychology of Atheism* (Minneapolis: Bethany, 1974), pp. 81-88.
9. Parker Tyler, *Magic and Myth of the Movies* (New York: Garland, 1985), p. xviii.
10. Quoted in Robert Short, *The Gospel From Outer Space* (San Francisco: Harper and Row, 1983), p. 15.
11. Quoted in *ibid.*, p. 65.
12. *Ibid.*, pp. 19-28.
13. Stanley Crouch, "Beyond Good and Evil: The Paradoxes of Jesse Jackson," *The New Republic*, June 20, 1983, p. 20.
14. See Will Eisenhower, "Your Devil Is Too Small," *Christianity Today*, July 15, 1988.

15. Quoted in David Shipman, *The Story of Cinema* (New York: St. Martins, 1982), p. 813.
16. Paul Johnson, *Modern Times* (New York: Harper and Row, 1983), p. 698.
17. Richard Grenier, *The Marrakesh One-Two* (Boston: Houghton Mifflin, 1983), p. 271.
18. See Roger Ebert, *Roger Ebert's Movie Home Companion* (Kansas City: Andrews, McMeel & Parker, 1985), p. 213.
19. Hortense Powdermaker, *Hollywood: The Dream Factory* (Boston: Little, Brown, 1985), p. 64.
20. Virginia Stem Owens, *The Total Image: Or Selling Jesus in the Modern Age* (Grand Rapids: Eerdmans, 1980), p. 80.
21. Malcolm Muggeridge, *Christ and the Media* (Grand Rapids: Eerdmans, 1977), p. 41.
22. Virginia Stem Owens, *Total Image*, pp. 11, 93.
23. Interview with Franky Schaeffer at Karson-Higgins-Shaw Communications, June 6, 1986, pp. 6, 7.

CHAPTER ELEVEN *Politics and Dramatic Film*

1. Mikhail Heller and Aleksandr Nekrich, *Utopia In Power* (New York: Summit Books, 1986), p. 54.
2. See Mark Litwak, *Reel Power* (New York: Morrow, 1986), pp. 105, 106.
3. Andrew Sarris, *Politics and Cinema* (New York: Columbia University Press, 1978), pp. 4, 10, 11.
4. Annette Insdorf, *Indelible Shadows: Film and the Holocaust* (New York: Random House, 1983), pp. xiii.
5. See David Satter, "Why Glasnost Can't Work," *The New Republic*, June 13, 1988, p. 19.
6. See "Morning Report," *Los Angeles Times*, August 5, 1988, Part VI, p. 16.
7. Quoted in William L. O'Neill, *A Better World* (New York: Simon and Schuster, 1981), p. 245.
8. Andrew Sarris, *Politics and Cinema*, p. 13.
9. See George Szamuely, "Did the U.S. Recruit Nazi War Criminals?," *Commentary*, June 1988, pp. 50-53.
10. "Morning Report," *Los Angeles Times*, May 12, 1988, Part VI, p. 2.
11. John Simon, *Reverse Angle* (New York: Clarkson Potter, 1982), p. 198.
12. Pauline Kael, *Kiss Kiss Bang Bang* (Boston: Little, Brown, 1968), p. 63.
13. Mel Gussow, *Darryl Zanuck*, p. 92.
14. See Pauline Kael, *Kiss Kiss Bang Bang*, pp. 151-153.
15. Quoted in Martha Bayles, "The Road to Rambo III," *The New Republic*, July 18, 1988, p. 33.
16. *Ibid.*
17. George Szamuely, "Hollywood Goes to Vietnam," *Commentary*, January 1988, p. 49.
18. William K. Lane, "Vietnam Vets Without Hollywood Tears," *Wall Street Journal*, July 26, 1988. See also the correspondence, August 4, 1988.

19. *Ibid.*
20. See Lloyd Billingsley, "Scheduled Slavery: The Misery of India's Untouchables," *Eternity*, November 1984.
21. Richard Grenier, *The Gandhi Nobody Knows* (Nashville: Thomas Nelson, 1983).
22. See David Roberts, Jr., "The ANC in Its Own Words," *Commentary*, July 1988.
23. Quoted in Bryan Brennan, "Walker Is an Amusing Hit in Nicaragua," *Los Angeles Times*, March 5, 1988, Part VI, p. 8.
24. Ellen Farley, "Flying South," *Los Angeles Times*, February 7, 1988, Calendar Section, p. 39.
25. Charles Krauthammer, "Singing the Sandinista Song," *Washington Post*, November 22, 1985, p. A-23.
26. Gregg Barrios, "The Murder of the Archbishop—Fade in," *Los Angeles Times*, July 3, 1988, Calendar Section, p. 4
27. "Morning Report," *Los Angeles Times*, February 2, 1988, Part VI, p. 2.
28. Steven Mufson, "Uncle Joe," *The New Republic*, September 28, 1987.
29. Stanley Kauffmann, "Under the Volcano," *The New Republic*, July 18, 1988, p. 26.
30. "Morning Report," *Los Angeles Times*, May 24, 1988, Part VI, p. 2.
31. Quoted in Andrew Sarris, *Politics and Cinema*, p 68.
32. *Ibid.*, p. 77.

CHAPTER TWELVE *Politics and the Documentary*

1. Quoted in Thomas W. Bohn and Richard Stomgren, *Lights and Shadows* (Palo Alto, CA: Mayfield, 1987), p. 375.
2. Quoted in Lewis Jacobs, *The Documentary Tradition* (New York: Hopkins and Blake, 1971), p. 29.
3. *Ibid.*, p. 383.
4. *Ibid.*, p. 381.
5. See Siegfried Kracauer, *From Caligari to Hitler* (Princeton, NJ: Princeton University Press, 1947), p. 301.
6. Lewis Jacobs, *The Documentary Tradition*, p. 138.
7. Mel Gussow, *Darryl F. Zanuck* (New York: Da Capo, 1971), p. 114.
8. *Ibid.*, p. 91.
9. Andrew Sarris, *Politics and Cinema* (New York: Columbia University Press, 1978), pp. 80, 82.
10. Malcolm Muggeridge, *Christ and the Media* (Grand Rapids: Eerdmans, 1977), p. 65.
11. Malcolm Muggeridge, *The Infernal Grove* (New York: William Morrow, 1974), p. 226.

CHAPTER THIRTEEN *The Hollywood Blacklist*

1. Quoted in Victor Navasky, *Naming Names* (New York: Viking, 1980), p. 79.
2. Quoted in Sidney Hook, *Out of Step: An Unquiet Life in the 20th Century* (New York: Harper and Row, 1987), p. 493.

3. See Judith Michaelson, "Blacklist Spirit Still Alive, Entertainment Leaders Warn," *Los Angeles Times*, June 23, 1988.
4. Quoted in Enrique Krauze,"The Guerrilla Dandy," *The New Republic*, June 27, 1988, p. 31.
5. William L. O'Neill, *A Better World: The Great Schism; Stalinism and the American Intellectuals* (New York: Simon and Schuster, 1982), p. 251.
6. Anna Louise Strong, *I Change Worlds* (New York: Holt, 1935), p. 224. See also Lloyd Billingsley, *The Generation That Knew Not Josef* (Portland: Multnomah Press, 1985), pp. 46-54.
7. Sidney Hook, *Out of Step*, p. 255.
8. Quoted in William L. O'Neill, *A Better World*, pp. 244, 245.
9. Quoted in Nancy Schwartz, *Hollywood Writers' Wars* (New York: Knopf, 1982), p. 88.
10. Elia Kazan, *Elia Kazan: A Life* (New York: Knopf, 1988), p. 130.
11. Quoted in William L. O'Neill, *A Better World*, p. 244.
12. Nancy Schwartz, *Hollywood Writers' Wars*, p. 89.
13. Morgan Y. Himelstein, *Drama Was a Weapon: The Left-Wing Theatre in New York, 1929-1941* (New Brunswick: Rutgers University Press, 1963), p. 3.
14. *Ibid.*, p. 4.
15. Quoted in Otto Friedrich, *City of Nets* (New York: Harper and Row, 1986), p. 73.
16. Victor Navasky, *Naming Names*, p 78.
17. William L. O'Neill, *A Better World*, p. 213.
18. John Cogley, *Report on Blacklisting: Movies* (New York: Fund for the Republic, 1956), p. 38.
19. William L. O'Neill, *A Better World*, p. 234.
20. See "Wall Street Uses Finland for War," *The Daily Worker*, December 1, 1939.
21. See Otto Friedrich, *City of Nets*, p. 51.
22. See Sidney Hook, *Out of Step*, p. 306.
23. Elia Kazan, *Elia Kazan: A Life*, p. 136.
24. Nancy Schwartz, *Hollywood Writers' Wars*, p. 185.
25. *Ibid.*
26. Bruce Cook, *Dalton Trumbo* (New York: Scribners, 1977), p. 131.
27. Morgan Himelstein, *Drama Was a Weapon*, p. 221.
28. John Cogley, *Report on Blacklisting*, p. 40.
29. Quoted in William L. O'Neill, *A Better World*, p. 243.
30. Dorothy Jones, "Communism and the Movies: A Study of Film Content," in John Cogley, *Report on Blacklisting*, p. 211.
31. Sidney Hook, *Out of Step*, p. 313.
32. Otto Friedrich, *City of Nets*, p. 154.
33. William L. O'Neill, *A Better World*, p. 362.
34. See Paul Potts, "Don Quixote on a Bicycle," in Audrey Coppard and Bernard Crick, eds., *Orwell Remembered* (New York: Facts on File Publications, 1984), p. 252.
35. William L. O'Neill, *A Better World*, p. 78.
36. See Bruce Cook, *Dalton Trumbo*.

37. Hilton Kramer, "The Blacklist and the Cold War," *New York Times*, October 3, 1976.
38. Robert C. Toth, "Soviets Concede Stalin Violated Yalta Agreements in Eastern Europe," *Los Angeles Times*, July 10, 1988, Part I, p. 12.
39. Hilton Kramer, "The Blacklist and the Cold War."
40. See Bruce Cook, *Dalton Trumbo*, pp. 165, 166.
41. John Cogley, *Report on Blacklisting*, p. 44.
42. Elia Kazan, *Elia Kazan: A Life*, p. 191.
43. Interview with Roy Brewer, May 13, 1988.
44. Jack Vizzard, *See No Evil* (New York: Simon and Schuster, 1970), p. 182.
45. Quoted in Nancy Schwartz, *Hollywood Writers' Wars*, p. 89.
46. Hilton Kramer, "The Blacklist and the Cold War."
47. *Ibid.*
48. Bruce Cook, *Dalton Trumbo*, p. 309.
49. Elia Kazan, *Elia Kazan: A Life*, p. 462.
50. William L. O'Neill, *A Better World*, p. 374.

CHAPTER FOURTEEN *The Christian Filmmaker*

1. Rumor has it that what attracted Fayed about the project was not the morally inspiring character of the story, but the fact that the Jewish runner, Harold Abrahams, lost a race.
2. Liz Smith, "Moviemaker Puttnam Fears for Fearful Hollywood," *San Diego Union*, March 18, 1988.
3. Tina Brown, "Hollywood Knives," *Vanity Fair*, April 1988, p. 99.
4. Exodus 35:31-33.
5. W. Somerset Maugham, *The Summing Up* (New York: Signet, 1964), p. 61.
6. Mollie Gregory, *Making Films Your Business* (New York: Shocken Books, 1979), pp. 18, 19.
7. See Nestor Almendros, *A Man With A Camera* (New York: Farrar, Straus and Giroux, 1984), p. 92.
8. Mark Litwak, *Reel Power* (New York: Morrow, 1986), p. 9.
9. See *ibid.*, pp. 311, 312.
10. See "$10 Million Bid Refused for 'Temptation' Film," *San Diego Union*, July 22, 1988, p. D-5. See also Pat Broeske, "Universal Asked to Destroy Scorcese's Film About Christ," *Los Angeles Times*, July 13, 1988, Part VI, p. 9.
11. John Simon, *Reverse Angle* (New York: Clarkson Potter, 1982), p. 6.

CHAPTER FIFTEEN *The Christian Film Viewer*

1. John Simon, *Reverse Angle* (New York: Clarkson Potter, 1982), p. 3.
2. Quoted in Diana Rigg, *No Turn Unstoned* (New York: Doubleday, 1983), p. 8.
3. Charles Hillinger, "Latinos Ask for Changes in IMAX Alamo Film," *Los Angeles Times*, December 31, 1987, Part VI, p. 10.

CHAPTER SIXTEEN *Conclusions*

1. Quoted in Stephen Farber and Marc Green, "Trapped in the Twilight Zone," *Los Angeles Times Magazine*, August 28, 1988, p. 33.
2. Pauline Kael, *Kiss Kiss Bang Bang* (Boston: Little, Brown, 1968), p. 334.
3. Virginia Stem Owens, *Total Image* (Grand Rapids: Eerdmans, 1980), p. 94.
4. Allan Bloom, *The Closing of the American Mind* (New York: Simon and Schuster, 1987), p. 81.
5. John Fowles, *Daniel Martin* (Toronto: Collins, 1977), p. 274.

MOVIE INDEX

INDEX